The government, which was designed for the people, has got into the hands of their bosses and their employers, the special interests. An invisible empire has been set up above the forms of democracy.

WOODROW WILSON

I am a firm believer in the people. If given the truth, they can be depended upon to meet any national crisis. The great point is to bring them the real facts.

ABRAHAM LINCOLN

THE BUYING
OF THE
PRESIDENT

THE BUYING

OF THE

PRESIDENT

CHARLES LEWIS
ALEJANDRO BENES
MEREDITH O'BRIEN
and the Center for
Public Integrity

AVON BOOKS ◆ NEW YORK

THE BUYING OF THE PRESIDENT is an original publication of Avon Books. This work has never before appeared in book form.

AVON BOOKS
A division of
The Hearst Corporation
1350 Avenue of the Americas
New York, New York 10019

Copyright © 1996 by the Center for Public Integrity
Published by arrangement with the Center for Public Integrity
Library of Congress Catalog Card Number: 95-44468
ISBN: 0-380-78420-3

Library of Congress Cataloging in Publication Data:
Lewis, Charles, 1953–
    The buying of the president / Charles Lewis and the Center for Public Integrity.
      p. cm.
Includes bibliographical references and index.
1. Campaign funds—United States. 2. Presidents—United States—Election—1996. 3. Presidential candidates—United States. I. Center for Public Integrity. II. Title.
JK1991.L49   1996   95-44468
324.7'8'097309049—dc20   CIP

First Avon Books Trade Printing: February 1996

AVON TRADEMARK REG. U.S. PAT. OFF. AND IN OTHER COUNTRIES, MARCA REGISTRADA, HECHO EN U.S.A.

Printed in the U.S.A.

OPM   10 9 8 7 6 5 4 3 2 1

The Investigative Team

Reporters

Rebecca Borders
George Clifford
Margaret Ebrahim

Researchers

Rachel Burstein
Karen Cooper
Jerry Dasti
Josh Zivo Feit
Joelle Goode
Thomas Greving
Sheryl Henderson
Alex Knott

Vicki Lorenz
Michelle McGrorty
Jennifer O'Brien
Jennifer Sarnelli
Robert Schlesinger
Paramita Sen
Paul Waldman
Douglas Weber

The Center for Public Integrity

Diane Renzulli, Senior Associate
Amy Bohm, Associate

The Center for Responsive Politics

Ellen Miller, Executive Director
Larry Makinson, Deputy Director
Joshua Goldstein, Research Director
Jacqueline Duobinis
Dave Royce

Special Thanks

To William LeoGrande, head of the American University Department of Government; Sanford Ungar, dean; professors Rose Ann Robertson, Chris Simpson, and Wendy Williams of the American University School of Communications; and to Reese Cleghorn, dean; and Christopher Callahan, assistant dean, of the University of Maryland College of Journalism.

Contents

Foreword

This book, in a nutshell, poses the $64 billion question of the 1996 election: Have *they*—the big contributors, the megalobbyists, K Street, Wall Street, the white-envelope crowd—bought the next president yet?

The hopeful answer is no, not yet, although they're certainly trying. But the cynic would say yes, realistically, because that's the way Washington and the two-party system have come to work.

Over the next 200-odd pages, however, readers can make up their *own* minds drawing on an unprecedented compilation of numbers, analyses, and revelations. For some, *The Buying of the President* will flesh out what they've always suspected. More Americans, though, will be stunned. They'll say, "I didn't realize it was this bad. I had no idea. What on earth do we do?"

This concern should become a central part of the 1996 debate. In the thirty-five-year cavalcade of presidential campaign books that began with Theodore White's landmark *The Making of the President, 1960,* no one has ever concentrated on the quiet but just as critical influence battle fought out with checkbooks—about how powerful patrons and interests invest in the people they expect to hold top offices, including the presidency, and what these donors expect to get (and worse, what they really *do* get) in return. Documentation like this has never before been compiled and published in advance of the election being described. *Never.* And the spotlight is scorching.

Executive Director Charles Lewis, the staff of the Center for Public Integrity, and the dozens of full-time and part-time researchers who backstopped them, have outdone themselves. Their individual chapters on President Clinton and other White House contenders or longshots go a long way toward documenting their all-too-provocative title. Moreover, not only is this buying of the president *bipartisan,* but, worse still, it's arguable that the entrenched two-party duopoly constitutes a damp and dark climate in which the mushrooms of capital corruption grow. And the top political contests that determine who will make federal policy, taxes, rules, and regulations—led, of course, by the race for the White House—are the ultimate mushroom beds.

When Chuck Lewis invited me to write the foreword, he gave me a preview of some of the factoids and tabulations found in this book. Among the more notable and new pieces of information is that the 1996 candidate/public official to raise the most special interest money for his own campaigns in the U.S. during the past twenty-five years is not Bob Dole, not Phil Gramm, but Pete Wilson, who has accumulated more than $80 million from these groups. Two presidential candidates, Bob Dole and Phil Gramm, have been close to fundraisers/contributors who have gone to prison. Two presidential candidates, Bob Dole and Phil Gramm, have been found by federal authorities to have taken *hundreds* of illegal corporate campaign contributions in the past. Three presidential candidates, Bob Dole, Phil Gramm, and Lamar Alexander, have entered into personal business dealings with wealthy contributors. No presidential candidate's net worth has increased more than Alexander's, whose net worth between 1978 and 1991 jumped 1,000 percent (300 percent between 1984 and 1994). Unsuccessful presidential candidate Pete Wilson's largest patron over his political career is an organization representing government employees directly affected by his policies. Wilson received $1.57 million in contributions and independent expenditure TV advertising from the California association of prison guards and other correctional employees. According to available records, Bill Clinton's inaugural was the most expensive in U.S. history, costing $32 million, and his Inaugural Committee sold the rights to everything except the Lincoln Memorial, and has $9.7 million sitting in the bank, left over. The Center for Public Integrity has compiled a database of practically every CEO to travel around the world with Commerce Secretary Ron Brown, whether they contributed to the Democratic National Committee, the date, how much, and the amount of federal cookie-jar financing and insurance they have received.

This is just the tip of the iceberg, and no other organization has the author's qualifications to measure it. Lewis launched the Center for Public Integrity in 1990, ending an eleven-year career in television journalism that had made him a top producer for CBS's "60 Minutes." He was determined to fill what he (correctly) saw as a central gap in Washington monitoring and muckraking: *No-holds-barred examination of the city's own political corruption.* Since then, some of the nonprofit organization's best-known reports and findings have documented how

- from 1974 to 1990, nearly half of all former senior White House trade officials went to work for the people they had negotiated against, namely foreign companies and governments;
- since 1979, 112 former members of Congress converted to personal use roughly $10.5 million in unspent campaign contributions;
- based on the first systematic look at unpaid policy advisers to presidential candidates, the vice chairman of the 1992 Bush-Quayle campaign and adviser to the Wilson campaign, James Lake, was also simultaneously a registered foreign agent on behalf of the owners of the scandalized Bank of Credit and Commerce International (BCCI);
- since 1977, half of the national political party chairmen have had conflicts of interest, simultaneously receiving fees from corporations, law firms, and other sources, with no one having more entanglements than then–Democratic Party Chairman Ron Brown;
- Mexican interests spent more than $30 million to pro-

mote the development and enactment of the North American Free Trade Agreement (NAFTA), hiring forty-four law firms, lobbyists, public relations companies, and consultants, including thirty-three former U.S. officials;

- in 1993 and 1994, hundreds of special interests cumulatively spent in excess of $100 million to influence the outcome of health care reform legislation with at least ninety-seven law, lobbying, or public relations firms hired by health care–related interests, including eighty former U.S. officials, and during 1992 and 1993, over eight-five members of Congress participated in 181 trips paid for by the health care industry;

- of the members of Congress who left between 1984 and 1993, eighty-one of the ninety-nine who stayed in Washington became—should anyone be surprised?—lobbyists.

Now Lewis and the Center have turned to the biggest influence-peddler target of all: the presidential campaign. *In theory,* ongoing study of Washington's dirty-laundry baskets should give the observer a cast-iron stomach. But *in fact,* the subject matter is one of never-ending revelations and new dimensions. Lewis admitted that, "We found far more than we even *imagined* might exist." Well, that's Washington. My own book, *Arrogant Capital,* published in September 1994, sought to explain why the nation's capital, in the half-century since the end of World War II, had become a massive enough entrenchment of lobbyists, special interests, and political professionals to take over the two-party system, neutralizing the ability of our national elections to clean house.

This conclusion, which some at the Center have come to share, grew in my mind as the data (and the historical precedents) on Washington's transformation mounted. What I found still seems extraordinary:

- Since the end of World War II, the number of people in greater Washington who are lobbyists or engaged in support of lobbying activities grew from several thousand to 91,000.

- The number of lawyers admitted to practice before the federal courts of the District of Columbia jumped from under 1,000 in 1950 to 61,000 in 1990. Washington is America's lawyer-central.
- The size of the staff of the U.S. Congress, roughly 2,500 in 1945, swelled to 21,000 in the early 1990s and remains over 20,000 today. No other major nation's legislature has even a quarter of that staff.
- Reflecting this same affluent buildup, by 1990 metropolitan Washington contained seven of the nation's twenty highest per capita income counties.

These numbers were stunning, too. But let me underscore a point: *They are an essential context for understanding the processes and corruptions described in this book.* Washington is a giant influence-mongery, and the buying of the president is the hottest game in town. At the risk of stating the obvious, the reason all this matters so much is that it detracts from American democracy and from your role as a citizen and voter.

The data and relationships laid out in this book just scratch the surface and the Center for Public Integrity has masses more documentation available on-line and in its files. But don't read about it and weep. Instead, *read about it and get angry.*

Kevin Phillips
Bethesda, Maryland
September 1995

Introduction

Theodore White wrote in his Pulitzer Prize–winning classic, *The Making of the President, 1960,* that the American presidential election is "the most awesome transfer of power in the world—the power to marshal and mobilize, the power to send men to kill or be killed, the power to tax and destroy, the power to create and the responsibility to do so, the power to guide and the responsibility to heal—all committed into the hands of one man."[1]

White did not write very much about the grubby issue of money back then. He made no mention of the amount of cold hard cash it took for Kennedy and Nixon to secure their parties' nominations and mount effective general election campaigns. Nor did he investigate where the cash came from, or what the donors sought in return from the next president of the United States. Back then, journalists generally did not write about such matters or ask impolite questions about money, and the candidates practically never discussed it. This book does.

The presidential campaign in the United States has become not so much a "beauty contest" or "horse race," but instead a giant auction, in which multimillion-dollar interests compete to influence and gain access to the candidates who would be president. That should not suggest that money is the *only* significant factor in presidential elections. There have been plenty of failed candidacies that were well-funded. In 1996, however, along with a resonant, timely message, a reasonably attractive, articulate presentation, and an effective organization, money is an essential ingredient of electoral success. If voters are to have access to relevant information about the candidates before casting their ballots, then the electorate needs to know and understand the real forces at play—the ones the candidates won't tell you about—in the 1996 presidential election, namely which special interests are best represented, and by which candidates.

Before the first vote is cast in a presidential primary, a private referendum has already been conducted among the nation's financial elites as to which candidate shall earn his party's nomination. In every election since 1976, the candidate who has raised the most money at the end of the year preceding the election, and has been eligible for federal matching funds, has become his party's nominee for the general election. Today more than ever before, it is commonly understood in national political circles that the "key to victory is a lot of money at an early date."[2]

This book is not intended as a personal indictment of those seeking the highest office in the land. Nor is it intended to provide *every* detail of the candidates' involvements with their contributors. That would take volumes to accomplish. This book is an investigative portrait of the nation's brutal, victimizing political process. Every major candidate campaigning for the White House becomes entangled in questionable dealings and relationships.

Alliances between political candidates and their financial patrons are certainly not uniquely American. Compromising relationships are endemic to politics generally. Not only does the country understand it, but for generations we all have come to *expect* it. However, it is unrealistic to expect our elected officials to operate in a system that requires each of them to raise millions of dollars in campaign contributions in order to get elected, and to raise those millions without any strings attached. As long as such a system exists and is tolerated, public reputations will become tarnished, and public skepticism and mistrust about government will continue. Apathy and disillusionment about politics have become so deep today that in 1992, 85 million eligible American adults did not vote in the presidential election, and in 1994, 114 million Americans did not participate in the political process.

Those U.S. citizens who actually *do* exercise their rights of political expression in this democracy are noticeably angry. Since 1992 an incumbent President and the entrenched Congress, Republican and Democrats alike, have been ejected unceremoniously from power.

The American people—Republicans, Democrats, independents, and that largest group, nonvoters—are growing more and more economically insecure and politically reactive, increasingly disempowered and disenfranchised. This era of discontent did not happen overnight, but as political columnist E. J. Dionne has written, it is the legacy of the past thirty years, "a polarized politics that highlights symbolic issues, short-circuits genuine political debate, gives discontent few real outlets, allows money a paramount role in the electoral process, and leaves the country alarmed over whether it can maintain its standard of living. Is it any wonder that Americans have come to hate politics?"[3]

Part of us may yearn for a return to simpler, more genial times, but one should be careful in wishing for something better. The system by which campaigns are financed in 1996 is the result of reforms arising from the deliberate deceit by the nation's highest government officials in the ultimate modern political scandal, Watergate. The American people learned that the 1972 presidential election was actually a sordid affair, involving burglaries, political dirty tricks, suitcases of illegal cash, mysterious bank accounts, and a multitude of official lies that began to be described simply as "the coverup." Among many other consequences, twenty-one companies—blue-chip firms including American Airlines, Goodyear Tire and Rubber, Gulf Oil—pleaded guilty to making illegal campaign contributions totaling nearly $1 million to five Democratic presidential candidates and the Nixon campaign.[4]

As a result of all the criminal investigations, the nation discovered that 1,254 individuals had contributed a total of $51.3 million in the 1972 campaign, an average of more than $40,900 per contributor. The biggest donor was W. Clement Stone, who gave more than $2 million to the Nixon reelection campaign.[5]

The country's moral outrage over Watergate resulted in the most significant political reforms in U.S. history. Limits were imposed on campaign contributions. Public disclosure requirements were strengthened through the creation of an independent Federal Election Commission. In 1974, presidential campaign money and politics became more accountable to the American people. Partial public funding of presidential campaigns was instituted for the first time in the history of the Republic. With $1,000 ceilings on individual contributions and tens of millions of dollars from the public provided to the major candidates, the goal was to take all of the "fat cats" out of the presidential campaign process. These reforms became law under a new president, Republican Gerald Ford, who said "the times demand this legislation."[6] Just weeks earlier, President Richard M. Nixon had resigned in disgrace.

Two decades later, the irony is that the well-intentioned Watergate-era political reforms have actually served to sanction and legitimize the influence of money on politics. For one thing, reform laws in the early 1970s permitted companies and labor unions to establish political action committees (PACs). PACs have proliferated wildly, frequently giving millions of dollars in unison as part of *de facto* industry-wide or union-wide coalitions, almost always to the congressional incumbents watching out for their special interests. Meanwhile, despite the limits, individual donors frequently encourage their spouses, friends, and children, some of whom are just learning to read in school, to each contribute a thousand dollars to the same candidate. Separately, lawyer/lobbyists and other vested interests host fundraisers at which scores or hundreds of maximum allowable contributions are "bundled," or given in one bunch. In 1996, all of this is legal under the "reformed" system.

In addition, it is commonplace for corporations, unions, or interested millionaires to each give hundreds of thousands of dollars to help elect a president. As one observer put it, "only now, skulking bagmen and offshore banks have been replaced by party committees."[7] In 1988, the presidential campaigns of Michael Dukakis and George Bush spent approximately $45 million combined in "soft money"—funds channeled on their behalf to state and local party organizations for voter registration, voter education, get-out-the-vote activities, etc.—

which is nearly half as much as the $92 million they received in public funds. This amount of soft money was more than *twice* the amount spent during the 1980 and 1984 elections combined.[8]

In 1988, 249 individuals each gave at least $100,000, achieving a total of $25 million, to help elect George Bush president. By giving that much, they became members of "Team 100" and not only had personal access to Bush and other members of the Bush administration, but many of them— from real estate and construction to finance, from manufacturing to agribusiness to oil and gas interests—received special favors during the Bush presidency.

The many *quid pro quo* relationships have been well documented by *Common Cause magazine* and others. The two largest donors were Archer-Daniels-Midland (ADM) and its chairman, Dwayne Andreas, who gave $1,072,000, and Atlantic Richfield (Arco) and its chairman, Lodwrick Cook, who contributed $862,360. Both companies made or saved hundreds of millions of dollars from their well-placed Washington investments.

Andreas—who with his company also contributed $270,000 to help Bill Clinton and the Democratic party capture the White House in 1992—is just one of dozens of the surviving "fat cat" donors to George Bush and the Republican Party who also gave substantial sums to the Nixon Committee to Reelect the President, better known by its now-amusing acronym, CREEP. Just as the 1992 Bush campaign had a Team 100 for its largest, six-figure benefactors, the 1972 Nixon campaign had its "100 Club." W. Clement Stone gave $2.3 million to the GOP and CREEP in 1970–1972, and in 1988–1992 contributed $103,000 to the party and the Bush campaign. Other Nixon-Bush donors include millionaire businessmen Walter Annenberg, Leonard Firestone, Jr., Max Fisher, Laurance Rockefeller, and Saul Steinberg, as well as the Phillips Petroleum company. In 1972, these Nixon CREEP donor names were kept in the desk drawer of Nixon's loyal secretary, Rose Mary Woods, and this secret list became known to White House staffers as "Rose Mary's Baby."[9]

Besides the fact that the names of such contributors are now publicly disclosed, little has changed. As former Watergate prosecutor Roger Witten told the *Wall Street Journal,* "It's a complete repeat of what went on in Watergate. It's exactly what we sought to prosecute in the early 1970s." Witten and others have tried, unsuccessfully, to shut off the soft money pouring into both political parties and their candidates.[10]

The Watergate parallels, the abiding sense of deja vu, and for some, unabashed sentimentalism, were all poignant for a single moment in March, 1992. At a hotel in Rancho Mirage, California, Richard Nixon addressed members of the Bush campaign's Team 100, looking out at many familiar faces whose pockets were still deep twenty years after the infamous 1972 Nixon reelection campaign. The elite gathering gave the former president a long and loud standing ovation.[11]

The garishness of money in politics has reached new levels of audacity, and all within the law. For years critics of campaign finance, such as the late Philip Stern, have described our legislators as "the best Congress money can buy." But these are truly glorious days in Washington for industry lobbyists and lawyers, who represent everyone from corporations that pollute and tobacco companies to the largest banks, real estate, and insurance companies. These corporate interests have raised and contributed vast sums of money—tens of millions of dollars—to those in power. Their representatives now sit in Capitol Hill hearing rooms side by side with the members of Congress they helped to elect, together drafting new laws on such issues as clean air, clean water, workplace safety, information technology, and public health that will affect every American. There is no longer even the polite pretense of an open, honest debate between opposing interests. Amidst Washington's mercenary culture, in which wealthy private interests play an increasingly crucial role, the impression is unmistakable and indelible that our government—theoretically of the people, by the people, and for the people—is actually being sold to the highest bidder.

During the past decade our national seat of government has been blighted by a plethora of abuses of power and the public trust too numerous to review here. Not surprisingly, public opinion polls indicate that most Americans do not trust their elected officials. Arguably as much as at any time in the contemporary, post–Civil War history of the republic, the American people feel significantly alienated from Washington, from national decision making, from the political process.

So, against this unusually volatile political backdrop the United States faces another presidential election. This race will likely be the most expensive presidential campaign in U.S. history. The consensus among political observers is that, with an unprecedented "front-loaded" selection process in which thirty-five state primaries are compressed into twenty-nine days in February and March 1996, each candidate needed to raise approximately $20 million—that's $54,794 a day—in 1995 alone in order to mount a viable campaign. The costs of seeking the White House thus have gotten so exorbitant as to be a real deterrent to serious national political figures. In early 1995, three major prospective Republican presidential candidates—former cabinet secretaries Richard Cheney and Jack Kemp, and former Vice President Dan Quayle—declined to seek their party's nomination in part because of the extraordinarily high sum of money that is now required to run.

Kemp explained the dilemma to the Center for Public Integrity, "It would be no secret that my passion—as I stated when I made my [withdrawal] announcement—is really for the ideas of the party, not for the fundraising of the party."[12]

He learned he would have to appear at between two hundred and 250 fundraising events in 1995. "I just decided that rather than spend 80 percent of my time on the phone or at fundraisers, which most of them [the presidential candidates] are doing, I would enjoy fighting for a cause I believe in." Kemp is co-director of Empower America, a relatively new conservative nonprofit organization in Washington. Some of his causes include studying and discussing ideas about "flat tax" reform, the Mexican peso devaluation, and the District of Columbia financial crisis. Kemp believes that "in no small way I'm probably more relevant out of the race than I am in the race."[13]

At age sixty, with nine grandchildren and a love of skiing, Kemp had no desire to endure the kind of personal sacrifice and commitment today's presidential campaigns require of a serious candidate and his family. To complicate matters, he ran unsuccessfully for the Republican presidential nomination in 1988, and he still owes more than $100,000 from that failed endeavor. The experience left him somewhat introspective about what it takes today to seek the highest political office in the land.

"I'm not compulsive. I was never compulsive about it [running for President]. When they said Kemp wasn't disciplined, it wasn't that I wasn't disciplined, I'm not compulsive. You've got to be compulsive . . . [Texas Senator] Phil Gramm has kept every name of every person to whom he has spoken for the last fifteen years. I respect that, I'm not a martyr . . . I don't criticize anybody who's going through this, but I'm glad I'm not. . . . I think the [presidential election] process is too long and too expensive."[14]

That is, of course, a common sentiment. Interestingly, no major 1996 presidential candidate seriously or sincerely proposes changing the role of money in politics today. Indeed, the men who would be president have all, without exception, accepted and embraced the current system of bankrolling campaigns. Some are more unabashed about it than others. In early 1995, with nearly $5 million from his last Senate race transferred over to his presidential campaign account and 160,000 names and addresses of potential donors he had collected over the years, Senator Phil Gramm (R-TX) announced what everyone had known for years, that he was a candidate for the 1996 Republican nomination for President. The night before his formal announcement speech, Gramm told thousands of supporters at a Dallas fundraiser which by itself brought in $4.1 million, "I have the most reliable friend you can have in American politics, and that is ready money."[15]

In 1991, the year before his election as president, candidate Bill Clinton raised $3.3 million in his drive for the White House. In 1995, three major Republican candidates—Bob Dole, Phil Gramm, and Lamar Alexander—vying to oppose Clinton in the 1996 general election had each raised that much or more *in the first quarter alone*. Gramm already had amassed more than $12 million!

In 1995, former Tennessee governor and Bush administration Department of Education Secretary Lamar Alexander

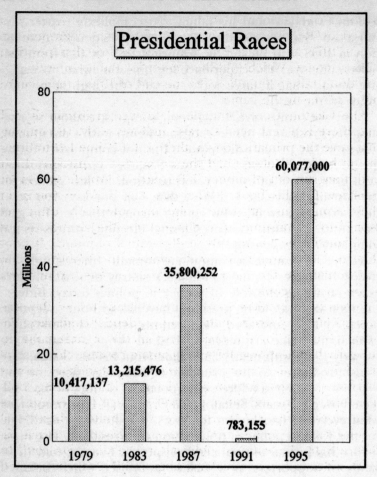

Presidential Races

Total receipts for all candidates through June 30 of each year.
Source: FEC.

planned to attend no fewer than 148 fundraising events nationwide during the year. That actually translates into double the number of trips because each event requires a "premeeting" with organizers. Alexander's goal was to raise $1 million every ten days. Led by veteran GOP fundraiser Ted Welch, who helped the Republicans first "discover" the soft money loophole in the early 1980s, Alexander has twenty-two national co-chairmen, including six of the seven men who served as Republican party national finance chairmen between 1977 and 1992. The principal task of that position: raising money. Welch told the Center for Public Integrity, "if you don't raise $20 million [by the end of 1995], then you're not a player in the game."[16]

The Clinton/Gore '96 national finance chairman agreed that there is a real need to raise millions early, recognizing that once the primaries begin, there is little time left to bring in the bucks. "I always had the saying that campaigns don't end, they run out of money," Terrence McAuliffe said in an interview for this book. "What happens is, when you're in these campaigns, at some point you physically can't get money to buy airtime, to get money for the airlines to put the plane in the air. You physically run out of money. It's not that your ideas aren't any good anymore, the problem is that you don't have the means to get your message, your ideas across to the people."

Fundraising prowess has become a litmus test of the seriousness and national viability of a presidential candidacy. Political reporters for the major news media organizations, in the early handicapping for an upcoming contest, closely scrutinize the cumulative incoming receipts to candidates, money that translates to television advertising, field organizing, polling, focus group and other political message refinement, political consultants, etc. A contender with limited wherewithal is relegated to "second tier" status and viewed somewhat pathetically by the national political and media *cognoscenti*. In 1995, aides to Senator Richard Lugar (R-IN) were frustrated when this occurred almost instantly to that Republican presidential candidate. Lugar was characterized frequently as "honest" and "quietly competent," but universally regarded as an unlikely victor in the critically important early caucuses and primaries because of his assumed lack of emphasis, experience, or proven national ability to raise double-digit millions of dollars.

As a southern governor who has not personally sought electoral office in more than a decade, the perception of national viability and visibility was absolutely vital to Lamar Alexander. He and his supporters helped create a nonprofit organization called the Republican Exchange Satellite Network (RESN) that televised Republican "neighborhood" meetings on a nationwide cable channel. Based in Nashville, the group existed for about two years leading up to Alexander's announcement for the Republican presidential nomination in 1995. The size of the budget and contributors—whose donations are not limited under the law—were not disclosed to the public, including the Center for Public Integrity. The organization was strategically useful to Alexander, keeping his name and presence in the public eye around the country. As he put it, "When I go to New Hampshire or Iowa or Texas, this gives me a framework in which to operate. I suddenly have a reason to be there, to build Neighborhood Republican meetings in those places."[17]

Bob Dole is, of course, the veteran presidential candidate. In his unsuccessful bid for the GOP nomination in 1988, he raised $20.8 million. Dole represents, revels in, and resists reform of the current campaign finance system. Very few political figures have raised more private money to run for public office since Watergate than Dole, who, before 1995, had cumulatively received more than $47.6 million over his long career from vested interests.[18] As much as any other presidential candidate, he is a creature of Washington. In his last Senate race, 79 percent of the Kansan's individual campaign contributors were from out of state.[19] And we found that only one of his ten largest career patrons since 1979 is from Kansas. That patron ranks in the top ten only when independent expenditures made on Dole's behalf are included in the contribution totals. Regarding the 1996 presidential contest, Dole, like Alexander, has also utilized and benefitted from a mysterious, now defunct, nonprofit entity called the Better America Foundation. In the days before the dramatic November 1994 elections, the group chaired by Dole bought $1 million in TV commercials on CNN, which featured Dole speaking in front of a fluttering American flag.

The entanglements and *quid pro quo* arrangements between politicians and special interests are not new, but voters are entitled to know what they are. United States history is adorned with examples of how our most revered presidents assisted and benefitted from certain individuals and interests. Take a closer look at our ultimate icon of moral probity and integrity, Abraham Lincoln. The fact is little known, but in the momentous presidential election of 1860, Lincoln outspent his opponent, Stephen A. Douglas, by a two-to-one margin, expending $100,000.[20] As a private citizen, Lincoln had been a lawyer for the growing railroad industry, including the Illinois Central Line. As Lincoln biographer Carl Sandburg has written, in 1860 the Lincoln presidential campaign forces planned an immense demonstration of "human force" at the Republican party national convention in Chicago. "Hour on hour the bulk of the 40,000 strangers kept up a shouting and a tumult for Abraham Lincoln, for Old Abe, for the Rail Candidate. [Lincoln friend and Rock Island Railroad attorney Norman B.] Judd had fixed it with the railroads so that any shouter who wished to come could set foot in Chicago at a low excursion rate."[21] Subsequently, the "Rail Candidate" became the "Rail President." Railroad industry officials joined the new administration in Washington, and it was during Lincoln's tenure as president that the federal government issued railroad land grants allowing the companies to acquire the most acreage in U.S. history.[22]

In one of this nation's most historically significant presidential elections, it was well understood in 1932 that Franklin Roosevelt was in favor of the outright repeal of Prohibition and restoring liquor control to the states. After just three weeks in office as president, Roosevelt signed the Beer Bill, and by the end of his first year, the Eighteenth Amendment was repealed and alcohol was flowing legally once again in the states.[23] In the 1936 presidential election, brewers and distillers gave FDR's Democratic party $73,000, and only $6,000 to the Republicans. "Liquor paid its debt of gratitude to the Democratic party by giving 5.7 percent of the large contributions . . . this group is also heavily represented in the small contributors, and numbered among the labor organizations were a conspicuous number of brewing unions."[24]

Whether opening up the West to the railroads or ending the Federal government's dubious role as regulator and moral arbiter over alcohol consumption, special interests made mil-

lions of dollars from these public policy decisions, and the
political leaders who promulgated these policies benefitted
tangibly. The problem in many money-politics discussions is
the imprecision and lack of nuance and sophistication. The
above-described policy judgments by Lincoln and Roosevelt
are generally regarded to have been the correct and logical
decisions then and now, and both men almost certainly would
have arrived at these positions regardless of the money contributed to their parties. However, such a congenial conflu-
ence of events in which private and public agendas neatly
coincide is, of course, not always apparent or true. The point
is that in a democracy, each instance involving politicians,
policies, and pelf must be weighed and considered separately,
on a case-by-case basis, and the people have every right to
know this information and place it in the larger context of
their voter preference decision.

All of the major 1996 presidential candidates are entangled
with those specific interests that have helped to make their
public careers possible. By using the available public records,
we have put together an individualized list of the "Top 10
Career Patrons" for each of those politicians who had declared their candidacies by September 15, 1995.

In addition, the Center for Public Integrity has studied the
personal financial dealings of each of the major presidential
candidates. We found that three of the most prominent Republican contenders—Bob Dole, Phil Gramm, and Lamar Alexander—have seen their families' personal net worth soar
during their tenures as public servants. Because of their official capacities in government over the years, they or their
spouses each have come into contact with millionaires who
have assisted them in improving their personal financial positions. That is part of the story. To be fair to all of them,
they likely would have done well financially regardless of their
chosen careers because they are all intelligent, well educated,
ambitious, and hard-working. And assessing the net worth of
public officials is further complicated by the fact that many
candidates' spouses are or have been substantial wage earners
in their own right.

In Bill Clinton's case, he might have done better had he
chosen another career. Clinton's net worth would have in-

creased 65 percent, from a 1983 estimate of $461,265 to at least $760,000 in 1994, if it were not for $1,025,000 in legal fees. As a result, his net worth is -$265,000.[25]

Conservatively calculating the generally limited financial information that each of the candidates has made available over the years, it is clear that Lamar Alexander's net worth has increased the most since 1984, by 300 percent, from at least $634,519 in 1984 to at least $2,540,000 in 1994. It should be noted that unlike the others mentioned here, Alexander worked in the private sector during part of this time. Phil Gramm's net worth has jumped 116 percent during his tenure in the Senate, from at least $265,305 in 1984 to at least $574,000 in 1994. Bob Dole's net worth has appreciated 48 percent, from at least $1,884,237 in 1984 to at least $2,789,000 in 1994, while serving in the Senate.

Life has not been nearly so lucrative for the rest of the nation. Most Americans have not seen their family's personal net worths—assets minus liabilities—appreciate substantially the past decade or so. And most probably do not believe that their elected officials should become wealthy from public service. Whatever they believe, the stark reality is that each of the presidential candidates (and their families) under discussion—Alexander, Clinton, Dole, and Gramm—has profited personally from his public associations.

We found, for example, that all four men, plus former candidate Wilson, have had advantageous business dealings with financial backers from their campaigns involving owned or rented property. Alexander rented a Hilton Head condominium to campaign contributors and also co-owned a large tract of land in Tennessee with contributors which would have likely appreciated from a parkway he proposed to build as governor. Governor Bill Clinton entered into a real estate venture, the Whitewater Development Corporation, with campaign fundraiser James B. McDougal, who reportedly absorbed most of the losses.[26] Senator Bob Dole benefits from a Florida condominium purchased on favorable terms from major contributor Dwayne Andreas, the chairman of Archer Daniels Midland (ADM). Senator Phil Gramm accepted more than $50,000 in "free" construction work on his Maryland vacation home from a Texas builder and savings and loan operator seeking and receiving Gramm's help with federal regulators. As governor and earlier as mayor of San Diego, Pete Wilson has lived "rent free" in apartments paid for by friends and contributors.

Private use of public life is legal and not uncommon. George Washington Plunkitt, the boss of New York City's notorious Tammany Hall machine, once said that he made his fortune in politics by buying property that he knew in advance would escalate in price because of a planned subway line. Plunkitt made a distinction between honest graft and dishonest graft; the latter was outright corruption. But as Plunkitt said about himself in 1915, "There's honest graft, and I'm an example of how it works. I might sum up the whole thing by sayin', 'I seen my opportunities and I took 'em.' "[27]

Too often lost these days, especially along the Potomac, is the fact that public officials, including those who would be president, work for us, the people. Their decisions and actions profoundly affect our lives. We hire these officials by voting for them. We, through the taxes we pay, compensate them for their services. They are our employees. As such, understanding precisely who it is we are hiring, and making sure that they are doing their jobs, is vital to the health of this democracy. The few we elect to public office are charged with representing our interests. The danger in any republic, as James Madison warned in the tenth of *The Federalist Papers*, is when, "Men of factious tempers, of local prejudices, or of sinister designs, may by intrigue, by corruption or by other means, first obtain the suffrages, and then betray the interests of the people."

The Buying of the President provides information, together in one volume, that the electorate can, and, dare we say, should use in determining which candidate it will allow to "obtain its suffrages" in an effort to assure that the one elected does not "betray the interests of the people."

Party Animals

A full assessment of the major candidates for the presidency is not possible without an understanding of the milieu in which they have been created and operate. The ideas, organization, and money behind the political parties substantially define what each candidate stands for today. The simple fact is that in this century, no one has been elected to the White House who has *not* been a member of either the Democratic or Republican party. Thus, before focusing our investigative attention upon individual contenders, we first must explore their moorings to these institutions.

President Bill Clinton is the leader of the Democratic Party today, and like all of his recent Oval Office predecessors, the national party's day-to-day activities are directed by the president's political operatives. Senator Bob Dole was once chairman of the Republican party, and has been the leader of the Republican members of the U.S. Senate for more than a decade. Senator Phil Gramm was chairman of the Republican Senate Campaign Committee. Lamar Alexander traveled nationwide in 1993 and 1994, televising Republican Neighborhood Meetings via cable and satellite to an estimated 20 million Americans and party faithful. Governor Pete Wilson received more than $1.4 million from the national Republican party in his 1990 California campaign alone.

All of the major presidential candidates for 1996 are inextricably intertwined with their political parties.

Interestingly, this republic was never predicated upon the existence of political parties. As Arthur Schlesinger, Jr., has observed, neither the Articles of Confederation nor the Constitution provided for parties. The United States began without party government. When George Washington gave his farewell address, he warned against "the baneful effects of the spirit of party."[1] Or as John Taylor wrote in a letter to John Adams in 1814, "All parties, however loyal to principles at first, degenerate into aristocracies of interest at last, and unless a nation is capable of discerning the point where integrity ends and fraud begins, popular parties are among the surest modes of introducing an aristocracy."

Despite this less than auspicious beginning, factions, and eventually parties began to coalesce. Political scientists have delineated five separate party systems or eras. Without recounting a detailed history of U.S. political parties, it should be noted that the mid-nineteenth century was roughly the heyday in which parties played the strongest role in American political life. As the nation evolved, parties filled an institutional void, as a way for groups and interests to win elections by forging coalitions, amidst an increasingly diverse, growing electorate.[2]

Political parties have been vessels for ideas, and as such they have contributed to the country's political education and helped to develop national purpose and policies. They have offered a mechanism to mediate and modulate bitter disputes at the national level. They have helped government to organize and have provided an accountability mechanism—the "loyal opposition."[3] Parties have drawn ordinary citizens into the political system, recruited and trained political leaders, and offered avenues of "upward mobility to vigorous newcomers debarred by class or ethnic prejudice from more conventional avenues to status. As agencies of 'Americanization,' they received immigrants from abroad."[4]

The twentieth century has seen the gradual decline of political parties. Party loyalty, discipline, and identification have all been deteriorating. There is no shortage of explanations put forth by academics and pundits to explain why political parties have become increasingly irrelevant to the average American. Progressive movement measures early in this century, such as creation of a civil service, dampened the potency of party patronage. Television and the high costs of media

campaigns, increased candidate independence, and political
action committees are but a few of the reasons frequently
cited for the erosion of the parties.

While partisan activities at the grass roots and precinct levels appear to be on the wane, at the national level in Washington, the Republican and Democratic parties have reasserted
themselves in recent decades. Their organizations, the size of
their budgets and staffs, the high-tech computer and polling
wizardry now being brought to political campaigning, and the
advent of sophisticated direct-mail communications reaching
millions of people all suggest a new aggressiveness in party
strategy.

To date, the amount of money the Democratic National
Committee (DNC) raises, through direct mail and other
means, is a mere fraction of what is raised by the Republican
National Committee (RNC). Both party committees have
clearly become organizationally and financially "national-
ized." So while party identification and other indices are stun-
ningly low by historical standards, the amount of money
raised and the actual scope of centralized party operations
from Washington is the highest in U.S. history.

Receipts of the Major Parties
*In millions of dollars

	1977–78	1979–80	1981–82	1983–84	1985–86	1987–88	1989–90	1991–92	1993–94
Democrat	$26.4	$37.2	$39.3	$98.5	$64.8	$127.9	$85.7	$177.7	$139.1
Republican	$84.5	$169.5	$215.0	$297.9	$255.2	$263.3	$206.3	$267.3	$245.6
Total	$110.9	$206.7	$254.3	$396.4	$320.0	$391.2	$292.0	$445.0	$384.7

*Includes national, state, and local committees. Source: Federal Election Commission.

Throughout the 1980s, as the Democratic party tried to
play financial catch-up with the Republicans by aggressively
soliciting millions of dollars from corporate America, there
was considerable discussion about the ramifications. As Robert Kuttner wrote, in *The New Republic*, "The Democratic par-

ty's poignant quest for philosophical moorings is complicated and compromised by its search for political money. It is one thing for the Democrats to abandon old themes because the majority of voters seem weary of government programs, labor unions, and needy people. It is another thing altogether to move right because that is where the money is . . . the danger is that the Democrats' natural identity as the party of the non-rich will be fatally undermined by the logic of campaign finance."[5]

According to Kuttner, in late August 1984, about seventy of Democratic presidential candidate Walter Mondale's biggest fundraisers nationwide told Mondale flatly to cease with the populist rhetoric. California businessman Irvin Kipnes recalled the meeting. "Several of us said, 'Fritz, quit knocking the rich; they're financing your campaign.'" According to Kipnes and others, Mondale replied "Oh my goodness, I'm so sorry. There's nothing wrong with wanting to be rich. I want to be rich."[6] There was consternation in liberal Democratic circles that Mondale would not endorse the Bradley-Gephardt tax reform bill that year, which would have closed most tax loopholes and cut tax rates drastically. Mondale's money men were against it, and the candidate never supported it.[7]

As author William Greider has trenchantly written, in the early 1980s, it was not Ronald Reagan who "opened the floodgates" of tax breaks for business interests, but the Democratic chairman of the House Ways and Means Committee, Representative Dan Rostenkowski of Illinois. And it was not the party traditionally associated with "big business," the Republicans, but the Democrats who first attempted to reduce the top tax rate on unearned income.[8]

When pollsters sample U.S. voter opinion about the Democratic party, the most common description has been "the party of average working people." Years ago, that was the response of 50 percent of the electorate, but now only 13 percent of Americans express that sentiment.[9] According to Greider, "the Democrats might more accurately be described now as 'the party of Washington lawyers'—lawyers who serve as the connective tissue within the party's upper reaches. They are the party establishment, to the extent anyone is, that has replaced the old networks of state and local political bosses. But these lawyers have no constituencies of their own and, indeed, must answer to no one, other than their clients.''[10]

Some of the biggest names in the national Democratic Party—former chairmen Robert Strauss and Charles Manatt, lobbyist Tommy Boggs, former LBJ aide Harry McPherson, former White House Counsel Lloyd Cutler, longtime Democratic presidential advisor Clark Clifford, and former Carter White House official Stuart Eizenstat—are all extremely wealthy, successful Washington lawyers whose clients include Fortune 500 corporations and banks. Meanwhile, the Democrats were notably silent about some of the debilitating financial failures in the 1980s. These party leaders "did not urge Democrats to go after Michael Milken's junk bonds and the leveraged buyouts that cannibalized companies, or the gutted financial regulations that produced bank failures and taxpayer bailouts, or the high interest rates and debt crises that devastated small business, farmers, labor, housing, and manufacturing."[11]

The 1992 election of Bill Clinton was significant because a Democrat had campaigned against the "politics-as-usual" and "influence-peddling" of Washington, a populist message which seemed to resonate throughout the U.S. But a closer look revealed that it was merely rhetoric. The Center for Public Integrity found that more than half of Clinton's campaign advisers were from Washington law and lobbying firms, and the Center for Responsive Politics discovered that the most generous donor group to the Clinton/Gore ticket was made up of lawyers and lobbyists.

The influencing role of money in political parties is not exactly a new public issue. Commenting acidly that " 'bribery' has existed in all ages, but it manifests itself in different forms," author Louise Overacker wrote in her 1932 book *Money in Elections,* "As the cost of campaigns has risen, parties have been forced to expand their resources. In the United States, meeting little response from the rank and file of the electorate, they have been forced to rely to an increasing extent upon large contributions from prosperous business interests."[12]

Overacker observed, "No party which is financially dependent upon the substantial business interests ... would feel free to embark upon an economic program which met with their hostility. Even a dog will not bite the hand that feeds it, and a political party will hardly 'sell out' the person whose money it accepts."

Today the political parties accept tens of millions of dollars annually from the "substantial business interests"—far more than they did in 1932. Indeed, more than 70 percent of contributions to the Democratic and Republican parties today comes from corporations.[9] According to the Federal Election Commission and the public interest group Common Cause, from 1991 through 1994, the Republican party raised 95 million dollars in soft money. More than 90 percent of the large donations (at least $20,000 each) came from business interests—corporations, executives, trade associations, and lobbying firms. During the same four-year period, the Democratic party raised 75 million dollars in soft money, more than 70 percent of that from corporate donors.

Today, while campaign contributions are meticulously documented and analyzed, most Americans do not know the specifics about who is paying the bills of either party, or what those who pay the bills get in return. There is public concern over individual, six-figure "soft money" contributions quietly pouring into the two political parties, but no one really seems to understand how that money is disbursed to the state and local levels, and most public discourse surrounds the donors and the candidates. Even less attention has been directed toward the party leaders, the national party machines, and their relationship to major Washington lobbyists and the large, multibillion-dollar interests they represent.

The political parties aim to win elections at the national, state, and local levels. That is their paramount mission. But the leaders of the Democratic and Republican National Committees, by dint of their position and status in Washington, also represent a back-channel route for corporations and wealthy individuals to achieve critical inside access to public officials. It is a largely hidden and unaccountable system by which powerful, monied interests can potentially bend and influence public policy for private benefit.

Party chairmen meet frequently with the president if they are from the same party, as well as with congressional leaders of the same party. In the 1980s, when the Republicans controlled the White House and the Democrats held Congress, the Republican chairman had frequent access to the president and his cabinet. The Democratic chairman was included in such exclusive gatherings as the speaker of the house's closed-door deputy whip meetings on Wednesday mornings in the Capitol, where legislative strategy, the upcoming agenda, and the vote counts were openly discussed.

According to the Center for Public Integrity, between 1977 and 1993 *half* of the national party chairmen received outside income from corporations and law firms—despite party charters expressly stipulating that the chairman's position is "full time." One ethical controversy involved RNC Chairman Frank Fahrenkopf, who was simultaneously earning $100,000 a year as a lawyer for the law firm Hogan and Hartson. On one occasion he set up and personally attended a meeting for his firm's clients, Toyota Motor Manufacturing USA, with the then Secretary of Commerce Malcolm Baldrige.[14]

But of the eleven chairmen elected in that period, none simultaneously wore more hats or raised more questions about conflicts of interest than DNC Chairman Ron Brown. While directing party activities, Brown also continued to receive income from his law firm, Patton, Boggs, and Blow, and he maintained business relationships with at least three private companies. He solicited government business for both the law firm and the company he headed. He traveled to Japan on law firm business.

In 1992, Brown was the only party chairman to decline to be interviewed by the Center, but the managing partner of his law firm, Timothy May, expressed frustration and incredulity that anyone would raise questions of a potential conflict of interest regarding Brown. It is ridiculous, he said, "that someone is chairman of a party and has influence and that they can't employ this influence to help clients."[15] Such are the ways of Washington, the standard practices understood and accepted by the political establishments of both parties and their nominees for president. Brown, for example, was

nominated by Bill Clinton and confirmed by Congress as secretary of commerce.

Government, parties, and political power and influence are
so meshed in Washington as to be indistinguishable. Consider
the anecdote once told to us by the late John White, whom
President Jimmy Carter chose to head the DNC in the late
1970s. In those years, the Democrats were in grim shape financially. Not only was the Democratic party still paying off
its longstanding multimillion-dollar debt from the 1968 presidential campaign, but the day-to-day situation had suddenly
become so dire that the DNC's *entire* staff might have to be
let go, and the prospect loomed that the DNC actually might
have to vacate its office space. Such a notion, White said,
would have been acutely embarrassing. And so the chairman
cast about, looking for a dependable Democratic donor who
would be able to write a very large check and help the DNC
avert further disaster and humiliation. White found such an
individual—Lew Wasserman, the chairman of MCA Inc., the
entertainment conglomerate.

What did Wasserman seek in return? Not anything really,
White said. But there was one occasion, he recalled, when
Wasserman was coming to Washington and couldn't get a
hotel room. He called White, who telephoned the owner of
Washington's expensive Madison Hotel, imploring him to accommodate Mr. Wasserman. Unfortunately no room was available. White smiled proudly and recalled that he finally found
suitable overnight lodging for the wealthy Hollywood
mogul—at the White House, in the Lincoln Bedroom. This
favor for Wasserman, White said, was "just a small thing."[16]

The average American never gets to meet the president,
much less sleep in the Lincoln Bedroom. Give a few hundred
thousand dollars to your political party, and if your party captured control of the White House in the last election, perhaps
something can be arranged. Nothing bears this out more than
the revelation in the summer of 1995 that the Democratic
National Committee—in a letter signed by party co-chairmen
Senator Christopher Dodd and Donald Fowler, and first disclosed by the *Chicago Sun-Times*—actually offered potential
supporters a "menu" of meals with President Clinton and

Vice President Gore and their wives.[17] The items were varyingly priced, but in essence, the less you give, the less you get.

Prizes for Donations

As part of its effort to recruit donors, the Democratic National Committee outlined events open to donors who give at certain levels.

• A $100,000 contributor would get two meals with President Clinton, two meals with Vice President Al Gore, a slot on a foreign trade mission with DNC leaders, and other benefits, such as a daily fax report and an assigned DNC staff member to assist with contributors' "personal requests."

• A $50,000 contributor would get invited to a reception with Mr. Clinton, one dinner with Mr. Gore, and two special high-level briefings, among other benefits.

• A $10,000 contributor would get invited to a presidential reception and a dinner with Mr. Gore and would get "preferred" status at the 1996 Democratic National Convention.

• A $1,000 contributor would get invited to events with first lady Hillary Rodham Clinton; Mr. Gore's wife, Tipper, and female political appointees.

DNC National Chairman Donald Fowler responded to charges that the party and the president were selling access and influence to contributors by saying that such fundraising efforts would continue until the law requires both parties to operate differently. "Until the system is changed, we will not unilaterally disarm," Fowler reportedly said, accurately reflecting the fact that every party and administration have given special treatment to its biggest supporters.[18]

Not to be outdone, the GOP had its own program for donors in 1995, the "Eagles" club.[19] The Republican offer was less expensive, just "$20,000 per family or $7,500 for members under age thirty-five," according to the *Washington Times*. A single membership costs $15,000 and gets you on special trade missions to places like China and Sweden; meetings with top Republican officials; access to a personal "regional representative in Washington;" an invitation to former President Gerald Ford's annual "Eagles Cup" tennis and golf tournament; a lithograph of an American eagle signed by former President George Bush; "VIP accommodations and preferential seating" at the convention; and an invitation to a "private" meeting with "the newly inaugurated president and vice president of the United States," if, of course, they happen to be Republicans.

RNC Chairman Haley Barbour dismissed comparisons with the Democratic plan, saying, "You get invited to the inauguration, you get invited to the convention. That's very different than saying you get to have dinner with the president."[20] Despite Barbour's dismissal, the Republicans have not been above enticing potential donors with influential keepsakes— among other favors, top donors to the Republican National Committee were offered special photo sessions with President Bush and Vice President Quayle, during their administration.

The candidate and the party have always needed and used one another. In the context of the 1996 presidential campaign, the undeniable reality is that no man or woman can win a major party nomination for president of the United States today without participating fully in the life of the parties.

The 1992 Political Party Conventions

Nowhere is the headlong rush for cash by the political parties more blatant than at the quadrennial national conventions. And no one has chronicled these excesses more thoroughly than investigative reporter Sheila Kaplan. In a series of articles, she illustrated the remarkably unabashed extent of the corporate connection to the political parties evident at the Republican and Democratic conventions in the summer of 1992.[21]

American Express Company, Time Warner, AT&T Company, and the New York Telephone Company, a subsidiary of NYNEX Corporation, for example, *each* contributed more than $400,000 in cash and other support to help pay for the

Democratic National Convention in New York City, at which Bill Clinton was nominated to be the party's candidate for president. In addition to scores of corporate receptions at posh restaurants and hotels in Manhattan, at which lobbyists and business executives could meet and talk with the nation's top Democratic officials, the most enterprising and colorful event was probably "Victory Train '92."

A sum of $25,000 or more paid to the party could get you three tickets on the special VIP train from Washington's Union Station to New York City, and according to promotional literature, "Once aboard, you'll be able to roam the train and enjoy the ride with Members of Congress, Democratic governors and mayors, and DNC contributors from across the country. Whether meeting new friends or enjoying the scenery through the glass wall of the observation car, the journey promises to be memorable."

Three hours of uninterrupted access to a Capitol Hill lawmaker is an alluring prospect for any lobbyist. No journalists or congressional staff were allowed on the special train chartered by the Democratic National Committee. Kaplan, however, was undaunted. She managed to board the train and took copious notes, as well as numerous photographs of well-known lobbyists and elected officials laughing and enjoying the rolling party. Later, in New York, the uninvited Kaplan visited several corporate receptions, where the same kind of exclusive, high-priced "schmoozing" was occurring.

Joan Baggett, the DNC chief of staff in the summer of 1992, discussed the Victory Train. For the previous year, she said, the DNC had tried "to get members for our finance council, labor council, business council, which are just regular contributors that contribute both federal and nonfederal dollars to the DNC. We tried to recruit members to that. As part of membership in those counsels, we said there would be activities at the convention that would essentially service our donors. You know, do receptions for them. And we viewed the train sort of as one long reception, quite frankly."[22]

When asked if such an event is "a lobbyist's dream," Baggett said, "Quite honestly, if somebody's given $5,000, or somebody's given $20,000, they can be on the train; I mean, along with all the [DNC] staff. So, there was no feel of exclusivity to it except to the extent they were donors . . . and there were members. But people go to fundraising receptions all the time here. Do they have a captive audience? No. But frankly, if a member of Congress doesn't want to talk to you if he's on a train, I've never seen it deter them to be rude to you if they need to.''

Perhaps most revealing was her opinion that it wasn't an unusual opportunity for donors with special interests. "The people who were on the train—quite honestly, I wasn't on the train, but I roughly know who they were—don't have any problem getting in to see members of Congress."[23]

The Republican National Convention in Houston had a similar matter-of-factness when it came to soliciting and servicing donors. Kaplan again documented the various corporate receptions and extravaganzas.

The Houston Host Committee raised more than $4 million from corporations to help support the many receptions and gala events. DuPont, Conoco, Exxon Corporation, Shell Oil Company, Pennzoil Company, and Enron Corporation each contributed at least $250,000. AT&T, which had earlier helped finance Democratic convention events, contributed $450,000 in cash and in kind contributions to the Republicans. Texaco, Inc., Occidental Chemical Corporation, and Tenneco Corporation all contributed at least $100,000.

At the climactic moment of an elaborate reception hosted by Atlantic Richfield (Arco), a small "Victory Train" appeared and chugged noisily into the crowd. Waving happily to the exclusive group from the caboose were none other than President George Bush and Vice President Dan Quayle.

Kaplan and *Legal Times* also reported other corporate celebrations, such as the *four* separate parties thrown for Senate Minority Leader Robert Dole of Kansas by RJR Nabisco, Southern Pacific Transportation Company, Coastal Corporation, and the Pharmaceutical Manufacturers Association. No industry had a higher profile than the major tobacco companies. Besides the RJR Nabisco affair for Dole, U.S. Tobacco reportedly flew former President Gerald R. Ford in for a breakfast. Philip Morris was a key sponsor of a major luncheon attended by Bush and Quayle, as well as a separate event at which Quayle and Housing and Urban Development

Secretary Jack Kemp spoke. The Houston convention manager was former Bush aide and senior vice president of Philip Morris, Craig Fuller (who worked in 1995 as campaign manager for Republican presidential aspirant Pete Wilson).

These tobacco companies, as well as BellSouth Corporation; Goldman, Sachs and Company, and Paine Webber Inc., sponsored events at *both* the Democratic and Republican conventions. Large corporations frequently hedge their political bets; in the end, party loyalty is ancillary to bottom-line commercial concerns.

The 1996 Campaign

The role of money in political parties is spiralling upward every year, and the soft-money donations to the Democrats and Republicans in 1996 will be substantial. The Democratic party convention in Chicago and the Republican party convention in San Diego will be lavish, corporate hospitality suite and reception affairs, and each of the major candidates will make dozens of personal appearances before their contributors in the span of four short days.

The last thing any of the candidates or their campaigns want to do is alienate the large corporate and individual donors who have the power to help buy them the keys to the White House. Of course, for the two likely party nominees arriving in San Diego and Chicago to be chosen by the convention delegates, the process of ingratiating themselves to the party's financial kingpins began long ago.

Bill Clinton

There is probably no case more instructive of the intersection of private and public interest and the incestuousness of Arkansas business and political elites than that somewhat complicated affair known as Whitewater. When Clinton was attorney general of Arkansas in 1978, he and Hillary Rodham got into a real estate deal with James B. McDougal and his wife, Susan, to develop 230 acres along the White River in Madison County. An unsecured loan of $20,000 was made by a Little Rock bank to Hillary Rodham as a down payment, and Governor Clinton later hired fellow investor McDougal onto the public payroll. To add conflict upon conflict, McDougal purchased a thrift, Madison Guaranty, represented by Hillary Clinton before state regulators.[1]

In what might be the clearest *quid pro quo* for McDougal, Governor Clinton apparently cleared the way for state agencies to move into a building owned by the S&L, for which they paid an estimated $200,000 in yearly rent. The Associated Press discovered an April 23, 1987 memo that recounted allegations made by Greg Hopkins, an attorney working for former Madison official Charles Peacock III.[2] The memo said, "Mr. Hopkins stated that a portion of the loan proceeds made to Dixie Continental leasing [Mr. Peacock's company] went to Bill Clinton's campaign, and that in return for the substantial campaign contribution, Bill Clinton assured Jim McDougal that a state agency would lease space from Madison at its headquarters on Main Street in Little Rock."

The Arkansas Development Finance Authority (ADFA),

headed by longtime Clinton aide Bob Nash (who served as director of presidential personnel in the Clinton White House), subsequently moved into the building despite protests from within the agency. Other state agencies were also housed in the building.

No one in Arkansas officialdom or the news media noticed anything peculiar about any of these dealings. As Arkansas columnist John Brummett observed, "Bill Clinton's Arkansas was a place without an opposing party, with a press that was . . . lax for years in coverage of the underlying financial angle of politics, with politicians and business people who had overlapping and sometimes intimately curious associations."[3]

President Clinton declined to be interviewed for this book or to respond to written questions submitted by the Center for Public Integrity.

In the context of this book, the point of Whitewater and Bill Clinton's public service career in Arkansas is that long before the presidential election of 1992, his political identity as an accommodator of the largest, most powerful monied

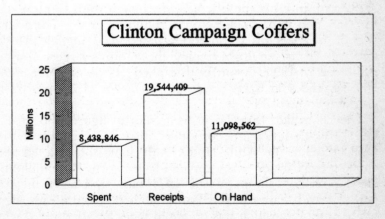

Reporting through September 30, 1995.

Spent figures include all purchases or payments made in connection with or for the purpose of influencing a federal election.
Receipts are anything of value received by a political committee.
On Hand figures include funds held in checking and savings accounts, certificates of deposit, petty cash funds, travelers checks, treasury bills, and other investments valued at cost.

interests was well established. While he was governor, millions of dollars in private favors at public expense accrued to various companies and individuals, and Clinton's professional career as a politician was supported by the Arkansas financial and political elites.

Clinton in Arkansas

Bill Clinton, who grew up without much money, has always understood the political importance of raising substantial campaign funds. What is most striking about his first campaign is how a 28-year-old assistant professor of law in Fayetteville, Arkansas, running for a seat in the Congress for the first time, could raise more money than the incumbent four-term Republican congressman. During that 1974 election Clinton raised $178,000, about $20,000 more than John Hammerschmidt, from traditional Democratic party sources.[4]

In 1974 as well as 1992, candidate Clinton has actually embraced powerful corporate interests and much of their agenda despite his rhetoric against them. When Clinton ran for Congress in 1974 the largest employer in the Third District of Arkansas was Tyson Foods, based in Springdale, which was well on its way to becoming the nation's largest poultry producer. In 1995, Tyson Foods ranked "110th on the *Fortune* 500 list, and sold 6,000 products in 57 countries, from fresh chickens to taco fillings."[5]

The chairman, Don Tyson, is a colorful figure who in the late 1970s designed his corporate office as a replica of the Oval Office in the White House, with doorknobs shaped like chicken eggs. Tyson was estimated to be worth $800 million.[6] He supported Clinton in the 1974 race, and according to author David Maraniss, the Tyson family donated a campaign telephone bank which was operated from an apartment near the University of Arkansas, although it should be noted that no such "in-kind" contribution was reported by the campaign to the Federal Election Commission. Clinton never talked much about the company itself publicly, but instead spoke empathetically about the plight of chicken farmers.

The Tyson-Clinton relationship continued in Washington,

of course, and it grew out of a special culture. Probably no one has better captured the real essence of the political-financial nexus in Arkansas than journalist Michael Kelly, who wrote that Arkansas

> ... has been ruled for almost all of its existence, and is largely ruled still, by a thin upper crust of Democratic party officials and Democratic legislative leaders and important landholders and businessmen. This elite, bound together not by party or even ideology but by mutually advantageous relationships, holds sway over a small and politically disorganized middle class and a large but well-beaten population of the poor. The contradiction is that Arkansas voters, in a class-based reaction against this condition, perpetually favor politicians who are "common" in touch, populist in theology, and reformist in policies.[7]

To be plausible and acceptable to the political and financial elite of Arkansas, a politician certainly can and must relate well to the people. But he or she must not substantially interfere with the daily commerce of the state, the business status quo. Every candidate in Arkansas instinctively knows this or learns it the hard way. Such is the theater into which Bill Clinton's political career was born.

Even though Clinton narrowly lost in his first race in 1974, Tyson was impressed. He backed Clinton in his successful race in 1976 for attorney general, and in 1978 when Clinton was elected the youngest governor in the United States, at the age of thirty-two. But before financially supporting his candidacy in 1978, Tyson had a private talk with Clinton. Tyson wanted the young politician to do a favor for him and his company, one that amounted to a deal worth millions of dollars. He wanted to get the state legal truck-weight limit raised from 73,000 to 80,000 pounds, enabling Arkansas poultry and trucking interests to better compete with out-of-state companies. According to Tyson, Clinton assured him he would get the limit changed. "Bill promised a bunch of us that he'd raise the weight limit on trucks. Damn right he did. He promised me, personally, in my car driving to the airport three or four months before the election. . . . He said he'd take care of it."[8]

Tyson was thrilled with the 1978 election day results. He was so supportive of the young politician that before the swearing-in, Tyson hosted a pre-inaugural party for Clinton at the Camelot Hotel.[9] But the thrill was gone very quickly.

Governor Clinton wasn't able to deliver Tyson's truck-weight change and Tyson was livid, convinced that Clinton "never even tried to get it through."[10] That wasn't the last of Clinton's first-term mistakes. Clinton not only alienated Tyson and the poultry industry, but the trucking companies, the timber interests, and the utilities. In 1980, all of these power-ful forces supported Clinton's opponent, Republican Frank White, and the youngest governor in the nation suddenly became the youngest ex-governor.

Tyson, the Stephens family, Arkansas Power and Light, Southwestern Bell, and much of the Arkansas business community actively worked to defeat Clinton. The loss made a profound impact on him. Over a period of weeks and months, in conversations with Tyson attorney James Blair and a savvy woman he had met during the McGovern Texas campaign, Betsey Wright, Clinton had an epiphany that "to be successful, a politician had to appear hugely concerned with bettering the lives of ordinary citizens, but had to be careful to avoid acting on those concerns so aggressively that they threatened the interests of the business elite . . . Clinton pondered how he could win votes as a populist reformer and still raise money as a businessman's Democrat."[11]

Brownie Ledbetter, a longtime civic activist and president of the Arkansas Fairness Council, knew and worked with Clinton for years. She told the Center for Public Integrity, "He began seeing himself as a mediator between and among various factions." Arkansas progressives began to see Clinton's positions become milder, and the young politician was transforming before their eyes from a crusader into an accommodator. "It was a heartbreaker. I felt very disappointed," Ledbetter said.

In 1982, a humbled Clinton was returned to the governor's mansion in Arkansas, and from 1983 until he resigned as governor in order to seek his party's nomination for president, Clinton never really threatened the interests of the business elite, in some cases directly servicing them. Almost immediately upon becoming governor again in 1982, Clinton found a way to get the truck-weight limit increased to 80,000 pounds, by coupling it with a special tax on the heaviest trucks to pay for anticipated road damage. Tyson was delighted. His investment in politician Clinton has repaid itself a thousand times over. As the state's largest employer with 22,000 workers, Tyson Foods received roughly $12 million in tax breaks during the years Clinton was governor.[12]

In 1984 and in subsequent races, Tyson backed Clinton, not only at election time, but by allowing the governor to travel frequently on the Tyson corporate jet, picking up the tab on expensive meals, among other favors.

For her part, Hillary Rodham Clinton was ensconced in the old, established Little Rock Rose law firm, which represented Tyson and other important corporate and financial interests in the state, including Stephens Inc., and Wal-Mart, among many others. It was Tyson's attorney, James Blair, who helped her make close to a 10,000 percent return on a $1,000 play in commodities trading. Blair had approached her with the "sure-thing" investment in October 1978, when Clinton was thirty points ahead of his opponent, a virtual certainty to become Arkansas's next governor.

Clinton achieved modest reforms as governor, from education to ethics, from lobbyist disclosure to minority hiring. It was Clinton who backed a comprehensive ethics and disclosure proposal on the general election ballot in Arkansas in 1988, and it became law. Clinton and his inner circle of advisers, however, exempted themselves from the conflict-of-interest disclosure requirements.[13]

Few of his reforms were opposed by Arkansas's corporate angels. Meanwhile, he and his administration were notably laggard and unaggressive in halting Tyson's polluting of rivers and streams. Clinton, according to Don Tyson, had "started running the state better and learned a few lessons. And, hell, my trucks were running full, 80,000 pounds."[14]

In 1991, a year after promising he would serve a full four-year term as governor if reelected, Clinton announced his candidacy for president of the United States.

The 1992 Presidential Campaign

Money was of paramount concern to the Clinton campaign, which raised more funds than any of the other Democratic challengers prior to the 1992 Iowa caucuses. If Clinton was to be regarded as a "serious" national candidate, then his fundraising base would have to reflect a breadth far beyond Arkansas interests. Wall Street, Hollywood, the high-tech "information highway," telephone, computer, and media conglomerate interests, and many other groups were heavily and successfully solicited.

Campaigning on the phrase "putting people first," Clinton did not accept political action committee (PAC) money, which meant that in the crucial pre-nomination phase he would have to depend on individual donations which are limited to $1,000 each. After the nomination was assured, much of the fundraising energy turned to soft-money donations of $25,000 and larger to the Democratic party, for "get-out-the-vote" and other permissible activities throughout the states which would obviously benefit Clinton.

Clinton was no stranger to Washington or its money politics. In the late 1980s, he had helped to form a conservative Democratic organization known as the Democratic Leadership Council (DLC) and its affiliated think tank, the Progressive Policy Institute (PPI). Headquartered in Washington, and famous for phrases such as "reinventing government," the DLC relied on undisclosed corporate contributions and unlike the Democratic party, generally eschewed labor union policy issues or support.

The most aggressive "anti-Washington" rhetoric in the caucus/primary season was made by candidates Pat Buchanan, Ross Perot, and Jerry Brown. It was not until the summer of 1992 that the apparent nominee of the Democratic party began to strike the same chord. Clinton announced that he planned to end "influence peddling" and "business as usual" in Washington, and the campaign issued a best-selling book of policy positions and ideas under the title *Putting People First*, which said "It's long past time to clean up Washington. On streets where statesmen once strolled, a never-ending stream of money now changes hands—tying the hands of those elected to lead." To the masses, Clinton was portraying himself as an outsider to the seat of power and government.

By contrast, in a study about the presidential candidates and their campaign advisers issued a week after the 1992 New Hampshire primary, the Center for Public Integrity discovered that more than half of Clinton's unpaid campaign advisers were from "inside the Beltway" of Washington. No fewer than six advisers came from the DLC or PPI. During their "day jobs," several of Clinton's unpaid policy advisers got handsome fees from foreign corporations and governments, tobacco companies, the insurance industry, oil and gas firms, investment banks, and other business interests.

Thomas Hoog was a vice chairman of Hill and Knowlton, and a policy adviser to the campaign. Former Carter White House aide Anne Wexler, chairman of the Wexler Group lobbying firm, acted as an adviser to the campaign at the same time her firm catered to the needs of numerous domestic and foreign corporate clients. Samuel "Sandy" Berger, an attorney at Hogan and Hartson who represented Toyota and the embassy of Japan, among others, advised Clinton closely on foreign policy issues, headed the national security transition team, and became White House deputy assistant to the president for national security affairs.[15]

Judging from the people around him it was plain to see that candidate Clinton was continuing the bipartisan Washington practice of putting lobbyists first. According to the Center for Responsive Politics, lawyers and lobbyists were Clinton's biggest campaign contributors in 1992, donating $3.1 million.

Banking and financial interests were not bashful about supporting the Arkansas governor. In 1992, candidate Clinton received at least $853,295 in campaign contributions from the financial sector, according to the Center for Responsive Politics. And the company that produced more than $100,000 and the largest number of individual contributors was the New York–based securities firm Goldman Sachs, whose chairman, Robert Rubin, contributed $27,500 in soft money to the Democratic National Committee and the Democratic Congressional Campaign Committee. Rubin currently is serving in his second cabinet position as treasury secretary. Goldman

Sachs has given Clinton $97,650 over the course of his career (see Top 10 list at the end of this chapter).

On the night he won the presidential election, Bill Clinton talked about a "new beginning," including the "need to reform the political system, to reduce the influence of special interests and give more influence back to the kind of people that are in this crowd tonight." Many in the crowd that night, however, represented special interests.

The Transition

Clinton ate his first supper as president-elect in the nation's capital at the home of his friend Vernon Jordan, a Washington partner at the law firm of Akin, Gump, Strauss, Hauer, and Feld, who also serves on several corporate boards of directors, including at the time RJR Nabisco. He was joined by super-lobbyist colleague and firm co-founder, Robert Strauss, former Democratic party chairman and U.S. Trade Representative. Also present was Ron Brown.

Soon Clinton started appointing his acquaintances to top positions. Jordan became co-chairman of the Clinton transition. Brown was nominated to be secretary of commerce. Veteran corporate lobbyist Howard Paster, head of the Washington office of Hill and Knowlton, joined the transition team and later joined the White House staff. Charlene Barshevsky, a registered foreign agent for Japan, Canada, and Mexico, became the deputy U.S. trade representative. There were many other such appointments, at all levels of the new administration.

Cabinet-level nominees requiring Senate confirmation were all prepared and "handled" by corporate lobbyists in Washington working in the Clinton transition. The Clinton cabinet appointment to draw the most news media attention and criticism was Brown's designation as secretary of commerce. In the 1980s, as a lawyer/lobbyist for Patton, Boggs, and Blow and also as deputy chairman of the Democratic party, Brown's clients included the country of Haiti under the Duvalier regime and about a dozen Japanese electronics companies interested in influencing pending copyright legislation. While party chairman, from early 1989 to late 1992, he continued as a full partner at the firm, and simultaneously engaged in numerous business activities.[16] Brown, who organized an impressive and successful nominating convention for Clinton and had done what no other DNC chairman had done since 1976 in helping to get a Democrat elected president, was rewarded with a cabinet position, commerce, which both parties have used as a plum for prominent fundraisers. Brown was easily confirmed.

The Clinton transition had two offices, in Little Rock and in Washington. It was funded by private contributions totalling $5,197,404, made up of funds from a Little Rock account based on donations of up to $5,000, and a direct-mail-based account located in West Virginia. At one point, the transition team actually organized an elaborate "economic summit," inviting hundreds of business, labor, government, and other leaders from around the nation to give their suggestions to the president-elect.

What public policy issues would dominate the fabled "first 100 days" of the Clinton Administration? Another less polite way of putting the same question was: Which special interests would make the *most* money from Washington's newest regime?

The Inauguration

It was described by President-elect Clinton as the "People's Inaugural." But it is unclear which people he was talking about. More private money was raised and spent for the Clinton inaugural than any previous such event, financed mostly by wealthy individuals and interest groups. Of the estimated $32 million spent on the event, about $14 million came from 192 corporations, individuals, and labor unions that loaned $100,000 each to a special fund. The loans were to be repaid from the sale of tickets, memorabilia, and television rights to inaugural events.

Donors loaning $100,000 to the Presidential Inaugural Foundation included vested interests directly affected by the regulatory process of the government. One such interest was

Loans Given to the 1992 Inaugural Committee

**$100,000 Loans from
Corporations/Labor Unions**

AFLAC, AFSCME, American Bankers Association, American Federation of Teachers COPE, American International Group, Anheiser-Busch, Atlantic Richfield, Beneficial Management, Boeing, Caddell & Conwell, Chevron, Coastal Corporation, Coca-Cola, Communication Workers of America, Consolidated Natural Gas, Discovery Communications, Dyson-Kissner-Moran, Enron, Edward Ricci & Associates, First Boston, Friedkin Industries, Fuqua Capital Corporation, Genentech, General Aviation Manufacturers Association, Gilardi & Co., Gilman Paper Co., Greenwich Capital Markets, Guilford Mills, Inc., Halstead Industries, Household International, IBM, ITT, Int'l Ass'n of Machinists & Aerospace Workers, Jim Walter Corp., Johnson & Johnson, Kal Kan Pet Care, Klett Lieber Rooney & Schorling, The Limited, Loews Clearing Corp. (Tisch family), M & M Mars, Merrill Lynch, Metropolitan Life Insurance, The Money Store, NRG Resources, National Association of Home Builders, National Education Association, New Hampshire Oak, Inc., New York Life Insurance Co., Occidental Petroleum, Paramount Communications, Philips Petroleum, Preston Gates Ellis & Rouvelas Meeds, Primerica Corporation, Proctor & Gamble, Public Securities Association, R & S Associates, Revlon, SGM & PIM Trust, SME, Inc., Shell Oil, Shorenstein Co., Sills, Cummis, Skadden Arps, Springs Industries, Stephens, Inc., Sun Co., Uncle Ben's, United Airlines Airlines, United Auto Workers, United Food & Commercial Workers, Valero Management Co., Warner Music Group, Waste Management, Wells Fargo

LOANS LESS THAN $100,000

Mortgage Insurance Company, Waite, Scheider, Bayless & Chesley

$100,000 Loans from Individuals

Albert Abramson (Bethesda, MD), Steward Bainum (Silver Spring, MD), Bernard Bergreen (New York), Philip Berman (Allentown, PA), William Brandt and Sondra Murphy (Greenwich, CT), Crandall Bowles (Bowles, Hollowell & Connor), Ann Cox Chambers (Atlanta), Barry Diller (Los Angeles), Jeffrey Epstein, Jane Eskind (Nashville, TN), Frederick Field (Los Angeles), Roy Furman (Furman-Selz, New York), Michael Gelman (Chevy Chase, MD), Arthur Goldberg (Somerset, NJ), Morris Goldings (W. Newton, MA), Richard Greenfield (Haverford, PA), T.M. Hoake (Washington, DC), James Hormel (San Francisco), Clifford Hudson (Oklahoma City), Robert Kaplan (New York), Jeanette Hyde (Raleigh, NC), Wallace Hyde (Raleigh, NC), Ayse Manyus Kenmore (Equivest, San Francisco), James Kinsey (America Online), Arthur Kobacker (Columbus, OH), Sidney Kohl (Pam Beach, FL), Joanna Lau(Lau Technologies), Bill Lerach (San Diego), John Moores (Sugar Land, TX), Lawrence O'Brien (Dewey Ballantine), Philip Odeen (BDM International), Jeffrey Picower (Palm Beach, FL), William Rainer (Riverside, CT), Sanford Robertson (San Francisco), Mack Robinson (Atlanta), Christopher Rogers (Washington, DC), Robert Rose (Credit Agricole Futures), Fred Rzepka (Bedford Heights, OH), Alan Sagner (Roseland, NJ), Robert Samuels (W. Hartford, CT), Rich Schibell (Asbury Park, NJ), Sheldon Seevak (Goldman Sachs), David Shaw (New York), Stan Shuman (New York), Jerome Siegel (New York), Leonard Simon (La Jolla, CA), Maurice Sonnenberg (New York), Richard Stern (Chicago), Thomas Tisch (New York), Barrie Wigmore (Goldman Sachs), Herbert Winokur (Greenwich, CT), O.S. Wyatt

---

LOANS LESS THAN $100,000

Lee and Carlie Sorensen Dixon (Washington, DC), Judi Trabulsi (Austin, TX), James Barker (Green, Stewart & Farber), William Dockser (CRI, Rockville, MD), Patrick O'Connor (Minneapolis), Dennis Nixon (International Bank of Commerce), Leah West (West Co.), Roy Spence (GSD&M), Stephen Swid (SCS Communication, New York), A.R. Sanchez (Sanchez-O'Brien Oil & Gas), Andrew Tobias (New York), James Wade (Washington, DC)

Total of all Loans: $14,242,500

---

the law firm Skadden Arps, whose managing partner, Neal McCoy, told *Legal Times,* "We think that in order to be a participant in public life, it was desirable to make the loan."[17]

The Center for Public Integrity was able to obtain the names of those who loaned $14 million to the inaugural foundation and the amounts they loaned, despite the fact that the Presidential Inaugural Foundation refused to disclose the information. Virtually all of the interests had business with the federal government.

The inaugural had a "for-profit" feel to it. The Disney Channel sponsored and exclusively broadcast two children's events at the Kennedy Center. The television networks had a prime-time gala evening also, broadcast by CBS, produced by the Inaugural Committee, which sold advertising time directly to Ford Motor Company, Anheuser-Busch, and many others.[18] Tens of thousands of people who gathered in front of the Lincoln Memorial couldn't see the Abraham Lincoln statue because of the hundreds of ticket-payers occupying seats on rows of makeshift bleachers, watching performances being televised on HBO.

The president-elect's half-brother, Roger Clinton, got into the act. A professional singer who arguably should not have quit his day job, he made his first appearance on live national television crooning with his band at the MTV Rock and Roll Inaugural Ball. Roger Clinton signed a $200,000 record contract with Time Warner's Atlantic Records.

Meanwhile, Commerce Secretary–designate Ron Brown gave his assent to a Kennedy Center "Friends of Ron Brown" gala paid for by dozens of large corporations and unions each ponying up $10,000 to honor him. First reported by the *Los Angeles Times* and followed up by other papers, the event was personally canceled by Bill Clinton, who overruled the objections of Brown and said, "There's a big difference between being chairman of a political party where people may be supporting your political party or the other one and having a Commerce job where you actually make decisions.... That made it a very different issue."[19]

Time magazine called the Clinton inauguration "a multimillion-dollar corporate sponsorfest" which was in stark contrast with his "folksy campaign."[20] Although it has not previously been reported, the Clinton/Gore inaugural forces raised a remarkable *$42 million*. After all the bills and loans were taken care of, the inaugural committee had made a profit of $9.7 million.

At the end of the "People's Inaugural," William Jefferson Clinton was sworn in as president of the United States, and in his relatively short inaugural address said, "Let us resolve to reform our politics, so that power and privilege no longer shout down the voice of the people ... Let us give this capital back to the people to whom it belongs."

The Franchise Presidency?

During the final two weeks of the transition, Clinton and his closest advisers had realized that his campaign promises had been unrealistic and economically impossible. There was no money in the national budget and ignoring that fact would alienate Wall Street. Clinton did not take the stark news well. His "face turned red with anger and disbelief. 'You mean to tell me that the success of the program and my reelection hinges on the Federal Reserve and a bunch of fucking bond traders?' " Suddenly the campaign was truly over, and it was soberingly clear that populist platitudes would no longer play in the money power centers of New York and Washington.[21] A new course was charted to accommodate the largest banks, brokerages, and corporations nationwide that would lead some critics to dub him a "Republicrat."

The Clinton administration has pursued and serviced the American business community more aggressively and more systematically than any previous administration. Clinton assiduously courted corporate support for his economic program after he arrived at 1600 Pennsylvania Avenue. Individual aides—White House officials Mack McLarty and political director Rahm Emanuel, Robert Rubin and public liaison chief Alexis Herman—were given assignments.[22]

It hasn't just been companies that have been accommodated, but the lobbyists who represent them as well. Herman, the former DNC chief of staff to Ron Brown, would meet on Wednesdays with a select group of Washington lobbyists, some who had served in previous administrations, that she has called "a gathering of elders"—Michael Berman of the Duberstein Group; Robert Healy, top Washington lobbyist for ARCO; Jody Powell, former Carter White House aide now with his own firm, Powell Tate; and Anne Wexler of the Wexler Group lobbying firm, among others. Herman considered Wexler a mentor and actually hired her son in the office. The lobbyists have assisted strategically on the NAFTA, the General Agreement on Tariffs and Trade (GATT), and budget legislation.[23] Separately, White House Chief of Staff Leon Panetta frequently has met on Thursdays with Washington lawyers and consultants.

All of the outreach and access is heady to lobbyists, who recall candidate Clinton's promise to "break the stranglehold of special interests" on Washington. Red Cavaney, former Reagan White House official and president of the American Plastics Council, said the administration's relationships with lobbyists are "as good as I've ever seen in my 20-odd years of doing this, in terms of their willingness to sit down and discuss issues." A Washingtonian since 1970, Edward P. Faberman, the top lobbyist for American Airlines, echoed the sentiment, "I don't remember an administration that has given as much opportunity . . . to discuss issues and work with them."[24]

As president, Clinton has talked about ethics and lobbying more than any chief executive in recent memory. He issued an executive order banning executive branch trade officials from going to work for foreign interests. He initiated the elimination of the long-standing tax deduction for lobbying. And he directed the attorney general to draft an executive order preventing anyone who has not disclosed their clients from lobbying the executive branch. The most significant administration initiatives to reform the campaign finance system and impose stricter lobbying disclosure, however, were defeated in the Democratic Congress in late 1994, largely because they were not a top legislative priority for Clinton.

Clinton embraced the access-and-influence Rolodex culture of Washington, to which elected federal officials become beholden because they all require huge sums of campaign cash. (On election night, 1994, outside of camera view, the president watched the sobering returns at the White House with, among others, the ultimate Washington insider and Democratic fundraiser, lobbyist Tommy Boggs.) Not surprisingly, the president opted to go slow on pushing campaign finance reform, ostensibly so as not to interfere with his other domestic programs, such as health care, in the Congress. Ironically, it was multibillion-dollar health care interests, pouring roughly $30 million into congressional coffers and spending far, far more than that on advertising and lobbying, that helped to kill health care reform. In May, 1993, during the same week that he introduced his long-awaited, modest campaign finance reform proposal, he also helped his party raise millions of dollars, largely from lobbyists.

Tripping with the Secretary

No administration official has received more attention for working closely with corporate interests than Commerce Sec-

retary Ron Brown, whose business liaison role there is not
vastly different from what it was as chairman of the Democratic party. More than any previous commerce secretary, he
has championed business interests and concerns at every
turn.[25] In speaking up for Brown after the Justice Department
recommended that an independent counsel investigate his
financial dealings, President Clinton said Ron Brown's leadership had resulted in "expanded opportunities for American
businesses in this country and abroad." By all appearances,
Brown's Department of Commerce continued to apply the art
of the deal the secretary had learned as a lobbyist and as
chairman of the Democratic party. American giants such as
AT&T and ARCO, among others, which made contributions
to the DNC or the 1992 Clinton campaign, got seats on
Brown's plane when he traveled to far-off lands to meet with
foreign governments in an effort to promote American
business.

A Center for Public Integrity database of the trips, compiled from the available information—showing who went on
them, how much they or their companies contributed to the
Democrats or the Clinton campaign, what deals they made
and whether they got additional support from the Overseas
Private Investment Corporation (OPIC) or the Export-Import
Bank—indicates that at least 187 companies participated in
fourteen trade missions.[26] Sixty-seven of those companies, just
less than 40 percent, contributed to the Democrats, not including contributions to congressional candidates. Between
1993 and 1994, at least twenty-six of the companies, or
roughly 14 percent, received OPIC or Ex-Im support totalling
$5.6 billion. Five companies got at least $2.6 billion. Those
five—Enron, U.S. West, GTE, McDonnell Douglas, and
Fluor—gave a total of $563,000 to the Democrats between
1991 and 1994.

Some information about the trips came to light only after
the Washington-based organization Judicial Watch sued the
Commerce Department and obtained 30,000 pages worth of
documents. They further support the notion that favorable
treatment was given to friends of Ron Brown, Bill Clinton,
and the Democratic party.

One of the illuminating documents is a letter from former

House majority Whip Tony Coelho to Melissa Moss, the director of commerce's office of business liaison and formerly the DNC finance director under Brown. Coelho, who contributed the maximum-allowable $1,000 to the Clintons' defense fund and was an unpaid adviser to the Clinton White House and senior adviser to the DNC until the 1994 election, served as the managing director of the investment banking firm Wertheim Schroder and Company after resigning from Congress under an ethical cloud. In the letter, Coelho expressed his appreciation for Moss' "willingness to help in having our Chairman and CEO, James A. Harmon, invited to participate in the Secretary's trip to China." Coelho was not shy in his letter to Moss, writing, "If you think there is anything more I can or should do to make this happen, including speaking directly to the Secretary, please let me know as this is very important to me."

In August and September of 1994, Ron Brown led a U.S. trade delegation to China. James Harmon was on the plane. Neither Coelho nor Melissa Moss returned calls from the Center for Public Integrity.

Another telling document is a June 1994 interoffice memo to the file at the New Orleans–based Entergy Corporation written by "J.C.B," who made a trip to Washington "to meet with Department of Commerce officials . . . regarding Entergy's China Projects." "J.C.B" was later identified as Chris Brown, business manager for Entergy Power Development Group in Hong Kong.[27] He wrote, "Met with Jude Kearney [deputy assistant secretary for service industries and finance in the International Trade Association at the Commerce Department and a staffer to Clinton when he was governor of Arkansas] regarding Secretary Brown's upcoming trip to China." The memo states that Kearney "indicated competitive nature of being selected to ride on the plane with the Secretary. Also indicated that politics of the situation were important and he as a political appointee would push those that were politically connected." Entergy certainly is "politically connected."

Entergy is the parent company of various U.S. electric companies, including Arkansas Power & Light (AP&L). President Clinton has maintained a long and politically prosperous relationship with AP&L for years. Beryl Anthony, a former Democratic congressman from Arkansas and former chairman of the Democratic Congressional Campaign Committee (DCCC), serves as one of the company's Washington lobbyists. Anthony is a partner at the Washington law and lobbying firm of Winston and Strawn and also represents the Hong Kong Trade Development Council.

In 1992, while Brown was chairman of the party, Entergy contributed $20,000 to the DNC Building Fund. Since 1993, Entergy has contributed $43,000 to the DNC and $20,613 to the DCCC. The Minneapolis *Star-Tribune* reported that Entergy also made a contribution to the Democratic Leadership Council (DLC) at the time that Clinton served as its chairman. Neither Entergy nor the DLC would disclose the amount. Arkansas campaign finance records are sketchy. The bottom line is the Center for Public Integrity has documented at least $83,613 in contributions during the past three years.

It's no surprise that Entergy chairman Ed Lupberger got his boarding pass to travel with Ron Brown to China and Hong Kong. Entergy signed two major contracts while on the China trip with Brown, who attended the first signing ceremony. In November of 1994, President Clinton and Brown led a trade delegation to Indonesia. Entergy also came home with lucrative deals from that trip.

In his press release announcing the deals in China, Entergy's CEO, Ed Lupberger, said, "This is an example of how U.S. business and industry and the governments of China and the U.S. can work together for the mutual benefit of everyone involved." From its China deals alone, Entergy will benefit to the tune of contracts worth an estimated $1.3 billion.

In later testimony before a Senate committee, Brown said press reports about Kearney's involvement and the Commerce Department's having done favors were wrong. "Jude Kearney has categorically denied the content of that [Entergy] memo," Brown said. "I do not think that that has any basis in fact."[28]

There are numerous examples of how companies that did as little as simply throw a cocktail party at the 1992 Democratic convention, to companies that contributed hundreds of thousands of dollars to the campaign and party, also had executives fly with Brown on foreign trips. In each case the company contributions or favors were done during, or subsequent to, Brown's tenure as chairman of the DNC. The companies involved include some of the country's largest.

Executives from the oil company ARCO, the Atlantic Richfield Company, got to go to China, Hong Kong, and South Africa with Brown. ARCO donated $278,317 to the DNC in 1991 and 1992 while Brown was the party chairman and from 1993 through 1994, ARCO gave $164,500 in soft money to the DNC. The total contribution to the Democrats between 1991 and 1994 was $442,817.

The Clinton sales team was in full force on behalf of AT&T in Saudi Arabia. In an April 1994 letter to King Fahd, the president recommended AT&T as the best choice to update that country's phone system, "I hope AT&T, which has long been a market leader, will receive every opportunity to establish itself as Saudi Arabia's preferred partner, both for quality and cost, in this project," Clinton wrote. Two trips to Riyadh by Ron Brown and one by Secretary of State Warren Christopher included pleading the company's case. On May 9, 1994, Saudi Arabia reached out and touched AT&T, choosing them over firms from France, Germany, Canada, and an alliance between a Swedish and a Japanese company. The contract is worth $4 billion.[29] "We've been pleasantly surprised right from the beginning with this administration and Commerce," said William Marx, CEO AT&T Networks.[30]

In 1992, while Brown was chairman of the DNC and head of the convention in New York, AT&T gave $400,000 to the DNC. AT&T executives traveled with Brown to Saudi Arabia, South Africa, Russia, and Indonesia. Not including undisclosed Russia deals, AT&T signed contracts worth at least $4.13 billion.

OPIC and Ex-Im Bank

The Brown trade missions would not have been so successful for some U.S. corporations if it had not been for the special government financing and support available to them from two government-backed entities: The Export-Import

(Ex-Im) Bank of the United States and the Overseas Private Investment Corporation (OPIC). Ex-Im and OPIC provided a total of $39.8 billion in financial backing in 1993 and 1994. President Clinton appointed long-time Arkansas political supporters to both organizations.

Lottie Shackelford, a former mayor of Little Rock, is one of the members of the OPIC board of directors appointed by Bill Clinton in 1993. During the 1992 Clinton-Gore campaign Shackelford held the position of deputy campaign manager, having previously worked in Clinton's first campaign for Congress in 1974. Today she is a vice chairman of the DNC.[31] Since April 1994, Shackelford has also worked as a lobbyist and registered foreign agent for the Washington-based firm, Global U.S.A. The firm is also registered to represent the Westinghouse Corporation.[32] As it turns out, Westinghouse is listed as a client of OPIC for 1994.[33] Shackelford told the Center for Public Integrity that no company represented by her firm had been before OPIC and that if one had been, she would have recused herself, and would not even have been in the room when the company was discussed.[34]

OPIC provides loans and loan guarantees for U.S. companies unable to obtain conventional funding for foreign projects. OPIC's 1994 annual report says direct loans are "reserved for small businesses and cooperatives and generally ranging from $2 million to $30 million."[35] OPIC, however, during 1994 financed loans to major American corporations for much more than the stated $30 million high end. A joint venture by GTE Corporation and AT&T got a $200 million loan from OPIC to finance a cellular telephone services deal in Argentina.[36]

The Export-Import Bank of the United States is headed by Clinton appointee Kenneth D. Brody. Brody was an early Clinton supporter and fundraiser in New York and a former partner of Treasury Secretary Robert Rubin when both were at Goldman Sachs. Ex-Im has played an active role in the Brown trade missions. In fact a bank representative traveled with the official delegations. Clinton also appointed his long-time Arkansas aide, Maria L. Haley, to the Ex-Im board of directors.

"We carry out our mission—to help the private sector create and maintain American jobs—by financing U.S. exports that would not have happened without us," Brody wrote in Ex-Im's 1994 annual report.[37]

S. Lawrence Prendergast, vice president and treasurer of AT&T, was a member of the 1994 Ex-Im Bank Advisory Committee.[38] From 1993 through mid-1995, the Export-Import Bank has guaranteed $917,451,897 in loans for AT&T. The Ex-Im Bank has also made $94,286,107 in loans to AT&T during the same time period.[39]

In 1993, the Ex-Im Bank's Advisory Committee was headed by Warren H. Hollinshead, chief financial officer of the Westinghouse Electric Company. During that same year, Ex-Im awarded $98,075,505 in loan guarantees and $58,348,099 in direct loans to Westinghouse.[40] Ex-Im also provided financing for and loan guarantees to the Westinghouse Corporation from 1993 through mid-1995 worth a total of $572,774,329.[41]

When asked what influence corporate contributions to the DNC might have on Ex-Im financing decisions, Christopher Dorval, Ex-Im's vice president for public affairs, told the Center for Public Integrity, "If you can find one [big donor] that has benefitted from an Export-Import decision, I'd be surprised. I don't believe there's any connection at all."[42]

Roger Altman, Robert Rubin, and Goldman Sachs

With the pressing need to maintain the trust and confidence of Wall Street, a significant force in the new education of Bill Clinton in late 1992 and early 1993 was Robert Rubin, a man worth an estimated $100 million who resigned as co-chairman of Goldman Sachs to join the Clinton administration. Rubin and his wife made a $275,000 contribution from their personal foundation to the New York Host Committee to the Democratic National Convention. Goldman Sachs helped to fund the Clinton campaign for the presidency, with its officers contributing more than $100,000 in so-called "bundled" money. "Bundled" is the term applied to the aggregate contributions of multiple employees of a single company. Rubin had been an effective emissary to Wall Street during the campaign, and that role continued in the administration.

Rubin, Goldman Sachs, and the Clinton crowd go way back. Rubin has known longtime Clinton friend and White House counselor Mack McLarty for a decade, and in the late 1980s, Goldman Sachs helped to underwrite $400 million in bonds for the Arkansas Development Finance Authority (ADFA).[43] Goldman Sachs has enjoyed very good relations, as you might expect, with the Clinton Administration since January 20, 1993. Not only did the firm's co-chairman join the president's cabinet, but Kenneth Brody, a Goldman Sachs general partner until 1991, was appointed by the president to be chairman of the Export-Import Bank.

Goldman Sachs, the president's top career patron, contributed $15,000 to the Democratic party since Bill Clinton's inauguration, and also has ties to the president's legal defense fund, which was begun to defray the Clintons' legal expenses from the Whitewater investigation and a sexual harassment civil lawsuit. Although the Office of Government Ethics looks unkindly on anyone who solicits contributions for the defense fund, a Washington lobbyist for Goldman Sachs, Michael Berman, has raised money for just that purpose maintaining that it was "totally on my hook." The general counsel of the President's Legal Expense Trust was Bernard Aidinoff, whose law firm, Sullivan and Cromwell, has done substantial work for Goldman Sachs, and has contributed $37,600 to Clinton.

Much has already been reported about Robert Rubin and his old firm's interests in Mexico, but there is one point that bears mentioning again. Rubin spearheaded Goldman's move into Mexico, and the firm had steered billions of dollars to that emerging market over the years. The peso crisis of 1993–94 came to a head just as Rubin was becoming treasury secretary. His one-year recusal from dealing in matters affecting Goldman Sachs had ended. By helping Mexico to make good on its commitment to bondholders, the $20 billion U.S. portion of the bailout was viewed by some as a publicly-financed insurance policy for Rubin and Goldman Sachs, along with other large investment houses and banks that were highly exposed in Mexico. Rubin was a partner in the firm and could be civilly liable for claims by investors. Mexico has already used the bailout money to pay back investment banks. If the bailout was not a guarantee, the investment community was further reassured by the "Framework Agreement For Mexican Economic Stabilization," signed by Treasury Secretary Rubin and the Mexican Ministry of Finance on February 21, 1995. The document gave the Department of the Treasury "the right to distribute, in such manner and in such order of priority as it deems appropriate" the Mexican export revenues it now controls. In other words, Robert Rubin had the power to grant first right of payment to whomever he chooses, including the holders of Mexican bonds purchased from Goldman Sachs.

THE SAVINGS AND LOAN DISASTER, RUBIN, AND ALTMAN

Estimates of the cost to the economy of the savings and loan crisis range from $150 billion to $1.3 trillion. When it came time for the Clinton administration to supervise resolution of the debacle, the president put in charge two men who came from the sector that would end up making money off the disaster: Wall Street. Both Rubin and Deputy Treasury Secretary Roger Altman, formerly of the Blackstone Group, joined the administration after their investment banking firms had made millions of dollars in the clean-up of the savings and loan disaster.[44] The government was relying on Wall Street to sell the failed thrifts and Goldman, in particular, was one of the early and biggest players, purchasing "several billion" in assets.[45] Neither Rubin nor Altman was directly involved in their firms' thrift work, but in one case that began while Rubin ran Goldman, a Resolution Trust Corporation (RTC) audit found, in general, that both Goldman Sachs and the RTC behaved improperly in pursuing the deal and concluded that the adverse effects were magnified by the RTC having given Goldman Sachs an increased role as underwriter. Essentially, Goldman Sachs was both buying and selling properties.[46] The RTC was created by an act of Congress in 1989 to clean up the savings and loan mess.[47]

"We believe the $10.1 million in fees that RTC paid to Goldman Sachs for assets that it did not sell were unreasonable."[48]

Roger Altman resigned his position as Deputy Treasury Secretary in August 1994. The resignation followed in the wake of his testimony before the Senate Banking Committee's Whitewater panel about his role in disclosing information to the White House of the RTC's investigation of Madison Guaranty. During a heated House Banking subcommittee hearing on June 19, 1995, Altman denied a close relationship with the institution he directed. "I did not run the RTC on a day-to-day basis. Everybody knows that," said Altman.

But he paid enough attention to make at least one significant decision. Thomas Burnside, a former RTC counsel, wrote, "The RTC's lapses became most pronounced when Roger Altman, the deputy secretary of the treasury, ran the agency from April 1993 until March 1994. Within a month of taking control, he reversed the RTC's longstanding request to Congress to extend the federal statute of limitation on investigating S&L wrongdoing [and prosecuting S&L operators]. He said that the RTC no longer needed any extensions."[49] The RTC was set to close up shop on December 31, 1995, a year before it was originally mandated to do so.

"Everyone knew that to buy RTC properties was to make a lot of money," Burnside said in an interview from his St. Louis law firm. "In fairness to Altman, everybody on Wall Street was doing it." Burnside calculates that the sale of RTC assets was an even bigger problem than the original S&L crisis.

The final chapter in the savings and loan debacle will not be written for years. The relevant point here is that several Wall Street firms have benefitted during the Clinton years. But no financial institution has probably fared better from the Clinton administration than NationsBank.

NationsBank

In December 1994, the *Wall Street Journal* reported, "The Democratic party expects to close 1994 not just with an historic defeat at the polls but with a near-record financial debt that insiders believe will be hard to erase."[50] The debt was $5 million, the biggest debt for the party since 1968, which was followed by more than a decade of digging out.

But the Center for Public Integrity has learned that the

party's debt was evident to the White House in late 1993 and, as was reported being the case in 1994, President Clinton was "furious over the shortfall" because the party fundraising efforts set records in 1993 and 1994 by receiving $70 million.

"Fundraising is still going strong," Terrence McAuliffe, the DNC finance chairman, told the *Wall Street Journal*, "and we are very optimistic about the future because of the fundraising base, especially from the business community, that we've built this year." Part of that was a $3.5 million loan from NationsBank at a very favorable rate of prime plus 1.5 percentage points.

That much-needed loan, we learned, was made two weeks before the mid-term elections, on October 14, 1994, and two weeks after the Democratic Congress passed the Fair Trade in Financial Services Act, signed into law on September 29 by President Clinton, who had worked hard for passage. Stalled for years, the new law allowed financial institutions to operate a single national bank instead of keeping at least one bank branch open in every state they conduct business. No one wanted it more than NationsBank and its president and CEO, Hugh McColl. Indeed, NationsBank lobbyists reportedly helped to draft the legislation.[51] McColl calculated it would save his bank $50 million a year. Critics of the law said big banks would just swallow up small ones.[52]

We learned that candidate Clinton's openness to considering NationsBank's interstate banking legislation apparently was a fundamental *condition* of support for McColl, who endorsed Clinton late in the 1992 campaign after the two had breakfast, and sent a personal check to the campaign for $1,000. McColl declined to talk to us, but his spokesman Joe Martin said, "There were conversations between Bill Clinton and Hugh McColl about banking issues." Martin denied that McColl ever sought a formal or written "pledge" of support for the interstate banking proposal, but "Hugh came to believe that Governor Clinton understood the issues."

In 1992, prior to the breakfast, Clinton campaign officials had unsuccessfully solicited a major Democratic party contribution from NationsBank representatives, who were terribly earnest and specific about candidate Clinton's commitment and policy position on interstate banking "reform." The min-

uet between Clinton and McColl quickened by late 1992, to
the point they eventually became friends.[53] McColl contributed the maximum allowable donation of $5,000 to the Clin-
ton-Gore Presidential Planning Foundation, which had been
set up to defray transition expenses.

McColl has become one of Clinton's closest advisors on
banking issues and Clinton has called McColl "the most en-
lightened banker in America."

On July 15, 1993, following remarks by the president,
McColl spoke at a White House media event to promote Clinton's community development lending program. An *American
Banker* editorial at the time groused that McColl had appointed himself banking's "official mouthpiece . . . on behalf
of bankers everywhere, he endorsed the lending plan, which
is about as bank-friendly as John Dillinger . . . McColl would
endorse any half-baked Clinton idea in return for the White
House's support for interstate branching legislation."[54]

McColl left nothing to chance with Congress either. NationsBank significantly increased its PAC contributions, giving
$626,800 to congressional candidates in 1993–1994, according
to FEC records. In 1991–1992 three NationsBank PACs gave
$513,567.[55]

When McColl and Clinton were seen sitting together in the
NationsBank box at the 1994 Arkansas-Duke NCAA basketball
finals in Charlotte, North Carolina, one banking industry
commentator said of McColl, "Based on what the president
has done for him lately, I would have expected to see Hugh
sitting on his lap . . . In days gone by, political *quid pro quos*
were usually paid off with stuffed ballot boxes. Laws were
passed to stop that sort of chicanery. Now it is done with
money."[56]

While the interstate bill was moving through conference,
on August 23, 1994, Clinton and McColl were present at the
White House Community Development bill signing, and the
president declared, "Today, I'm proud to announce commitment from two of the nation's leading banks to help us in
this effort—$25 million from NationsBank and $50 million
from Bank of America over the next four years."[57] Five weeks
later the interstate banking bill was law; the $3.5 million loan
to the DNC came two weeks afterwards.

Martin said, "As far as we're concerned, [the loan] was just a routine business decision."[58] Martin said that neither he nor McColl nor NationsBank's lead lobbyist knew about the loan before it was made. The DNC's chief financial officer Brad Marshall and chief counsel Joe Sandler insisted that the loan was a legitimate, "arm's-length transaction."[59] They said that the DNC has kept its bank accounts with NationsBank, or a predecessor bank it absorbed, for years. "We felt very fortunate that they made the loan," Marshall said.

"NationsBank has been a pretty important force in the Clinton game plan," Tom Schlesinger, director of the Southern Finance Project, a consumer advocacy group on banking issues, told the Center for Public Integrity. "McColl is a dominant influence on this administration."

Even though Clinton, on signing the bill in the ornate Cash Room at the Treasury Department, said McColl "had a lot to do with my interest in this issue . . . who stayed up with me half the night once," McColl downplays his relationship with Clinton, telling reporters, "While I know the president, it would be an overstatement to say that I have any influence with the president."[60]

At the same time the interstate branch legislation was being lobbied by McColl and NationsBank, in May 1994 Clinton White House Senior Adviser George Stephanopoulos, who makes $125,000 a year, received a controversial 25-year, $668,000 loan at 6.375 percent interest from NationsBank. By industry standards, Stephanopoulos would appear to be unqualified for the loan based on his salary and net worth. In an interview with the Center for Public Integrity, Stephanopoulos said that charges of preferential treatment from NationsBank "are totally false." Administration ethics officers found nothing untoward, and NationsBank described the loan as routine. Regarding the interstate branch banking legislation, Stephanopoulos said that "I didn't work on the bill at all."[61]

The NationsBank relationship with Clinton is just one example of what to look for with respect to the financial industry's influence on the president and his party generally in 1996. In 1992, the Clinton/Gore campaign received more than $800,000 from financial interests.

The Telecommunications Companies

Of course, the financial industry has not been the only business group to capitalize on the Clinton Washington bonanza. Many of the nation's high-tech industries supported his candidacy. By late September, 1992, the campaign boasted that it had signed up no fewer than two hundred leaders of "fast-growing, 21st century, high-tech kinds of companies."[62]

During the 1992 campaign and as vice president–elect, Al Gore advocated a nationwide fiber-optic "information highway" as a *public* investment project, meeting the needs of not only companies, but also of schools, libraries, and public health facilities. He said he did not believe a *privately* funded, managed, and controlled electronic superstructure that would revolutionize our daily lives would ultimately serve the public interest. In December 1992, at the economic summit in Little Rock, Gore outlined his vision of the information superhighway as a publicly funded system along the lines of the public works projects of the 1930s and the interstate highway development of the 1950s. "[W]ith the advanced, high-capacity network, like the National Research and Education Network, it does seem to me that government ought to play a role in putting in place that backbone, just as no private investor was willing to build the interstate highway system, but, once it was built, then a lot of other roads connected to it. This new, very broad-band high-capacity network . . . ought to be built by the federal government and then transitioned into private industry."[63]

A year later, on December 21, 1993, Gore outlined a completely different vision: "Unlike the interstates, the information highways will be built, paid for, and funded by the private sector . . . And so I am announcing today that the administration will support removal, over time, under appropriate conditions, of judicial and legislative restrictions on all types of telecommunications companies: Cable, telephone, utilities, television, and satellite."[64] Gore added that the administration would encourage private investment.[65]

Gore's dramatic reversal got little media play, but did not go unnoticed by the telecommunications industry. On the exact date of his speech, Gore's Democratic party received

$92,000 in soft-money contributions from key industry players. MCI wrote twenty-three checks to the DNC between 1991 and 1994, averaging $11,696.96 per check. Among those checks was one for $50,000, written on December 21, 1993, the same day that Gore changed his position. On the following day, MCI kicked in another $20,000. Other major donors to the Democrats that busy day were Comptel, $2,000; NYNEX, $15,000 with another $10,000 the following day; Sprint, $15,000; and U.S. West, $10,000. Total giving over the two-day period from the industry was $132,000. Earlier that month, Bell Atlantic, whose average annual soft-money donation to the Democrats is $10,000, made a $50,000 contribution to the Democratic party on December 7, 1993.

The electronic technology *cognoscenti* certainly understood what had happened. Alan Pearce, a Washington economic consultant who served as the senior policy telecommunications adviser to President Carter, chief economist at the Federal Communications Commission (FCC), and economist for the House Telecommunications subcommittee, told us, "Between November [1992] and April [1993] Gore had done a 180 on public funding of the superhighway."

Gore declined to talk to the Center for Public Integrity, but Greg Simon, the vice president's chief domestic policy advisor, told us flatly, "There is no 180 degree switching" by the administration. But it was clear that the Clinton/Gore administration had modified its ambitions. "In terms of building the superhighway, there's really not a way for the government to build the big picture superhighway," Simon said.[66] As the administration had learned in other cases, campaign rhetoric collided with the budgetary realities of governance.

When asked about all of the telecommunication industry contributions made the same day as Gore's important policy speech, Simon bristled. "If our policy is following our politics then we really fucked up. There's no one-to-one correlation [of money to policy] that I'm aware of, especially any rumors of any money given anywhere on any given day of his speech."

That may well be, but it is also relevant that in the late 1980s and early 1990s, then-Senator Gore was a strong and active lawmaker on behalf of the phone companies. In 1989

and 1991, he introduced legislation that could potentially
bring the industry millions of dollars in new revenues by
allowing telephone companies to enter into cable television
service. Gore said, "deregulation [of the cable industry] has
allowed too many cable companies to gouge consumers and
has left too many consumers as unprotected victims."[67] At
one point, in 1991, Gore publicly criticized the largest cable
company, Tele-Communications Industry, Inc. (TCI), as an
unfair monopoly, and referred to TCI chairman John Malone
as "Darth Vader."[68]

From 1983 through 1990, the Tennessee senator received
$60,950 in campaign contributions from telephone compa-
nies, including Bell Atlantic. So in the early months of 1993,
as the cash-rich telephone companies began intensively lobbying the new administration, the industry and one of its
leaders, Bell Atlantic, sought out the Vice President. Gore
had been designated by President Clinton as the administration leader formulating telecommunications policy on the information superhighway.

Gore was "impressed" by a policy paper written by Bell
Atlantic CEO Ray Smith and a colleague. It called for a privately funded and controlled information highway, unfettered
by government restriction or regulation. A meeting was held
between Gore and representatives of the Regional Bell Operating Companies (RBOCs), on April 15, 1993. In the meeting, as echoed in the policy paper, Smith offered to pump
$125 billion into the data highway if, and only if, it was a
private project. Two weeks after the meeting, Smith said his
position was "Lift all the restrictions and we'll invest $125
billion in the data highway by the end of the decade . . . keep
the restrictions and we could only afford $25 billion."[69]

Ray Smith wouldn't talk, but Bell Atlantic spokesperson Jay
Grossman said of the meeting, "Ray would wrestle down anyone who was willing to listen to his vision." Gore aide Simon
added, "Ray Smith has no special relationship with the vice
president that is a unique one. He hasn't met with him more
than anyone else. The long distance people, the cable people,
the broadcast people, the public interest people, each of
those groups have met with the vice president in one form
or another."

Gore's chief of staff at the time was Roy Neel. Just a few months later he left to represent the RBOCs as the executive director of the Baby Bells' Washington-based lobbying organization, the U.S. Telephone Association.

The pressure and peddling from the phone companies continued during the week of the meeting. They descended on Washington wired with their policy paper and money, $34,000 given to the DNC: Bell Atlantic gave $7,500; BellSouth chipped in $5,500; MCI dialed up $15,000; and Southwestern Bell accounted for $6,000.

Foreshadowing the administration flip-flop to come, the president's nominee to head the Commerce Department's National Information Infrastructure Administration, Larry Irving, testified at his confirmation hearing on May 25, "I do not believe that the government should own, operate, or manage telecommunications or information networks that compete with the private sector."

Telecom contributions to the DNC jumped that week, with a total of $16,790 coming from the key authors of the industry policy statement. Ray Smith's Bell Atlantic, the most outspoken lobbyist, kicked in a $12,500 share.

Beyond the general issue of public vs. private funding of the information highway, economist Pearce told us, "The *quid pro quo* was to take away the restrictions on RBOCs which keep them out of the long distance market." In 1995, the Republican-controlled Congress removed those restrictions, by preliminarily passing and sending to conference the historic, sweeping telecommunications legislation.[70]

Of all the companies that will benefit from the new telecom laws, perhaps none has sought to become more "vertically integrated" than the Walt Disney Company. In the summer of 1995, Disney bought Capital Cities/ABC for $19 billion. In August of 1995, the company announced that it had hired superagent Michael Ovitz—who has put together deals involving Bell Atlantic, Nynex, and Pacific Telesis to produce shows and deliver them over home telephone lines—to become its president, and serve under Disney Chairman Michael Eisner.[71] Disney had formed a similar relationship with Ameritech, BellSouth, SBC Communications (formerly Southwestern Bell).[72] "Most significantly," the *New York Times* reported, "the move concentrates power even further among a handful of men, who will control not just the movie and television businesses but also enhance their influence over broader popular culture through their dominance of theme parks, publishing, and emerging new forms of interactive home entertainment expected to blend films, computer services, and telecommunications."[73]

In 1992, according to FEC records, the three media entertainment conglomerates to contribute the most to the Democrats were Time Warner, which gave $515,114 to the 1992 Democratic national convention; veteran donor Lew Wasserman of MCA, who gave $260,000; and four executives of the Walt Disney Corporation—Michael Eisner, Jeffrey Katzenberg (who has since left), John F. Cook, and the late Frank Wells—who together contributed $158,672 to the DNC. Additionally, Katzenberg gave $5,000 to the transition fund.

Disney donated another $50,000 to the Democratic party in the 1992 election year.[74] Disney donated no money to the Republican National Committee in 1992. The Clinton campaign didn't accept PAC contributions, but eighteen individual donors from Disney gave a total of at least $7,800, second only to sixteen Time-Warner employees who gave at least a combined $11,000.[75]

While the president has carefully cultivated liberal, wealthy Democrats who comprise the media industry in Southern California, Clinton has simultaneously courted the multibillion-dollar weapons manufacturers.

Defense Dollars and Deal Making

Despite the president's previous anti-war inclinations and his much-publicized avoidance of military service, President Clinton has consistently backed policies favorable to the defense industry. In February of 1995, the administration announced that for the first time it would consider the financial state of U.S. defense contractors when negotiating overseas arms sales. The administration has also pushed to relax export restrictions on high-tech equipment used to manufacture sophisticated weapons systems. Part of what has ingratiated the Clinton administration to weapons manufacturers has been the presence of William J. Perry, first as deputy secretary and later as secretary of defense.

Perry is a former defense consultant who headed Technology Strategies and Alliances (TSA) between 1985 and 1993. TSA's 1994 clients included Boeing, Grumman, Lockheed, Martin Marietta, McDonnell Douglas, Northrop, Textron, Texas Instruments, TRW, Westinghouse, and twenty other defense contractors.[76] While Perry severed his ties with the company, he had amassed more than a million dollars in consulting fees from TSA's clients. Not long after he joined the Defense Department, Perry began going to bat for the industry.

One of Deputy Defense Secretary Perry's extra base hits came when he and then–Defense Undersecretary for Acquisitions and Technology John Deutch quietly agreed to provide U.S. defense contractors with taxpayer-financed subsidies for mergers and acquisitions. That was a dramatic shift in Pentagon policy. Usually, such issues are taken before Congress. Instead, Deutch, in a July 21, 1993 memo, reversed the Pentagon's ban on the subsidies and underwrote $270 million worth of TSA client Martin Marietta's acquisition of General Electric's Aerospace Division.[77] Just seven weeks earlier, on June 3, 1993, industry CEOs, including Martin Marietta's Norman Augustine, had sent a letter to Perry and Deutch asking for DOD funding of "restructuring costs" for mergers and acquisitions. Perry also approved Northrop's $2.1 billion acquisition of Grumman. Both were TSA clients. The Pentagon called the policy shift a "clarification" that did not require congressional consent.[78]

Three weeks before the Augustine letter, General Electric, which had just sold Martin Marietta (now Lockheed Martin) its aerospace business, gave $25,000 in soft money to the DNC. Between 1993 and 1994 the company donated $101,500 to the party. In April and May of 1993, Martin Marietta pitched in $18,000 to the DNC and DCCC. FEC records indicate, its total for the election cycle was $49,250.

The policy shift required both Perry and Deutch to seek ethics waivers from rules that call for a one-year "cooling off" period before Pentagon officials can deal with former clients.

They got them from then–Defense Secretary Les Aspin, whom Perry replaced in February 1994. Paul Kaminski got an ethics waiver in November of 1994, when he was named to head the Pentagon's acquisitions and technology department, replacing Deutch. Deutch remained in the Pentagon loop a while longer and became deputy secretary of defense before moving to the CIA. Kaminski, who worked at TSA, is responsible for awarding $43 billion in defense programs to Pentagon contractors.[79] The Kaminski appointment marked the first time former defense industry consultants filled the Pentagon's top three policy posts.[80]

While the Pentagon was busy waiving ethical guidelines and rewriting the rules for funding corporate mergers, Commerce Secretary Ron Brown was out touting the virtues of U.S. weapons systems and pushing to deregulate licensing requirements for weapons-related technology exports, helping an industry that has been generous in return.[81]

Between 1993 and 1994, thirteen of the nation's largest defense contractors gave $448,500 in soft-money contributions to the DNC, compared to $328,340 to the RNC. During fiscal year 1993, the United States actively brokered $59.915 billion of arms exports, a large percentage of which went to developing countries.[82]

Brown's unabashed advocacy has generated claims that promoting big defense business is coming at the expense of other concerns, namely global weapons proliferation. Last year, the General Accounting Office chastised the Commerce and State Department for granting export licenses to repeat violators of U.S. arms and exporting laws. Brown has maintained that his policy "strikes the critical balance between nonproliferation concerns and economic interests."[83] Brown also aggressively promoted U.S. arms manufacturers by opening a pavilion at the annual Paris Air Show, the industry's international bazaar.[84]

Brown has also promoted defense contractors on his trade missions and a $1.4 billion Raytheon deal in Brazil was cited by Brown before Congress as proof of the indispensable role Commerce plays in assisting American companies.[85] The Sivam project Raytheon successfully bid on, or the Amazon Surveillance System, would build a network of radar and satellite stations designed to monitor two million square miles of Brazil's rain forest.[86]

In June of 1994, Commerce learned that the contract was about to go to a French company. The department kicked into gear, getting ten U.S. agencies to lobby Brazilian contacts on Raytheon's behalf *and* to convince a reluctant Ex-Im Bank to top the French financing proposal by underwriting the deal with $1.4 billion in credit despite Brazil's poor credit history.[87] According to one Ex-Im spokesman, the generous financing package was "by far the largest subsidy Ex-Im has ever made."[88]

Raytheon had been generous to the Democrats. During the 1991–1992 election cycle, Raytheon and its subsidiary, Beech Aircraft Co., gave $181,450 to the Democratic party and $104,875 to the Republicans. In January of 1995, after winning the Sivam deal, Raytheon kicked in another $15,000 to the DNC, according to FEC records.

In 1994, the same year Raytheon was vying for the Brazilian contract, Saudi Arabia chose Boeing and McDonnell Douglas over European Airbus to share a $6 billion jetliner order after President Clinton had called King Fahd on August 17, 1993, and urged him to buy American.[89] McDonnell Douglas contributed $95,850 to the Democratic party and Boeing gave $307,950 between 1991 and 1994, according to FEC records.

Or take the case of Vice President Al Gore and Export-Import Bank chairman Ken Brody, who in 1994 along with others in the administration urged the Czech Republic to award Westinghouse a contract to finish building a nuclear power plant. The Czechs are funding the overhaul using a U.S.–backed loan worth $317 million from the Export-Import Bank. Gore, who as a senator wrote a bestselling environmentalist book entitled *Earth in the Balance,* supported the loan and contract, reasoning that if Westinghouse did not get the contract, it would have gone to a Western European firm instead.[90] The contract caused some tensions, not only between the administration and environmentalists, but also with the government of Austria, which believed the facility, located roughly 100 miles upwind from Vienna, posed an environmental hazard. Westinghouse contributed $140,400 to the Democratic party in 1991–1992, according to FEC records.

Most Americans generally support the idea of U.S. officials assisting American firms abroad. But which companies are "serviced" first, or most, by the administration? Corporate interests have no doubt discerned that their "loyalty" to the current regime, quantitatively measured in terms of cold cash contributed to the Democratic party, is frequently rewarded.

All of this attention to the needs of America's largest trading corporations is a bone in the throat to millions of union workers nationwide, who helped get the Arkansas governor elected in 1992 and then watched him enthusiastically ramrod two of George Bush's trade agreements through the Democratic-controlled Congress. But labor has not been left out.

Clinton and Labor

Clinton's staunch support of the North American Free Trade Agreement and the General Agreement on Tariffs and Trade was not particularly surprising to anyone familiar with his business-labor positions in Arkansas, or his status as a founder of the conservative, heavily corporate-funded Democratic Leadership Council (DLC). As early as November and December 1992, two of Mexico's paid lobbyists worked in the Clinton presidential transition. Joe O'Neill helped his old boss, Senator Lloyd Bentsen, set up his office as treasury secretary, while at the same time he and his firm, Public Strategies, were making more than $30,000 a month to lobby for Mexico. Gabriel Guerra-Mondragon and his firm, Guerra and Associates, were on retainer to Mexico while he served as a transition adviser to the president-elect on national security issues.[91]

Governor Bill Clinton was not exactly beloved by organized labor in Arkansas, and the AFL-CIO Executive Council endorsed him for president only after he had secured the nomination. Nonetheless, from 1991 through 1994, labor unions nationwide continued their traditional support for the Democratic party, contributing $7.8 million, according to public records.[92]

NAFTA was one of the most bitter, divisive debates in Washington in years, and many union leaders are still angry over what they saw as a fundamental betrayal by Bill Clinton and his "New Democrats" of basic job-security concerns. To them, Clinton and Gore did the bidding for hundreds of multimillion-dollar corporations operating or seeking to operate cheap labor facilities south of the U.S. border, and no NAFTA proponent denied that there wouldn't be some "displacement" following enactment of the agreement.

Beyond the polarized trade issue, what is not generally understood is how the rapproachment occurred between the AFL-CIO leadership and the Clinton administration after the intense NAFTA showdown. Several weeks after the NAFTA rift, AFL-CIO President Lane Kirkland met privately with Clinton, in an effort by both men to put NAFTA behind them.[93] Clinton told Kirkland that he wanted him to develop regular, frequent contact with his close assistant, George Stephanopoulos. Kirkland and Stephanopoulos began having lunch every few weeks, sometimes joined by Robert Rubin. In May 1994, the entire AFL-CIO Executive Council went over to the White House and met with President Clinton. In July 1994, President Clinton asked Kirkland to travel with him to Poland, in light of the AFL-CIO's well-known, steadfast support for Lech Walesa and the Solidarity movement there. For the administration's massive health care reform effort, the AFL-CIO devoted organizers nationwide and at least $10 million to help build public pressure for the reform measure in Congress.[94]

While Clinton may not be labor's favorite Democrat, and never has been, his ascension to the White House in January 1993 returned labor leaders to the corridors of power in Washington for the first time since the Carter administration. The presidents of large national unions got their calls returned for the first time in twelve years, and found themselves socially and politically back as "players" in Washington. That is intangible, but certainly not insignificant.

The overriding point is that substantively, after the NAFTA humiliation, labor was delighted to join forces with the administration in the health care reform campaign. AFL-CIO leaders had complained about the need for national health care insurance for decades, and now a president was taking up the flag. Even more direct to union concerns were Clinton's call for an increase in the minimum wage, and his executive order banning the use of replacement workers by federal contractors.[95]

Of course, by 1995, there was no better reminder to Bill Clinton or to the labor unions of how much they needed each other than the 1994 elections. Suddenly they faced a hostile majority in both houses of Congress. The Clinton administration pledged that the president would veto attempts to repeal the Davis-Bacon Act, which sets wage rates on federal construction projects, among other Republican legislative initiatives vehemently opposed by labor.

Four independent counsels have been appointed to investigate members of the Clinton administration and the president himself. The Whitewater investigation has resulted in at least a dozen indictments. As Bill Clinton found his political career ironically bookended from Watergate to Whitewater, from outsider reform candidate for Congress complaining about scandal in 1974 to embattled incumbent staving off scandal in 1996, his old friend from Arkansas, Don Tyson, was counting his chickens as they hatched in Washington. In 1992, Tyson family members and company executives contributed $29,000 to Clinton's presidential campaign and Tyson was one of the few corporate executives who spoke at the Clinton transition economic summit in Little Rock.[96]

After Clinton took office, Tyson, as he had done for Governor Clinton, provided Agriculture Secretary Mike Espy with plane rides, meals and lodging, as well as $6,000 from Tyson and company employees to help retire the campaign debt of Espy's brother, Henry, who lost a bid for Congress in 1993.[97]

That same year the Department of Agriculture shelved work on new poultry inspection regulations. As *Time* magazine reported, "an uncooked chicken has become one of the most dangerous items in the American home. At least 60 percent of U.S. poultry is contaminated with salmonella, campylobacter or other micro-organisms that spread throughout the birds from slaughter to packaging, a process that has sped up dramatically in the past twenty years. Each year at least 6.5 million . . . people get sick from chicken . . ."[98]

Espy was forced to resign his position in the Clinton cabinet and an independent counsel began to investigate him. Espy has denied any impropriety, and Tyson company officials maintain they favor stricter inspections and were certainly not trying to influence Secretary Espy or the Clinton administration.[99]

To Don Tyson, who has reportedly *again* become disenchanted with Clinton and is giving money to Bob Dole in the 1996 campaign, the business of politics has never been particularly complicated. It consists of "a series of unsentimental transactions between those who need votes and those who have money . . . a world where every *quid* has its *quo*."[100]

In many ways, Washington seemed just like Arkansas, writ much, much larger, with many more opportunities.

BILL CLINTON
TOP 10 CAREER PATRONS*

1. Goldman Sachs, investment banking, New York, New York	$107,850
2. Voice of Teachers for Education Committee on Political Education of New York State United Teachers, PAC	$101,819
3. Jackson Stephens family, Stephens Inc. & Affiliates and Stephens Production Company, holding company and oil, Little Rock, Arkansas	$53,600**
4. Willkie, Farr & Gallagher, law firm, Washington, D.C.	$50,075
5. Gallo Family, wine, Modesto, California	$50,000
6. Sullivan & Cromwell, law firm, New York, New York	$37,600
7. Covington & Burling, law firm, Washington, D.C.	$33,200
8. The Hernreich family, broadcasting, Ft. Smith, Arkansas	$31,695
9. The Gillespie family, oil/well services, Magnolia, Arkansas	$28,904

10. Harvard University, employees, Cambridge.
Massachusetts $28,225

*Figures are compiled from contributions made to Clinton's gubernatorial campaigns between 1981 and 1990, as well as from donations to his 1992 presidential campaign—according to FEC and Center for Responsive Politics data—and donations to the President's Legal Expense Trust and the Clinton-Gore transition fund.

Based upon incomplete Arkansas election records, Bill Clinton has contributed $64,890.31 to his own campaigns; however, $50,000 of the total was either a donation specifically made by Clinton to his 1984 gubernatorial run or a personal loan to the campaign from Clinton later repaid by the Arkansas Democratic Committee—as was the case during Clinton's 1974 congressional race.

**The Stephens family also owned a 25 percent interest in Worthen Bank. The Worthen Bank has donated $24,000 to Clinton's campaigns.

Lamar Alexander

If anything distinguishes Lamar Alexander's career as a public official, it is how much that career has benefitted Lamar Alexander. After his 1982 reelection as governor of Tennessee and the 1983 Nashville inaugural festivities, several thousand dollars remained unspent from the campaign. Governor Lamar Alexander, with more than a little help from his friends, turned those leftover campaign funds and contributions of $5,000 and less made after the election into a personal fund for himself and his wife Leslee, better known as Honey. According to Tennessee election records, from 1983 until March 1989, Alexander and/or his wife spent $313,012 from the "Alexander Committee" on travel—to everywhere from China to Super Bowl XVI in Pontiac, Michigan—consulting, gifts, and other personal matters. Having a personal fund created by contributions from private sources is not illegal in Tennessee. In fact, despite the fact that Alexander had just won his second term and could not run again, money kept pouring into the campaign treasury. According to Susan Simmons, Alexander's finance director for the 1982 campaign, "There are times when the governor has expenses and he doesn't want the state to pay for it. His close friends don't want him to assume that financial burden."[1]

When Alexander was leaving office in January 1987, four of Alexander's biggest campaign contributors—Pilot Oil owner Jim Haslam; former *Nashville Tennessean* owner Amon Carter Evans; chairman of Ingram Industries, E. Bronson Ingram; and a partner of J.C. Bradford Co., W. Lucas Simmons—signed and sent a letter to 150 business executives, soliciting $1,000 contributions to the Alexander Committee. The mailing, which thoughtfully included self-addressed, stamped envelopes, asked that the money be forwarded by January 17, 1987, the day Alexander would leave the gover- nor's mansion. Throughout the seven-year life of the fund, expenditures were not dated or regularly accounted for. On March 15, 1989, for example, Alexander campaign treasurer Jim Lattimore filed a statement with the Tennessee Election Commission covering the preceding two years, and in the cover letter he wrote, "[I]t recently occurred to me that his political campaign [sic], The Alexander Committee, still has an obligation to file a Campaign Financial Disclosure Form."

The now-defunct Alexander Committee illuminates the puzzling paradoxes of this Republican presidential candidate: An earnest, innovative public servant who has reaped a small fortune because of the people he has met along the way; an intelligent man who has seen the ugliest American political scandals up close and yet seems unconcerned about the ap-

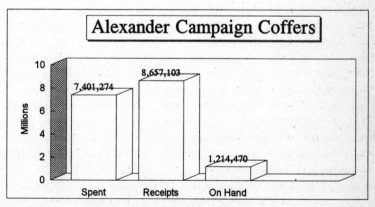

Reporting through September 30, 1995.

Spent figures include all purchases or payments made in connection with or for the purpose of influencing a federal election.
Receipts are anything of value received by a political committee.
On Hand figures include funds held in checking and savings ac- counts, certificates of deposit, petty cash funds, travelers checks, treasury bills, and other investments valued at cost.

pearance of conflicts of interest; a red-and-black flannel-shirted "populist," famous for walking hundreds of miles amidst ordinary voters, who is actually a millionaire, personally and politically closest to society's wealthiest interests.

One of Alexander's first and enduring mentors was Howard Baker Jr. Alexander managed Baker's 1966 Senate campaign, and went to Washington as his legislative assistant. A couple of years later, with Senator Baker's help, Alexander was hired as an assistant to the savvy Bryce Harlow, the head of congressional relations in the Nixon White House.

Just two years later, at the age of thirty, Alexander decided to return to Tennessee to become campaign manager for the GOP gubernatorial candidate and to lay the groundwork for seeking his first public office. Before he left the White House, a memo we obtained from the National Archives shows Harlow set up a farewell meeting between Alexander and Nixon. In a memo to Nixon, preparing the president for the August 13, 1970 meeting with White House staffer Alexander, Harlow wrote: "I had him positioned to be our White House anchor man for the Agnew campaign this fall. . . . Lamar's plans following the campaign are, first, to become a good lawyer in Tennessee—second, to remain active in political affairs—third, I suspect, to run for office in due time. He already has powerful support, state-wide."

But not enough. Alexander's maiden voyage into elective politics, in 1974, was unsuccessful. Running for governor against Democrat Ray Blanton, Alexander could not overcome the nation's revulsion for Watergate and many Republican politicians. Blanton used Alexander's connection to the Nixon White House. "Blanton never let anyone forget it," wrote Peter Maas. There had been a photograph published that showed Alexander standing next to a seated Nixon. A Blanton campaign poster pictured Blanton in the same pose alongside an empty chair. The line with it said "This Chair Is Not For Sale."[2]

Alexander returned to practicing law, but by 1978, he was ready to enter the fray once again. He hired political consultant Doug Bailey, who advised that he strike a more folksy pose. So Alexander donned the now trademark red-and-black flannel shirts, and took a 1,000-mile "populist" walk across the state. He was elected governor, defeating Jake Butcher. The same day that a young Bill Clinton was sworn in as governor of Arkansas, in January 1979, Alexander was sworn in as governor of Tennessee. His coming to power, however, had been rushed ahead of schedule, three days early, at the request of the U.S. attorney and the FBI, who had reason to believe that the incumbent governor, Blanton, had accepted cash in exchange for granting clemency to three state prison inmates who had been convicted of murder. Blanton was eventually convicted for selling liquor licenses. Such political corruption in Tennessee was not an isolated occurrence. Alexander's 1978 gubernatorial opponent, Butcher, was later convicted of banking fraud.

By comparison Alexander was widely viewed as impeccably honest, a man of unquestioned integrity. He went so far as to disclose his and his family's financial holdings, including his personal income tax returns, even though the law didn't require it.

As a 1996 presidential candidate, Alexander has asserted that during his tenure as governor "Tennessee began increasing family incomes faster than any state, became the only state to pay teachers more for teaching well, and moved from last place in auto production then to third among the states." When he left office in January 1987, Alexander said Tennessee had "fewer government employees, less debt, a AAA bond rating, and the nation's fifth lowest tax rate."

In Tennessee Alexander is generally perceived as having been an effective, competent, and at times creative governor. And his popularity proved to extend beyond state lines: He was elected chairman of the National Governor's Association in 1985. John Siegenthaler, the retired editor and publisher of the *Nashville Tennessean*, said, "As governors come and go, he was a good governor." Calling Alexander "innovative," Siegenthaler said, "I felt for too long he neglected the prison system, but aside from that, I felt his administration was a progressive one." Siegenthaler told the Center for Public Integrity that he was "surprised when I looked at the number of instances in which people close to him contributed to his financial success."[3]

A linchpin of Alexander's 1978 economic strategy for a

stagnant Tennessee was to seek Japanese and other foreign investment in his state. Indeed, since the 1970s, probably no U.S. governor more assiduously courted Japanese investment than Lamar Alexander. Not only did Governor Alexander make numerous trips to Japan, he recently said, "I spent more time in Japan than Washington, D.C., because it would help our state more."[4] By 1987, Tennessee had become the national model for foreign investment in a state: Japan had established forty-seven manufacturing facilities in Tennessee, employing 10,000 people, and Japanese assets in Tennessee were suddenly 10 percent of its total manufacturing investment in the entire United States.[5] In March 1986, during Alexander's last year as governor, Tennessee celebrated Japan Week.[6] That same year, Alexander wrote a book called *Friends: Japanese and Tennesseans*, in which he advised that states could attract Japanese investment if they "learned Japanese manners." First and foremost in his suggestion to officials in other states: "Never mention the war [World War II]."[7]

Alexander declined to be interviewed for this book, and did not respond to written questions submitted by the Center for Public Integrity.

In 1985 many observers blamed Alexander when prison riots broke out at several institutions throughout Tennessee. It was Alexander's greatest crisis as governor. As a candidate, he had appealed to "law-and-order" sentiments by proposing a plan known as "Class X," which basically extended the amount of mandatory prison time served for several specific felonies. Neither he nor the legislature, however, allocated additional funding for the ballooning prison population. Two federal judges, who happened to be conservative Republicans, criticized the Alexander administration, ordered that a court-appointed "special master" take over the state prisons, and required a special session of the state legislature to handle the emergency.[8]

As Gordon Bonnyman of the Tennessee Legal Aid Society remembered it, "Prisoners were backing up jails in counties all over the state. Not only did his Class X proposal not do a thing to control crime, the inhuman overcrowding that it caused gave us the most violent prison system in the country, as measured by the number of homicides . . . Alexander was all high-glitz and sloganeering; his only solution was to put prisoners to work and propose privatizing the prisons."[9]

Not long after, the way was clear. In September of 1985 Alexander, saying it was the only way to reduce the burden on taxpayers, endorsed and began advocating the $250 million proposal put forth by a private company called the Corrections Corporation of America (CCA) to build and operate two new 500-bed facilities in Tennessee's prison system. CCA was founded by his friend and former state Republican party chairman (1977 to 1980) Tom Beasley, who years earlier, while a Vanderbilt University undergraduate, had rented a garage apartment from the Alexanders.[10] The new firm was backed financially by Kentucky Fried Chicken millionaire, co-founder of the Hospital Corporation of America, and Alexander pal Jack Massey (since deceased) and his partner Lucius Burch.[11] This whole cast of characters gave new meaning to the phrase "friendly takeover." Besides Massey and Burch, other company stockholders included past Alexander campaign contributors: Alexander administration state tourism commissioner Etherage Parker Jr., Doc Crants, and the state insurance commissioner John Neff.

In 1984, Honey Alexander, the governor's wife, purchased $8,900 in CCA stock. Concerned about avoiding a conflict of interest, Honey Alexander exchanged her CCA stock for 10,000 shares in a life insurance company called South Life Corporation through a venture-capital firm called the Massey-Burch Investment Group, run by Massey. In 1989, Honey Alexander sold her shares in South Life for $142,000.[12] In 1995, one observer of this financial maneuvering quipped that "Hillary Clinton made only $100,000 on cattle futures; Honey did even better on what one could call prison futures." The future didn't change much for the state's inmates; the CCA privatization idea did not work and virtually all CCA-run institutions were returned to state stewardship.[13]

While Alexander was governor, he and Honey Alexander personally displayed an uncanny knack for reaping almost outlandish returns on very minimal investment, to the net effect of acquiring substantial wealth during his public service. Numerous news organizations have reported on it, and in 1991 the Senate Labor and Human Resources Committee delayed Alexander's confirmation to become George Bush's secretary of education for weeks because of questions surrounding Alexander's financial activities. Alexander has continuously denied any impropriety, saying, "I have spent about twenty years going out of my way to make sure that if anyone is going to offer me favorable treatment, I wouldn't take it."[14] To put it bluntly, the facts don't support that statement.

In 1981, while governor, Alexander and six other investors, including Alexander's close friend and mentor Howard Baker, who was Senate majority leader at the time, each paid $1 for the option to buy the *Knoxville Journal* newspaper for $15 million. After the owner of the *Knoxville Journal,* Charles Smith, died, his heirs gave Alexander and the other investors the option to buy the paper. The new partners decided not to exercise their option to buy, and they instead began searching for a buyer and found one: Gannett Co., which agreed to pay $15 million for 94.8 percent of the newspaper's stock. Alexander walked away with Gannett newspaper options and stock worth $620,000.[15] According to Alexander, "I held onto the stock longer than anybody else and between 1981 and 1987, when I sold it, it had dramatically increased and I made a very good profit."[16]

Most investors, of course, do not net $620,000 from $1, or have the opportunity or information to reap such rich rewards. Precisely who invited Governor Alexander to participate in the transaction has never been revealed. His glib explanation for the entire episode was not particularly illuminating: "We all had the same idea at the same time. The *Knoxville Journal* is a great asset, a newspaper we all admired, and all of us dreamed of owning a little piece of it one day."[17]

His little piece of Blackberry Farm, a resort-conference center on the southern edge of the Smoky Mountains, became something of a nightmare. Alexander bought one-third interest in the lodge for $9,516 from Sandy Beall in 1976, resold it to Beall in 1977 when he became governor, then bought it back from Beall in 1987 when he left office.[18] But what Alexander did *not* relinquish control of during his governorship were some 991 acres of potential development land, upon which Blackberry Farm was situated. The acreage was owned by Alexander and five friends, including major campaign contributors Beall and Jim Haslam. In January 1986, Governor Alexander proposed opening up an interstate highway, part of what's known as the Pellissippi Parkway, that would intersect the Blackberry Farm land. When the *Nashville Tennessean* exposed the conflict, Governor Alexander said it was "preposterous" to link the state road program with his ownership of the land, which he insisted would not be developed commercially.[19]

Interestingly, it has never been reported that Alexander called the publisher of the *Nashville Tennessean,* John Siegenthaler, before the investigative story appeared. "He called me and said the story would be unfair to him and . . . he asked me to hold the story," Siegenthaler told us. "I said I couldn't do that." Siegenthaler told Governor Alexander that from what he had seen, the situation "does suggest that this is self-serving." Alexander ended the conversation angry and frustrated, Siegenthaler recalled. Within hours of the exposé appearing on the front page, Alexander halted the state road program, saying, "If there was a question yesterday about that part of the Pellissippi Parkway, there cannot be one today because there is now no proposal from me to build it."[20]

Alexander got into another jam over Blackberry Farm a few years later, when it was discovered that as president of the University of Tennessee he had steered university business to the inn. Following a state audit, the Tennessee comptroller of the treasury revealed that Alexander had informed senior university officials that he had "disposed" of his financial interest. Subsequently, "the university held fourteen functions costing $64,626.49 at Blackberry Farm. Only after the president [Alexander] left his position at the university and various facts about Blackberry Farm had been publicly disclosed, did university officials learn that he had apparently transferred Blackberry Farm stock he owned into a trust for the benefit of his wife."[21]

Alexander claimed that he had been advised by university lawyers and the state attorney general that a conflict of interest would be avoided if he merely transferred his interest to his wife. Lewis Lavine, a longtime friend and former aide, told us Alexander often checked with the attorney general.

"It's more difficult to keep the private life and public life separate," Lavine said. "When he became governor, he disclosed everything; where every dollar came from." Alexander has been "in private life about half the time and in public life about half the time," Lavine added. "If he were to have been in private life full-time, he would be a multimillionaire."[22]

Relationships

How Alexander became the president of the University of Tennessee is unusual, but epitomizes the politician's propensity to receive and to give favors to his Tennessee friends in the 1980s. While the Alexanders were spending six months in Australia in 1987, three members of the University of Tennessee board of trustees—vice chairman William Johnson, James Haslam, and Amon Carter Evans—took it upon themselves to hire a consulting firm called the Ingram Group, presumably to assist them in searching for a university president. But the board had already retained a Chicago-based "headhunting" firm, Heidrick and Struggles, to conduct a nationwide search to fill the vacancy.

The Ingram Group consists in part of two former chiefs of staff to Governor Alexander, Thomas Ingram and Lewis Lavine. At one point, Lavine said, the Ingram Group believed it was "to help the Chicago headhunting firm be introduced to the state."[23] Bill Bowen, the vice chairman of Heidrick and Struggles, did not recall any contact between his firm and the Ingram Group.

When asked if the Ingram Group was in fact hired to lobby the university board on Alexander's behalf, Lewis Lavine disputed that he and other Alexander friends tried to persuade the board to approach Alexander. He said it was Alexander who needed to be persuaded to take the job. "He had no desire to be U.T. president," Lavine told us, "but the trustees persuaded him." After becoming U.T. president, Alexander said he wanted the Ingram Group to assist him in the transition process. The three generous trustees continued paying the firm for its "consulting services" to Alexander, as well as paying Alexander's own commuting travel expenses from his Nashville home to the Knoxville campus, prior to his relocation.

Soon after becoming university president, Alexander took actions that helped his friends. When local amusement taxes levied on admission sales to sporting events were causing the university some problems, Alexander recommended that the athletic department retain the Ingram Group for its "consulting services." The firm was paid through another company called Host Communications because, according to state auditors, "the appearance of a direct contract arrangement with the Ingram Group might be criticized."[24]

During Alexander's tenure as U.T. president, Johnson—one of his three board of trustee sponsors—held two top positions at Dominion Bank, which in 1991 loaned Alexander $650,000. Haslam and Evans, the other two sponsors, were two of Alexander's most generous contributors, and Haslam had been appointed to the state university board by Alexander when he was governor.

Alexander also brought his favorite media consultant, whom he had used in past political campaigns, Doug Bailey, of Bailey, Deardourff, and Associates, into the lucrative loop. The firm received approximately $30,000 to produce radio and television commercials for the University of Tennessee in 1989 and 1990, but "in an apparent attempt to avoid any negative appearances of a conflict" there were never "written contracts" prepared, said the state's comptroller.[25]

The comptroller referred his report to the district and state attorney general, although no prosecutorial actions were taken.

Moving to Washington

In 1990, Lamar Alexander was nominated by President George Bush to be secretary of education. His nomination was unanimously approved by the U.S. Senate Labor and Human Resources Committee, which sent it to the Senate floor. Alexander's biggest critic was Senator Howard Metzen-baum (D-OH), who complained of the nominee's "incom-plete disclosures," and the appearances of conflicts of interest, and said, "I'm still not certain I understand this blurred and complex series of professional positions and busi-ness transactions . . . however, I cannot conclude that any eth-ical violations occurred and for that reason I will support his nomination."[26] Alexander was overwhelmingly approved by the Senate on March 14, 1991.

For several weeks, the nomination had stalled because of a steady stream of revelations in the print media regarding Alexander's intertwining friendships and financial dealings. As the *Nashville Tennessean,* the *Wall Street Journal,* and other news organizations pointed out, from 1981 to 1988, Alexan-der had invested a total of $20,000 with friends involved in the following businesses: the *Knoxville Journal,* Corrections Corporation of America, Corporate Child Care (with Robert Keeshan, alias "Captain Kangaroo"), and Whittle Communi-cations, and he had made profits of $1.9 million.

Alexander seemed unfazed. "I'm not a stick in the mud," he said, but "an adventuresome person" who takes risks. "I think that some people think that I have made too much money and they don't understand how."[27] According to Alex-ander, "Some people have the idea that people who are elected governor are somehow rendered totally incompetent to do anything else after they get out."[28]

Just two and a half weeks after Alexander "got out" as governor, Corporate Child Care, Inc., was incorporated in Nashville with his help, along with investment capital from his longtime patron Jack Massey and others; today it is a successful company with 1,200 employees in more than a dozen states. In political speeches, presidential candidate Alexander is fond of distinguishing himself from his rivals on the basis of his business experience as an entrepreneur. What Alexander does not mention is that he had very lim-ited personal involvement in the venture, which in the be-ginning relied heavily upon insight, marketing information, and personnel from the state government, paid for by Ten-nessee taxpayers.

Whittle Communications

Both in Tennessee and across the nation, the confirmation process and resultant news coverage afforded a particularly fascinating glimpse into Lamar Alexander's relationship with one man, entrepreneur Christopher Whittle and Whittle Communications. Testifying at his confirmation hearing, nominee Alexander said that Whittle "has been a good close friend for twenty years. I think he is tremendously creative. I have done some work for the company ... You would not rank me as the most objective witness on Whittle Communication activities, and as a result of that, I would expect to recuse myself from acting on their activities while I'm secretary and probably not try to be out front in discussing them."[29]

Whittle, in an interview with the Center for Public Integrity, remembered that the two had worked for Senator Howard Baker in the late 1960s.[30] In the mid-1980s, "When I was deciding where to headquarter my company," Whittle said, of the time when he was torn between moving to New York or staying in Tennessee, "he was instrumental and worked hard to keep our business in Knoxville. That was in his economic development role as governor." He added, "I've known [Lamar] for twenty years," but said they have never been close personal friends.

But Whittle and Alexander were hardly strangers. Indeed, in a series of brainstorming sessions, three of which Whittle attended with other Alexander friends, the proposals that became known as the Bush administration's "America 2000" education goals were established, along with a "voucher" system.[31] According to Freedom of Information Act records obtained by the Center for Public Integrity, on February 28, 1991, just three weeks after assuring the Senate that he would recuse himself from Department of Education dealings with Whittle Communications, and a full fortnight before his actual confirmation, Alexander received a telephone call at the Department of Education offices from Chris Whittle. At about this time, former Alexander chief of staff Tom Ingram, while working as an executive vice president of Whittle Communications, was helping to set up Alexander's transition office. Another former chief of staff to Alexander, Lewis Lavine, head of the Ingram Group, one of whose largest clients was Whittle Communications, also helped Alexander get settled in. Lavine was actually hired by Alexander as a paid adviser for a few months.[32]

Just three days after his Senate confirmation, Lamar Alexander sold his Knoxville home for $977,500. He had bought it a year earlier for $570,000. The buyer was Gerald Hogan, a vice president of Whittle Communications, who received a $780,000 mortgage from First Tennessee Bank at the time that Alexander was on the board of the bank's holding company. Alexander explained to inquisitive reporters that expensive renovations had been made to the property, and that actually, "I lost money."[33]

A check of the Knox County, Tennessee, construction permits for the duration of the Alexanders' tenure at 3801 Topside Road, showed there were two permits obtained: One for $21,000 to build a swimming pool, and the other for unspecified renovations to the home, valued at $200,000. Adding the $221,000 in renovations to the original cost of the house, $570,000, comes to $791,000. In other words, it appears that the Alexanders made a profit of $186,500 from the sale of this house for $977,500. An interesting aspect in this whole transaction is that the house at 3801 Topside Road was appraised in 1991 to be worth $345,910, and it was assessed for taxes (at 25 percent of its appraised value) at $86,478.

Hogan disputed this assessment of the transaction in a telephone interview from his home today in Clearwater, Florida, saying the permits do not reflect the true amount of work done on the house he purchased from Alexander. Hogan was not able to provide other receipts. Neither Alexander nor anyone on the campaign committee would address the issue.

In the late 1980s Chris Whittle was developing a project to put television programming, including commercials, into public schools nationwide with something called "Channel One." Associating publicly with the "education reform governor" could only lend credibility and cachet to the venture. So Alexander joined Whittle's advisory board, Whittle paid Alexander $125,000 as a consultant, and Alexander was given the opportunity to buy four shares of Whittle stock for $10,000. A year later, as he became president of the University of Tennessee, to avoid a conflict of interest Alexander transferred the Whittle stock to his wife. It turns out that Alexander's $10,000 check paying for the stock had not been cashed—Whittle claimed it had been misplaced by a secretary in a desk drawer—and it wasn't cashed until after Whittle sold part of his company to Time Warner for $185 million. In late 1988, after the sale had been completed, Whittle purchased the stock back from Honey Alexander for $330,000, a $320,000 profit.[34]

"It's absolutely true that [the Alexanders] got a spectacular investment return," Whittle said. "I'd love to have done that for every investor in all my ventures. I'm an entrepreneur . . . Lamar didn't have any special treatment at all. A lot of people made money." Of the check in the drawer: "I said, 'Lamar, send me a check.' The check was not something I worried about depositing. I didn't get around to doing it."

What did Lamar Alexander do as U.S. secretary of education that was helpful to his old friend Chris Whittle? He did plenty, but in a subtle, complementary way. No federal money found its way to Whittle or his education-related programs, and in approximately fifty-six speeches or testimony given by Alexander as education secretary, he only once publicly mentioned Whittle by name. Instead, Alexander, as the nation's premier public official on education, and Whittle, as probably the most visible private-sector education entrepreneur, sang the same song, reinforcing each other. Alexander talked about the Bush administration school "choice" and voucher program, the controversial proposal that citizens be given public money so they can send their children to the school of their choice, public or private. Alexander spoke of school "choice" the first day he became secretary of education, in his swearing-in ceremony speech, and he mentioned it a dozen more times in major statements and speeches while a member of the Bush cabinet.

On May 6, 1991, in a speech at Washington's Brookings Institution, Alexander cited "choice" as his first priority as secretary of education, and he singled out Whittle by name, among others, for his role in "reinventing the American school." Just ten days later, on May 16, 1991, Whittle announced the Edison Project, his ambitious plan to create a nationwide private school system, which would give millions of dissatisfied Americans more choices about where to send their children to school. Six days later, on May 22, 1991, Secretary Alexander announced his support for the America 2000 Excellence in Education Act, which would allow some federal funds to "follow" eligible students to the public or private school of their parents' choice.

In July, 1991, Alexander and the Bush administration announced the creation of a private, nonprofit organization, the New American Schools Development Corporation (NASDC) funded by business and corporate leaders to provide research and development funds for America 2000 schools. To have the CEOs of companies such as Xerox, IBM, Eastman Kodak, Boeing, and Alcoa supporting the notion of private sector involvement and entrepreneurialism in education added credibility and momentum to the choice and voucher concept.

Alexander and Whittle's Tennessee waltz got noticed. Alexander, according to the *Chicago Tribune*, "is pushing a 'New American Schools' program to create schools remarkably similar to Whittle's."[35] Whittle told *The Nation* that "Ultimately we are trying to do the same things. He [Alexander] is taking the public route. I am taking the private route."[36]

The Professional Presidential Candidate

In 1992, there were signs that Alexander was growing restless in his cabinet job, although he had been secretary of education for barely a year. It was well understood in Washington that Lamar Alexander had grander ideas about his future, that his eyes were on the prize at 1600 Pennsylvania Avenue.

But even before attempting to run, there were things to do. He had to set up a personal income flow. He needed to develop and hone the political ideas and a 1996 message that would best resonate with the masses and enhance his appeal. Finally, he needed to establish a political and financial base, a springboard for the grueling 1996 marathon that would require a savvy, loyal, experienced staff and thousands of financial contributors from around the nation.

In June of 1993, Alexander started a PAC called Republican Fund for the '90s and has raised $398,099, according to its 1993 and 1994 disclosures. Among the contributors to this PAC, in addition to $5,000 from Lamar Alexander, are $5,000 contributions from friends James Haslam, Lewis Lavine, David K. Wilson, Thomas Beasley, Lucius Burch, and $10,000 from John Parish and his wife.

Within days of leaving the federal government in January 1993, Alexander also began a nonprofit, tax-exempt organization, the Republican Exchange Satellite Network (RESN), and in 1994 began getting help from the Hudson Institute and Empower America. Old friend and mentor Howard Baker set Alexander up in his law firm—a base from which Alexander was able to collect directors' fees from several corporate boards. All of it was done to enable his run for the White House.

Like Bob Dole, Alexander used a nonprofit to further his political aspirations. RESN was incorporated in Nashville in January, 1993, and dissolved on March 9, 1995, a few weeks after Alexander announced his candidacy for the Republican nomination. RESN even employed a full-time organizer in Iowa, Dick Redman. Few people doubted the real purpose of the organization and the physical and personnel ties to the formal presidential campaign are substantial.

According to IRS and FEC documents, the office space was rented from Howard Baker's law firm in Nashville, and today the space is being utilized by the presidential campaign. One of Tennessee's wealthiest commercial real estate developers, Ted Welch, was the treasurer and fiscal officer for RESN— and became the campaign's national finance chairman. The executive director of RESN, Colleen Pero, became the campaign's deputy director and general counsel, and her husband, Dan Pero, became Alexander's campaign manager. Agnes Warfield, who was Alexander's deputy chief of staff at the Department of Education, became the finance director for RESN and also was employed by Alexander's PAC, Republican Fund for the '90s. She became the campaign's finance director. Kevin Phillips (not the same one who wrote the foreword for this book) was RESN's spokesman, and became the Alexander campaign press secretary. Lewis Lavine, the original president of RESN, became a paid consultant to the Alexander presidential campaign.

Lavine, who in 1995 coordinated Alexander's walk in New Hampshire, also coordinated Alexander's drive around the country in a red Ford Explorer. The trip was paid for by RESN and the Hudson Institute. "The idea was to energize the Republican Party," Lavine recounted, and it "enabled Lamar to get out of the tunnel that candidates get into."

RESN, as mentioned earlier, has refused to release its contributors or expenditures, but we do know that the group raised $5.5 million, and thirteen individuals each contributed $100,000.[37] In 1993 and 1994, the organization subsidized Lamar Alexander's 1996 campaign-related travel around the nation, to New Hampshire, Iowa, California, and five of the "Super Tuesday" primary states, for monthly "Neighborhood Meetings" which aired nineteen times until January 1995, when Alexander turned the nationally televised cable television program over to the chairman of the Republican National Committee, Haley Barbour.

Alexander himself said that RESN gave him the opportunity to "create a political and financial base. And most importantly, it's given me a chance to focus on the issues, say what we're for, and develop my message for where we're going to take the country."[38]

Given his personal financial pattern over the preceding fifteen years or so, it will come as no surprise that Lamar Alexander's golden touch didn't fail him in 1993, 1994, or 1995. Soon after leaving public service, Alexander joined the board of directors of defense contractor Martin Marietta. He was paid $46,800 a year, plus $1,000 for each meeting he attended. When the company merged with Lockheed Corp., in March 1995, Alexander received $236,000 for no longer being a director of the new Lockheed Martin Corp.[39] His buyout was part of a $92 million compensation package paid to several former Martin Marietta executives and directors. One-third of the payment to Alexander, or $78,677, reportedly was taxpayers' money from the "government-subsidized merger."[40] The Alexander settlement was based in part on what he would have received in his term as a director, which was to expire in the spring of 1996. In Alexander's FEC financial disclosure covering the period from 1994 to 1995, signed on May 12, 1995, he listed $93,922 in income from Martin Marietta in "director's fees and other compensation."

Beginning in 1993, Washington superlobbyist Howard Baker placed his friend on the law firm payroll, making $295,000 as a "contract" lawyer. The national salary average for partners at large law firms was $310,644. Bud Adams, the firm's managing director, told us that Alexander works on retainer for three clients and not on "a billable hour approach," adding that he also "helps open doors and solidify client relationships." Adams called Alexander a "rainmaker," meaning he attracts money to the firm—far more than his salary. According to Baker, "I tried to design the best system I could to let him work with us and earn some money and stay free to run."[41]

Frustration over Alexander's large salary, and the cost of "hiring his personal retinue, including a secretary, scheduler, and an administrative aide," contributed to the breakup of Baker, Worthington, Crossley, and Stansberry. One former partner said the firm, which is now known as Baker, Donelson, Bearman, and Caldwell, had no illusions about Alexander's work schedule there, "I think it's clearly an investment in case he becomes president."[42]

Alexander does not participate in the profits of the firm and does not do any lobbying or any work in Washington. Adams maintained that the firm does no campaign work for Alexander, although a memo to "all employees" states "that the firm must be reimbursed for any campaign-related expenses."[43]

Should that happen, no one will be more important or worth more in Washington than Howard Baker, whose law firm includes such clients as Lockheed Martin, AT&T, Federal Express, Salomon Brothers, Schering Plough, U.S. Tobacco, National Soft Drink Association, United Technologies, Waste Management, and scores of other corporate clients. Howard Baker has been generous and worked very hard to get his friend and protege elected president. Ted Welch, who has raised millions of dollars for both men in their presidential bids—Baker in 1980 and Alexander in 1996—told us, "Some would say if Howard Baker worked as hard for himself [in 1980] as he is for Lamar Alexander, he'd be president today."

Alexander's other friends are working and giving hard too. David K. "Pat" Wilson has been a supporter from the start and he and his family have donated more than $80,000 over Alexander's career. Alexander's old pal, John L. Parish, has donated $30,165 to Alexander and between December 27, 1994, and January 4, 1995, he and his family gave $8,000 to the presidential bid. James Haslam II has contributed more than $20,000 to Alexander over the years, and between December 1994 and March 1995, the Haslam family donated $9,000 to the run for the White House.

Individuals, however, are not the only ones who have befriended Lamar Alexander. Executives at J.C. Bradford, the company that handles Alexander's stocks, have come together to help out their client. Lucas Simmons, a partner in the firm, began the contributions on January 9, 1995, and by March 31 at least seventy other employees had chipped in with at least $65,350 more. Simmons was one of those who, in 1987, signed a lettter that was sent to 150 businessmen asking for contributions to Alexander's political fund.

The contradictions and paradoxes of this continue to perplex the self-proclaimed Washington outsider who was a cabinet secretary. The strong leader, as the *Nashville Banner* once put it, "is not without an Achilles heel. He has long tended to place substantial importance on material possessions and capital accumulation."[44] Alexander is the millionaire who makes more money in one year than most Americans make in twenty, and who insists that he knows what the voters "out there" are thinking.

As vexing as it must be to him, the questions about money and his friends linger. At a National Press Club luncheon speech in 1995, several reporters submitted cards with the same question, "You've made a lot of money with very small investments and with very large help from your friends. Doesn't this represent the old style of politics that voters have grown to hate?"

In response Alexander said, "While I've been outside public life I've done what most Americans do, which is to try and earn a living and try to make some money. And I've been successful at it. I would think we would want a president who would help, who made more good investments than bad ones."[45]

The candidate never really answered the question that day at the National Press Club, nor did he address the peculiarity that his personal net worth soared during his public service. From 1981 to 1988, while he was governor and two years afterward, Alexander made four financial transactions putting up $20,000 and grossing a return of $1.9 million.

The people rarely get such an opportunity, but the particular people who helped Lamar Alexander will be in an excellent position to cash in their chips should their candidate make it to the White House.

LAMAR ALEXANDER
TOP 10 CAREER PATRONS*

1. David K. "Pat" Wilson Family, real estate/banking, Nashville, Tennessee — $83,750
2. Amon Carter Evans Family, media, Nashville, Tennessee — $43,782
3. Jack C. Massey Family, investment/finance, Nashville, Tennessee — $30,350
4. John L. Parish Family, manufacturing, Tullahoma, Tennessee — $30,165
5. Wine and Spirits Wholesalers, Nashville, Tennessee — $28,000
6. John T. Lupton Family, industry, Chattanooga, Tennessee — $25,000
7. James Haslam II Family, oil, Knoxville, Tennessee — $21,100
8. Wholesale Assn. Political Campaign, Nashville, Tennessee — $18,000

9. John P. Wade Family, consultant, Gallatin,
   Tennessee $16,150
10. Ben Rechter, investment, Nashville, Tennessee $14,700

*Includes 1978 and 1982 gubernatorial campaign contributions to the Alexander Committee, the Alexander Inaugural Committee, and the Lamar Alexander Williamson County Campaign. Contributions to the Republican Fund for the '90s, an Alexander PAC, from 1993–1994 are also included. Based on FEC records and Tennessee election data.

Pat Buchanan

Probably none of the current presidential candidates has come closer to the political abyss, and survived than Pat Buchanan. At the young, ambitious age of thirty-two, he was approached to head the infamous Watergate plumbers unit inside the Nixon White House. He turned down the opportunity.

In 1971, with Nixon preparing for reelection, White House superiors Charles Colson, H.R. Haldeman, and John Ehrlichman asked Buchanan to start the secret squad to investigate the president's enemies. Buchanan said it was a waste of time. "I have yet to be shown what benefits this would do for the president, or for the rest of us, other than a psychological salve," Buchanan wrote in a July 8, 1971 memo. Instead he preferred to deal with the issue directly. "Right out in the open . . . head-on. That is our forte."[1] Twenty-four years later he confirmed to the Center for Public Integrity, "I told Haldeman it was nonsense."[2]

Buchanan is properly perceived as a blunt no-nonsense politician. His association with Richard Nixon began in December 1965 when the former vice president spoke in St. Louis. An editorial writer for the *St. Louis Globe–Democrat*, Buchanan wanted to meet Nixon and when he did, he said, "Sir, I'd like to get aboard early." Soon after, Nixon invited Buchanan to New York for an interview. After a three-hour meeting Buchanan was in Nixon's camp with a starting salary of $10,000.[3]

The story of Buchanan's years with Nixon is, not surprisingly, complicated. Clearly from 1966 to about 1974, Buchanan was a loyal, fiercely partisan aide to Nixon. Bob Woodward and Carl Bernstein, the *Washington Post* reporters who broke the Watergate story, described Pat Buchanan as a "hard political realist, the gut fighter, the resident expert in media manipulation." Buchanan told Nixon to "destroy the tapes" after the White House Oval Office recording system first came to light in the summer of 1973. Nixon didn't and three months later, when the Watergate special prosecutor Archibald Cox was getting too persistent about the tapes, Buchanan recommended that Nixon fire Cox for insubordination. Nixon did, triggering the infamous "Saturday Night Massacre."[4]

Buchanan was close to Nixon and his family, almost like a son to the president. August 5, 1974, marked the release date of Watergate tape transcripts of conversations that occurred just six days after the break-in. The tapes came to be known as the "smoking gun." These June 23, 1972, tapes made it apparent that the president had repeatedly lied to the country about his involvement in the coverup for two full years. It was the ultimate betrayal for Buchanan.

As Theodore White portrayed this devastating realization of abject defeat and humiliation, "Now for the first time both [speechwriter Raymond] Price and Buchanan read the transcripts, and there was no doubt in the mind of either. They were bitterly angry. If the president wanted their reaction, their reaction was unanimous: the president should resign."[5]

Although Buchanan distanced himself from Watergate, he stayed at the president's side until the end and helped persuade Nixon to resign. At the height of the scandal, Pat Buchanan got a call from his father. "Pat, why aren't you fighting?" his father asked. "That was the right question," Buchanan wrote. "Whether Nixon was wrong was not the relevant issue. Even if he had booted it he had the right to be defended; and his friends had a duty to be there."[6] Buchanan stayed on with President Ford for a short time and later served with President Ronald Reagan.

Buchanan's strongly held, sharply defined beliefs can be traced back to his conservative upbringing. William and Elizabeth Buchanan were strict parents and their nine children were brought up in accordance with their Catholic faith. They wrote A.M.D.G. *Ad Majorem Dei Gloriam,* For the Greater Glory of God, on the top of each test in school; it was the motto of the Jesuits.[7] They learned the virtue of loyalty and the necessity of fighting back rather than backing down. "To Pop, fighting was concomitant of man's existence," Buchanan wrote.[8] The senior Buchanan was inspired by various conservatives, including Senator Joseph McCarthy, Spanish dictator Francisco Franco and General Douglas McArthur.[9]

Pat Buchanan reflected "conservative" views as a multimedia commentator. Television appearances and newspaper columns provided the forum through which Buchanan made his most controversial comments. AIDS, he said, "was nature's awful retribution against homosexuals."[10] On immigration, "Americans had to decide whether the United States of the 21st century will remain a white nation," he said.[11] Buchanan's attacks on Israel and its lobby in the United States, his views on the Holocaust and Jews have led to people calling him anti-Semitic, a charge he denies. "There hasn't been a nasty name in American politics that I haven't been called," Buchanan told the Center for Public Integrity. "Anyone out on point, from left to right, when he first goes out is called dreadful names: Barry Goldwater, Martin Luther King. Ronald Reagan was a hate monger. I think that goes with the territory. It does not bother me."

He promises to stop all foreign aid, get tough on immigrants, abolish affirmative action, and ban abortion. Buchanan has vowed to lead a "cultural war" against the entertainment media which he said were "polluted with lewdness and violence."[12] Portraying himself as the champion of working Americans, Buchanan said his 1996 campaign is "for those who want to make our country America the beautiful again."[13]

His personality and his willingness to express his vision have made him a rich man. He lives in a million-dollar house in McLean, Virginia, and made more than $800,000 in 1991 including $438,000 from "CNN Crossfire," according to a financial disclosure form he filed during the campaign. He owned a Mercedes-Benz, which became a campaign embarrassment in 1992 when he was vociferously attacking foreign lobbyists working for foreign auto manufacturers, and advocating an "America first" platform. Since 1992, he has gotten rid of his Mercedes and now drives a Cadillac.[14]

In 1992, when Buchanan left his pundit perch and declared his candidacy for the GOP presidential nomination, his first electoral effort, he embarrassed a sitting president, George Bush, by winning 37 percent of the New Hampshire Republican primary vote. Buchanan ran in thirty-three state primaries and won three million votes. At the 1992 Republican National Convention in Houston, Buchanan struck a strident note in his address to the GOP delegates by declaring "there is a cultural war going on in our country for the soul of America. And, in that struggle for the soul of America, Clinton and Clinton are on one side, and George Bush is on our side."[15] He said, "It was the best night not only of the [Bush] campaign, the convention, but of the whole year. I don't apologize for a word of it. It's one of the most famous speeches of any convention in history now."

As a conservative protest candidate, he raised a total of nearly $14 million in the course of the 1992 campaign, of which matching funds constituted $5.2 million.[16] "Matching funds" are payments made by the U.S. Treasury to qualifying presidential candidates. The money is raised from the public when they contribute to the Presidential Primary Matching Payment Account by checking a box on their tax returns. This system was established in 1974 after the Watergate scandal. Much of the money Buchanan raised came from direct-mail receipts that the campaign obtained from rented mailing lists of more than 70,000 donors.

A Federal Election Commission audit report on June 20, 1995, "made a final determination that Patrick J. Buchanan and Buchanan for President, Inc., repay $379,470 to the United States Treasury"—$344,423 in matching funds received in excess of the candidate's entitlement, and a pro-rated repayment of $35,047 for nonqualified campaign expenses. On March 31, 1995, the committee made a partial repayment in the amount of $5,032, leaving $374,438 owed to the U.S. Treasury.

Although the mainstay of Buchanan's money is still small contributions solicited over the radio, an "800" telephone

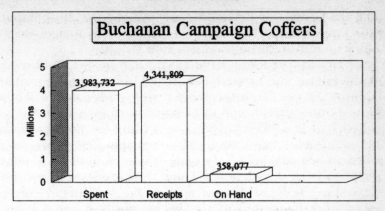

Buchanan Campaign Coffers

Spent: 3,983,732
Receipts: 4,341,809
On Hand: 358,077

Reporting through September 30, 1995.

Spent figures include all purchases or payments made in connection with or for the purpose of influencing a federal election.
Receipts are anything of value received by a political committee.
On Hand figures include funds held in checking and savings accounts, certificates of deposit, petty cash funds, travelers checks, treasury bills, and other investments valued at cost.

number and an aggressive direct-mail operation, he has attracted several wealthy business leaders to his campaign advisory team. They include Tom Monaghan, chairman of Domino's Pizza; W. Grover Coors, heir to the brewery; John G. Breen, chairman of the Sherwin Williams paint company; Mark DeMoss, president of the DeMoss Group; and former Reagan White House aide Richard Allen. Buchanan noted that Allen hasn't endorsed him, but only agreed to serve on his advisory committee.

When asked by the Center for Public Integrity if this is the same Richard Allen who has earned hundreds of thousands of dollars as a foreign lobbyist for China, Japan, and other countries, exactly the kind of thing "America First" Buchanan railed against in 1992, the candidate replied, "A lot of folks came with me to Washington with Richard Nixon to do good and stayed on and did well." The campaign hopes that these business types will be able to collect larger amounts of money than the usual $40 contributions. "This is to try and send a signal to folks that we got support," Buchanan told the Center for Public Integrity. Among the more important support Buchanan attracted for 1996 was that of Roger Milliken and the protectionist textile industry.

An ardent free trader until 1987, when he left the Reagan White House, Buchanan has switched his position to protectionism. "I was the most militant free trader in the White House other than Ronald Reagan," Buchanan said. He recalled that in 1985 or 1986, Roger Milliken, the chairman of the textile corporation, Milliken and Company, once came to see him in the Reagan White House about some piece of trade legislation. "I said, 'We can't help you because I'm the biggest free trader in the building.'" When asked what happened to change his position about trade, he said, "Ideas sort of change when you see what is happening in this country." Buchanan insisted that it was not conversations with people that helped him change his mind and adopt an aggressive, protectionist trade posture. "It's the books I read," he said, and "the loss of jobs and real income among ordinary folks."

In 1995, Roger Milliken, worried for decades about the influx of cheap overseas textiles to this country and its impact on his company and industry, joined the Buchanan campaign as a senior adviser. Buchanan told the Center for Public Integrity, "Mr. Milliken hosted a very gracious fundraiser for us. From our standpoint it was very successful and it was down at his place. He took me on a tour of his plant. He's got a wonderful company."

Since 1992, Buchanan has been one of the leading national public figures to oppose NAFTA and GATT. Although meager in comparison to the large, U.S.-based, multinational corporations that favored and lobbied for the enactment of those agreements, there are financial interests that bitterly opposed those measures. In 1992 and since, some of those interests, such as the textile companies, have aligned themselves with Buchanan, whose voice is consonant with theirs.

Buchanan believes that "both parties are very beholden to money power." He decried how NAFTA and GATT were passed despite public opposition. "The only reason Phil Gramm and Bob Dole and all those fellows would sign on to that was the presidential election. This was done for the big boys. It's appalling and that's why if you can do that you can raise $4 million in a dinner."

Buchanan has gotten closer to the big money now. At the March 7, 1995, fundraiser hosted by Milliken in Spartanburg, South Carolina, Buchanan collected at least $30,000 from various textile companies, employees, and industry supporters. As of June, Buchanan received $6,000 from Milliken and his family and at least $7,000 from Milliken employees. It was President Bush's lack of support for textile quotas and trade protections that led many textile executives to turn to the conservative commentator.[17] "Buchanan is listening," said John Nash, Washington counsel for Milliken and Company in Spartanburg, South Carolina. "You gotta love someone who is listening."[18]

Buchanan said that other politicians are now listening to him. He believes he is a visionary, and that others are just catching up: "I honestly believe that many of the ideas I advanced in 1991 or 1992, and have over the years, are very mainstream in the Republican party right now."

PAT BUCHANAN
TOP 10 CAREER PATRONS*

1. The Vopnford family, recreation, Blair, Nebraska $10,000
2. The Cheval family, Hinsdale, Illinois $6,500
3. America's Political Action Committee, $5,000
   Herndon, Virginia
4. Bart Stanley, Citizens for American $5,000
   Restoration, Houston, Texas
5. The Zignego Family, road construction, $5,000
   Milwaukee, Wisconsin
6. The McKinley Family, Fitzgerald, Georgia $4,975
7. Conservative Caucus Political Action $4,850
   Committee, Vienna, Virginia

8. The Ledbetter Family, geologist, Norman, $4,300
Oklahoma

9. The Flocken family, Anaheim, California $4,000

10. The McKissick Family, textile manufacturer, $4,000
Greenville, South Carolina

* Through 1994. Based on the 1992 presidential campaign. Includes individual and PAC contributors. Based on Federal Election Commission records and Center for Responsive Politics data.

Bob Dole

In Yorba Linda, California, on an overcast spring afternoon in 1994, Senator Bob Dole delivered one of the eulogies at the funeral of former President Richard M. Nixon. "The American people love a fighter and in Dick Nixon they found a gallant one," Dole said. "Today our grief is shared by millions of people the world over, but it is also mingled with intense pride in a great patriot who never gave up and who never gave in." With tears welling in his eyes, Dole ended by saying, "May God Bless Richard Nixon and may God bless the United States."[1]

What the senior senator from Kansas said about his mentor and friend that day could be just as accurately said about Dole himself. Bob Dole has been "kicked around" and like Richard Nixon has never given up. Evidence of that sat before Dole as he spoke, in the form of U.S. presidents Gerald Ford, Jimmy Carter, Ronald Reagan, George Bush, and Bill Clinton. All have confounded or supported Dole throughout his career. Nixon did both to Dole.

Dole was Ford's vice presidential running mate in 1976, when the Republicans lost the White House to Jimmy Carter and Walter Mondale. In 1980, Ronald Reagan edged out Dole for the GOP nomination and went on to be elected to two terms as president. Bush, who had been chosen by President Nixon to replace Dole as Republican National Committee chairman in 1973, later defeated Dole in the 1988 presidential primaries. And Bill Clinton, the incumbent Dole would like to replace, was just four years old when Dole began his political career in 1950, getting elected to the Kansas state legislature.

Regardless of the hardships Dole endured as a result of Nixon's political decisions, Dole still looked upon Nixon as a hero. As Richard Ben Cramer put it in his book on the 1988 presidential race, *What It Takes*: "Dole had such respect for Richard Nixon, it was near reverence. . . . In Nixon, Dole saw a man who'd been knocked down by life. But he was too tough to stay down. . . . He saw strength in Nixon, and nobility."[2]

But as he sought to emulate Nixon, Dole's campaigns came closer to resembling Nixon's than perhaps he wanted. In the not-so-noble world of campaign finance, on a much more modest scale than Nixon, Dole campaigns have solicited and accepted illegal contributions and have even seen one senior advisor hauled off to prison. The think tank Dole established in 1993 abruptly shut down amid a flurry of bad press regarding its secret contributions. What most people don't know about Bob Dole is that from 1973, the middle year of the Watergate scandal, through 1994, he has raised at least $47,612,125 for his Senate and presidential campaigns and his leadership PAC. Of that total he received at least $5,445,595 in PAC money.[3] Between 1981 and 1993, when it was legal for senators to accept money for appearances, Dole received $1,326,771.53 in honoraria for speeches. Now, in an era of anti-Washington fervor, Bob Dole is a consummate Washington insider and dealmaker, realities which are usually veneered by political euphemisms such as "experienced" and "effective." Those interests that have given most heavily to the Kansas senator have reaped magnificent returns on their investments.

Few citizens have the indomitable spirit and stubborn resilience, in life as well as politics, possessed by Robert Joseph Dole. He is an authentic American hero who put his life on the line for his country and nearly died in World War II. But Bob Dole has always fought back, especially in 1974 during the Watergate fallout.

Dole in Washington

For Bob Dole, who had already invested nearly twenty-five years of his life in public office and was in his first term in the Senate, the stakes were very high in 1974. As the chairman

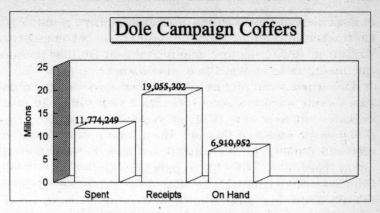

Dole Campaign Coffers

Reporting through September 30, 1995.

Spent figures include all purchases or payments made in connection with or for the purpose of influencing a federal election.
Receipts are anything of value received by a political committee.
On Hand figures include funds held in checking and savings accounts, certificates of deposit, petty cash funds, travelers checks, treasury bills, and other investments valued at cost.

of the Republican National Committee and resident of the Watergate apartment complex since the winter of 1972—nearly six months prior to the Watergate break-in at the Democratic party's offices—Dole appeared vulnerable to questions about what and when he knew of the burglary and the slush funds.[4] Dole, nevertheless, continued to doggedly defend his idol, President Nixon, against Watergate allegations. Despite the fact that Nixon had unceremoniously dumped Dole from the Republican National Committee chairmanship in 1972 after Republican congressmen fared poorly in the election, Dole introduced a Senate resolution in September 1973 to pull the plug on television coverage of the Senate Watergate hearings, arguing that they were distracting the public from important national issues.[5]

Many folks in Kansas, disgusted by Watergate and the shenanigans involving Nixon's Committee to Reelect the President, CREEP (Dole actually came up with that nickname), had come to believe that Dole was out of touch, had been intoxicated by the power and prestige in Washington and forgotten about the concerns of farmers in Topeka and Wichita. It was in this context that the squeaky-clean Congressman William R. Roy, a doctor, sought to defeat Dole by running ads linking Dole to Watergate and Nixon.[6]

Dole tried to emphasize what he had done for his native state serving on the Senate Agriculture Committee. It wasn't working. On Sept. 21, 1974, at the Kansas state fair, Dole changed the mood of the race and in the eyes of many forever sullied the political sensibilities of Kansans. His approach would later exemplify his reputation. During a Lincoln-Douglas–style debate with Dr. Roy, Dole exploded: "Why do you do abortions? And why do you favor abortion on demand?"[7] He then asked the doctor, who had performed abortions since the previous year's Supreme Court decision in *Roe v. Wade* legalizing the procedure, how many he had done. According to media reports, the shocked crowd booed Dole's question. But Dole had found an opening to swing attention away from Watergate and shrewdly took advantage of the opportunity.

Foreshadowing the manner in which Dr. Henry Foster's nomination for surgeon general would be torpedoed twenty-one years later, the drumbeat against Roy continued with fliers and ads bearing skull and crossbones and the words "Vote Dole."[8] The abortionist image stuck. Dole has said he tried to prevent the ads.[9] But a member of the right-to-life group that placed the advertisements said in 1976 that a Dole staffer had approved the ads. And a Dole for Senate campaign finance report filed in 1976 actually listed the ads as in-kind contributions to the campaign. Dole, who had been behind in the polls, barely beat Roy—by just more than 13,000 votes—to win his second Senate term.

As he rose in power and stature on Capitol Hill, Dole became an accomplished fundraiser. Throughout his political career, Dole, like Nixon, saw his campaigns for various national offices scrutinized by federal authorities, sometimes resulting in large fines for illegal contributions. David Owen, the close friend of the Dole family who ran Dole's 1974 senatorial race and played key roles in Dole's 1980 and 1988 presidential bids, but later went to prison for tax fraud, observed,

"He was obsessed by money and power. There are a lot of personality traits in Dole that parallel Nixon."[10]

Dole's 1980 presidential campaign was forced to refund more than $50,000 to various companies and to the Federal Election Commission for undocumented campaign disbursements.[11] During that same campaign, the FEC filed a complaint against Dole's wife, Elizabeth Hanford, for loaning his campaign $50,000. The $50,000 loan had been requested by Dole's campaign. Elizabeth Dole got the money from David Owen's bank at below the prime rate.[12] At the time, Owen was also chairman of the Dole for Senate Committee and Elizabeth Dole's financial adviser, later handling her blind trust. A letter from Jo-Anne Coe, assistant treasurer of Dole's leadership PAC, to Owen on Dec. 17, 1979, written on Dole's U.S. Senate stationery, said, "[T]hese funds are needed at the earliest possible time, and I will therefore appreciate your expediting the bank transfer." The campaign had only $14,709.04 in the Dole for President account at its Virginia bank.[13] The FEC dropped the charges and levied no fines, citing "the unique nature of Kansas law at the time of the transaction."[14]

During Dole's 1988 presidential campaign, allegations emerged that Owen, a former Kansas lieutenant governor and close Dole aide, had employees and executives of a Kansas company—to which he served as a $3,000/month consultant and in which he held stock—make $24,000 in contributions to Dole's 1986 Senate campaign. Employees reportedly were ordered to contribute and later got reimbursed by the firm, Birdview Satellite Communications. Steven Small, one of Birdview's founders and a former company vice president told the *Kansas City Star*, "I didn't feel right about [the contributions] but what could I do? I wasn't in a position to say no."[15]

When the story broke in the midst of the 1988 presidential primaries, Dole's staff denied that he had done anything wrong. The senator, who said he knew nothing of the donations, called for an internal and a Federal Election Commission probe into the matter and the staff promised that if any illegal money was received from Birdview employees, it would be returned.[16] FEC officials, however, have no record of any request from Dole to look into the Birdview matter.

Owen resigned from the 1988 campaign and told the Center for Public Integrity that Dole knew about the Birdview donations. He said Dole was present at a private fundraiser at the home of the former president of the now-defunct Birdview, Charles Ross, whom Owen said knew Dole well. Owen said Dole's reaction, in calling for an FEC probe, was "very typical of the way Dole operates, just sic an agency on someone to clear himself . . . He just cuts and runs whenever the heat gets hot. He leaves his friends out to dry."[17]

Owen landed in prison in 1994 as a result of an earlier situation similar to the Birdview episode. Owen's tax fraud conviction stemmed from two counts of filing false income tax returns. One count stated that Owen "disguised political contributions [about $11,000 worth bundled through his companies] to the [1986 Kansas Governor Mike] Hayden campaign as business expenses and that these were improper deductions."[18] Owen spent just over seven months in Leavenworth Prison and maintains that Dole had tried to strong-arm him into raising the money for Hayden, whom Owen credited with destroying his own 1982 gubernatorial bid by backing Owen's opponent. "I told him [Dole] why I was not supporting Hayden," Owen said in an interview. Nonetheless, Dole had pressed him to raise the money, Owen said, because Dole wanted a Republican governor in Kansas. Owen claimed he has done nothing illegal.

Dole declined to be interviewed for this book, but his press secretary, Nelson Warfield, in a letter responding to questions about the senator's relationship with Owen and these incidents said:

> As to David Owen, neither Senator Dole nor his wife knew of Owen's involvement with Mrs. Dole's blind trust [in the 1988 campaign]. When this came to light, Senator Dole promptly requested his resignation from his post with the campaign. Mr. Owen's subsequent conviction was for conduct unrelated to any activities he undertook on Senator Dole's behalf or that of his wife.[19]

"We don't need that in this campaign," Dole said after Owen resigned from the 1988 race amid controversy about his handling of Elizabeth Dole's trust. "In our campaign, if there is an appearance of bad judgment or misjudgment, or somebody has a problem, I think you should just step aside."[20]

Still more problems plagued Dole's 1988 presidential bid when it was later learned that the campaign had accepted more than $350,000 in illegal contributions and in-kind contributions of trips and services from corporations, individuals, and Dole's own leadership PAC, Campaign America.[21] As a result, in 1993 the FEC fined Dole's presidential campaign and Campaign America $122,975, to that date the largest penalty levied against a campaign.

From Dawson's to Capitol Hill

The posh offices of the Senate majority leader are a far cry from where Dole grew up. Back in Russell, Kansas—with an estimated 1920 population of 1,700 that grew to 4,781 in 1990—there wasn't much in the way of luxury. Dole was born on July 22, 1923, a few years prior to one of the most influential events of his life, and that of his peers: the Great Depression. During that bleak time, the Dole family of six was forced to rent out the top floor of their tiny two-room home and moved into the concrete-floored basement, using the rent money to pay the mortgage.[22]

One of the more popular tales of Dole's youth is that of his near-fatal World War II wound. Dole was hit by enemy fire in the back.[23] "I lay face down in the dirt," Dole recalled. "Unable to see or to move my arms, I thought they were missing."[24] In fact, after dire predictions by doctors that he would never walk again, Dole recovered, but his right arm was immobile. He underwent numerous operations, but it was only after the townspeople of Russell dropped nickels and dimes into a cigar box at Dawson's Drug Store, where he worked as a youngster, that Dole could afford the surgery that restored some movement.[25] To this day, the cigar box sits in Dole's Senate desk.[26]

During his rehabilitation, Dole met and later married Phyllis Holden, an occupational therapist. He resumed the college education he left for the war, and earned a law degree. While Dole was in law school, the local state representative's post opened up. Members of both the Democratic and Republican local parties in Russell County tried to persuade Dole to run on their ticket. Dole made the pragmatic choice. Even though his parents were both Democrats, the county was overwhelmingly Republican, so he chose to run with the GOP. In 1951, at age twenty-seven, he walked into the Kansas state legislature as one of the youngest state representatives in history.[27]

Dole stayed in local politics until 1961, when he entered the national scene as a U.S. representative. Within the span of a decade, Dole had gone from being a struggling student to a congressman.

In 1968, at age forty-five, Dole decided he was ready for an even bigger stage, that of the U.S. Senate. He got his chance when Kansas Republican Senator Frank Carlson personally informed Dole of his plans to retire and then made him his heir apparent.

By 1970, Dole had impressed President Richard Nixon enough that he made Dole the chairman of the RNC. Two years later, Nixon dumped Dole and had him fly to New York to offer the job to George Bush, then-ambassador to the United Nations. Dole said he felt like he had been pushed off a cliff.[28] The rigors of chairmanship and of the Senate office took a toll on Dole, not only professionally, but also personally; political life was credited with destroying his 23-year-old marriage. In late 1971, Dole flatly told his wife, "I want out."[29]

Dole gradually rebounded, winning re-election in 1974. Despite the fact that the infamous break-in occurred during his chairmanship to the Republican party, he escaped being pinned with any responsibility for Watergate or the CREEP slush funds. His common refrain regarding the break-in was, "Musta been my night off."[30]

Dole Runs

By December 1975, after years of courtship, he married Elizabeth Hanford, a talented Washington insider who was then a commissioner for the Federal Trade Commission. But there wasn't much time for the senator to devote to his new marriage. Nearly nine months later, Dole's career took another meteoric step. President Gerald Ford—who had ascended to the Oval Office after the unprecedented resignation of Richard Nixon on August 9, 1974, and had secured the 1976 Republican presidential nomination—called Dole and offered him the number two spot on the GOP presidential ticket.

At the time there was speculation that Dole had been selected to aggressively challenge Democratic nominee Jimmy Carter and his running mate Walter Mondale. During a heated vice-presidential debate with Walter Mondale, in which Mondale tried to associate Dole with the Watergate scandal, Dole said he didn't think Watergate would be considered an election issue . . . any more than the war in Vietnam would be . . . or World War II, or World War I, or the Korean War—all Democrat Wars . . . all in this century.''[31] Many labeled Dole's outburst as extreme and unwise. Some even blamed his so-called "hatchet man" image for Ford's loss, although Ford's pardon of Nixon likely alienated more voters.

It didn't take Dole long to regroup. In 1979, after a few years of jetting across the country making speeches and contacts, he announced his plans to run for president and take on the much-beleaguered President Carter. His wife resigned her job at the FTC to help her husband run. He vowed to run a positive campaign. "Above all, I mean to say what I stand for and speak plainly," he told a crowd of thousands in downtown Russell.[32]

What Dole didn't see coming was the Ronald Reagan tidal wave and it crushed him. After getting fewer votes in New Hampshire than any of the other candidates—only 607—Dole's campaign was considered dead. "Sometimes I think I never really ran for president in 1980," Dole later remarked.[33]

But after Reagan assumed office, Dole's power and influence grew. In 1984, Dole became Senate majority leader, and between 1984 and 1986 he sat on many key committees including Finance, Agriculture, Judiciary, Rules and Administration, and a Joint Committee on Taxation. In 1982, he wrote the Tax Equity and Fiscal Responsibility Act, TEFRA, which was designed to lower the deficit and close some tax loopholes. He exhibited leadership skill in getting a tax hike of more than $90 billion signed by Reagan.[34]

In 1987, when the GOP lost its majority status in the Senate and Dole became the minority leader, he decided to make another bid for president. But this time, he said, it would be done right, with professional staff and ample funds. There was no Reagan revolution to combat, no major scandal to taint his campaign. And it appeared there was a good chance that front-runner Vice President Bush might become mired in the Iran-Contra scandal.

Dole viewed this campaign almost as a grudge match to make up for the 1980 presidential primary in which Bush dismissed him as irrelevant, and his humiliation over losing the RNC chairmanship to Bush in 1971. Dole's political message emphasized his ties to the common folks, as a stark contrast to Bush's privileged upbringing. This tactic, however, backfired. The Bush camp called attention to the fact that Elizabeth Dole, who had been Reagan's transportation secretary, was independently wealthy and had helped boost Dole's overall net worth. Bush's campaign aides, who had a better organization in place than Dole, soon unleashed personal attacks on the Kansan, questioning the handling of his wife's blind trust and demanding the release of his tax returns going back five years.

It was as if a hornet's nest had been stirred. The Office of Government Ethics, an independent agency regulating the ethical conduct of the executive branch, launched a probe into a real estate transaction between Elizabeth Dole and David Owen, who served not only as the general finance director of the Dole 1988 presidential campaign, but also as Elizabeth's personal financial adviser. In addition, that same office began to investigate Owen's handling of her blind trust, which included several investments in various companies owned by Owen.[35]

Though Dole won the South Dakota primary, the Iowa caucus, and the Minnesota caucus, Super Tuesday loomed and his campaign didn't have the funds its staffers thought would be necessary to be competitive. He even lost North Carolina, Elizabeth Dole's home state where she had tirelessly campaigned for her husband. It was over.

Still the Doles recovered. Again it didn't take him or his wife very long. Bush appointed Elizabeth Dole secretary of labor, and Dole remained Senate minority leader and, ironically, President Bush's most important ally in the Senate. By November 1994, Elizabeth Dole had left government and assumed the helm of the American Red Cross. Her husband once again found himself Senate majority leader after the Republicans took over control of both houses of Congress for the first time in four decades. The family began its preparations for a third shot at the Oval Office.

Dole on Money

One legislative issue Dole has rarely championed is the reform of the political process. Because of his leadership role in Congress, good-government citizens' groups have viewed Dole as a major impediment to any serious effort at cleaning up Washington. According to Fred Wertheimer, who was the head of Common Cause until his retirement in 1995, "The past decade, Bob Dole has been in the forefront to block every serious effort to reform the campaign finance system."[36]

In 1971, as the Republican National Committee chairman, Dole made a long speech before the Senate Commerce Committee, promoting open and fair campaigns that he said both he and Nixon believed in:

> It is a regrettable but pressing fact that statutes presently in force provide no effective and comprehensive control or oversight of campaign financing or campaign conduct. No coherent, tightly drawn, enforceable body of laws governs or guides either contribution or expenditure of campaign funds. The forces of politics in effect run wild, with little or no protection of the public interest ... But they [campaign finance regulations] are so subject to abuse and avoidance that the public rightly lacks confidence in them. They are an annoyance to honest candidates and political organizations. They are a joke to the dishonest and devious. And they fail to achieve even token protection of the public's right to information and candor.[37]

He added, "American voters are entitled to know where candidates for public office and the organizations supporting them get their money and what they spend that money for."[38]

In July 1982, Dole made a statement which has been used over and over again in many different forms to capture his real sentiments on the influence money can have over politics. "When the political action committees give money, they expect something in return other than good government," Dole told the *Wall Street Journal*.[39] On another occasion, Dole said, "PACs give to incumbents, and that is me and other incumbents in this [Senate] chamber, because access to an officeholder is more important than a member's party, ideology or even voting record on the issues, and I never knew you had to buy access."[40]

In response to the Center for Public Integrity's question as to whether a candidate can receive millions of dollars from specific groups, allow those groups better access to power, and not feel indebted to them, Dole's campaign spokesman responded:

> The cynical view that everyone and everything is for sale is routinely rebutted in daily life in this country ... [T]he ultimate test of integrity for a reporter or a public official or anyone else must be individual conduct.
>
> So the proposition is false that successful fund-raising necessarily burdens a candidate with an obligation to yield to the undue influence of donors or provide benefactors with improper access. It depends on the individual. And in the case of Bob Dole, no contributor has ever improperly benefited [sic] by supporting any of his campaigns.
>
> Bob Dole has served in the Congress for over thirty years and has never been called before the Ethics Committee to answer charges of wrongdoing. Politics is partisan. Critics and opponents have leveled charges from time to time—several of which your organization now apparently seeks to resurrect. But the fact remains that Bob Dole has never compromised his personal ethics or broken the law to provide any benefit to any campaign contributor. So clearly, money does not necessarily buy access or influence. Certainly not in the case of Bob Dole.

But the man given to these conscientious public utterances has recently raised millions of dollars in secret contributions to a nonprofit foundation he founded, raised millions for his own leadership PAC, and was among the top honoraria recipients in the Senate. For each year between 1980 and 1986, except for one, Dole was the top honoraria recipient. Between 1978 and 1986 he received $825,266.[41] Dole's affinity for traveling on corporate aircraft has also made him vulnerable to criticism that he is out of touch with the average American who flies coach or doesn't fly at all. In April 1995 *Newsweek* reported, "Dole seeks [corporate plane rides] more than anybody else." Dole has traveled on ADM corporate planes at least thirty-five times between 1983 and 1995.[42]

His leadership PAC, Campaign America, "tailored after a similar venture Richard Nixon established in the 1960s," is likewise booming.[43] According to the FEC, during the 1993–94 election cycle, it had the largest increase in donations as compared to other PACs and raised the second-highest amount of money: $8.6 million.

In 1993, Dole formed yet another pocket into which patrons could deposit money and win influence when he started the Better America Foundation (BAF), a nonprofit, tax-exempt organization that was ostensibly designed to develop, analyze, and promote conservative public policies. Its only high-profile activity was the production of a national television commercial, for about $1 million, featuring Dole in front of a fluttering American flag, promoting the balanced-budget amendment prior to the 1994 elections.

BAF later came under attack for its policy of refusing to disclose the names of its donors, who gave a total of $4,978,900 by the end of 1994. Its slick brochure highlighted two points regarding gifts: first, that "there are no limits on the amounts an individual or corporation may contribute." Second, BAF's 1995 brochure promised, "There is no requirement for public disclosure or contributors; and names of the donors will not be disclosed."

Jim Whittinghill, former Dole aide and executive director of BAF, said in an April 1995 interview that he was not concerned about any criticism that the foundation was simply another tool for Dole to use in his 1996 presidential bid, despite the fact that its honorary chairman was Bob Dole, its staff was comprised of former Dole aides, and four of the five pictures on the wall in the office reception area included Dole.

"I worry about staying legal. I worry about crossing the line . . . I don't worry about some goofball organization making allegations," he said, referring to the Center for Public Integrity's questions about BAF.[44] Two months later, under fire from public interest groups, news organizations, and the DNC for allegedly using BAF polls and research material for Dole's presidential campaign, the board of directors decided to dissolve the foundation, make known the contributors, and return $2.5 million in contributions. Don Angell, a North Carolina businessman who gave Better America $10,000 on August 29, 1994, said he regretted the closing. "This was something where you can give large amounts. Now we're hung up on $1,000."[45]

It was not surprising to discover that those who gave large sums of money to BAF, including the Archer Daniels Midland Company and the Gallo Winery, were the same vested interests that have given hundreds of thousands of dollars to Dole's other political efforts, as well as to his charitable organization for the handicapped, the Dole Foundation, created in 1983, which has raised in excess of $7.5 million over the past six years and a total of at least $11,622,567 since 1984. The Better America Foundation benefactors are listed in the following table.

Contributors to the
Better America Foundation 1993–1995

Donors Giving $200,000 or More

Koch Industries, Inc. ($225,000); Pride 21 Corp. ($250,000)

Donors Giving $100,000 to $199,999

American Financial Corp.; AT&T; Anschutz Corporation; Atchison Topeka and Santa Fe Railway Co.; BankAmerica Corp.; Beechcraft; CSX Corp.; E & J Gallo Winery; Theodore J. Forstmann (NY); Massachusetts Mutual Life Insurance Co.; MBNA Corp.; Mesa; Metromedia Co.; Northrop Grumann Corp.; Philip Morris Management Corp.; RJR Nabisco Washington, Inc.; Julian H. Robertson, Jr.; Schering Corp.; G.D. Searle and Co.; Tele-Communications, Inc.; The Limited Service Corp.

Donors Giving $50,000 to $99,999

AFLAC Incorporated; Andreas Foundation; Archer-Daniels-Midland Co.; Atlantic Richfield Co.; Barrick Goldstrike Mines, Inc.; Cessna Aircraft Co.; Bill Daniels (Denver); Founders Asset Management, Inc.; Charles Gates (Denver); Thomas Gosnell (Rochester, NY); GTE Service Corp.; Forrest E. Hoglund (Houston); Jones Intercable; Kohlberg, Kravis, Roberts and Co.; Manville Corp.; Marriott International, Inc.; Metropolitan Life Insurance Co.; Ruan Corp.; Starr Technical Risk Agency, Inc.; C.V. Starr and Co., Inc.; Stephens Group, Inc.; Storage Technology Corp.; Textron Inc.; Time Warner Inc.; Torchmark Corp.; US West Inc.; UST Inc.; Dennis Washington (Missoula, MT); WMX Technologies Inc.

Donors Giving $25,000 to $49,999

Abbott Laboratories; American Medical Security; Stephen D. Bechtel, Jr. (San Francisco); Boyd Gaming Corp.; Dean L. Buntrock (Oak Brook, IL); C.S. Brooks Canada Inc.; Sheila and Herbert F. Collins (Gloucester, MA); COMSAT Video Enterprises; Contran Corp.; Coors Brewing Co.; Federal Express Corp.; Fidelity Investments; GE Financial Operation; Adele Hall (Shawnee Mission. KS); Donald J. Hall (Shawnee Mission, KS); Harbert Corporation; James M. Hoak (Dallas); Robert Ludwig (Bronxville, NY); M S Investments; James A. Ortenzio (NY); Ryan Holding Corp.; UtiliCorp United; Vulcan Materials Co.

Donors Giving $10,000 to $24,999

Don G. Angell (Bermuda Run, NC); Astra USA, Inc.; Baxter Healthcare Corp.; Coca Cola Co.; Cortlandt S. Dietler (Denver); Eaton Metal Products Corp.; Freeport-McRan Inc.; Stephen Friedman (NY); Belton K. Johnson Interest; William R. Jordan (Fayetteville, NC(; Yong C. Kim (Fremont, CA); Mutual of Omaha Companies; PepsiCo.; Anthony L. Soave (Detroit); Thomas W. Weisel (San Francisco)

Donors Giving Less Than $10,000

Abelson-Taylor Inc.; American Investors Life Insurance Co.; Michael E. Aylward (Chanute, KS); James Jay Baker and Assocs.; Baxter International Inc.; Robert A. Becker, Inc.; Dallas Fan Fares, Inc.; Jeanne M. Dugan (Holdel, NJ); Frank Dunlevy (San Francisco); Edelman Public Relations Worldwide; Electrophoretic Pump Co.; Seth J. Gersch (Hillsborough, CA); Seymour Graham (Hazelton, PA); James C. and Donna Hale (San Francisco); Bryce L. Harlow (Vienna VA); Harris Chemical North America Inc.; Tom C. Korogolos (DC); Scott and Lisa Kovalik (Orinda, CA); Casey A. and Julie L. Lair (Neodesha, KS); Mark T. Lair (Chanute KS); The Lenfest Group; Jack G. Levin (Hillsborough, CA); Scott Levin Assocs. Inc.; Kent A. Logan (San Francisco); James and Linda McMahon (San Francisco); J. Sanford Miller (San Francisco); Willard J. Overlock, Jr. (NY); Oxford Health Plans, Inc.; John E. Palmer (Overland Park, KS); Henry M. Paulson, Jr. (Chicago); Jay A. Precourt (Houston); John W. Rollins (Wilmington, DE); Lewis Rudin (NY); J.V. Saeman and Co.; Joseph M. Schell (Lafayette, CA); Seneca Meadows Inc.; John K. Skeen (San Francisco); Richard A. Smith (San Francisco); T.A. Thornhill (San Rafael, CA); Triax Communications Corp.; Mark Winkelman (NY)

When asked by the Center for Public Integrity if Watergate had an impact on the way he raised campaign contributions, and whether there was a difference between Nixon's Committee to Reelect the President and the Better America Foundation receiving millions in secret contributions, Dole's press secretary Nelson Warfield said:

> Senator Dole has been in the forefront of efforts to curb special interests in the political system. Back in 1974, he supported the Federal Election Campaign Act which required the public disclosure of contributors and their contributions. This sweeping legislation certainly represented a lesson learned from Watergate.
> ... Senator Dole voluntarily released complete and comprehensive contributor and expenditure records for his conservative think tank, the Better America Foundation. A tax-exempt 501(c)4, the organization was under no legal obligation to disclose this down-to-the-penny information. Indeed, similar organizations such as the Democratic Leadership Council (an organization that did much to boost the early presidential prospects of then-Governor Bill Clinton) have consistently refused to disclose the same information.
> The Better America Foundation went far above the requirements of the law to provide full disclosure. CREEP fought to avoid any such thing. There is simply no comparison between the two organizations.

Working from the timeless journalistic dictum "follow the money," the Center for Public Integrity set about attempting to further illuminate the more telling relationships between Dole and his donors. Senator Dole has taken public policy actions as a lawmaker which have helped each of the following companies—Ernest and Julio Gallo Winery, Archer Daniels Midland (ADM), and Witchita, Kansas–based Koch Industries—reap millions of dollars.

Ernest and Julio Gallo Winery

One of the most surprising discoveries about Dole's fundraising efforts is that his most generous patron since 1979 is the Ernest and Julio Gallo family. They have written checks to his campaigns and PAC totaling $381,000. Include the $790,000 contributed to the Dole Foundation from 1985 to 1994, as well as the $100,000 to the Better America Foundation in 1993, and the total amount of Gallo contributions tops $1 million.[46] Dole, in return, has worked hard for the Gallos.

Take for instance the customized inheritance tax matter, innocuously called the "generation-skipping transfer." By its name, no one could really tell that it was legislation tailor made for two California gentlemen getting on in years who just happened to produce one out of every three bottles of wine purchased in the United States. As part of the 1986 tax reform bill this "transfer" tax measure—which eventually became known as the "Gallo amendment"—would save the largest wine makers in the world $104 million in inheritance taxes when the two principles, Ernest and Julio Gallo, died and their heirs received the money.[47] Dole, who was then Senate majority leader, a senior member of the tax-writing Senate Finance Committee, and a member of the House-Senate conference committee on the 1986 tax bill, received $20,000 in one day from the Gallo family.[48] On March 31, 1986, during the writing of the bill, Ernest and Julio Gallo and their wives Aileen and Amelia each gave the maximum-allowable donation of $5,000 to Campaign America. And with the help of Dole and others, the provision passed.

Considering that the Gallos started in the wine business by reading books they borrowed from the Modesto Public Library in 1933, at the end of Prohibition, the two brothers were quite successful in building an unrivaled wine empire. Julio died in an auto accident in 1993, and in 1994 Ernest's fortune was valued by *Forbes* at more than $300 million.[49] The relationship between the Gallos and Dole began in the mid-1980s and as Dole's clout in the Senate grew, so did the Gallo donations.

MARKET PROMOTION PROGRAM

One of the largest agricultural subsidy programs from which the Gallo winery has benefitted is the Market Promotion Program (MPP). This initiative, which some have called "corporate welfare" almost since its inception in the 1985 Farm Bill, has yielded Gallo more than $23.8 million between 1986 and 1994.[50] The goal of the program is to "encourage the development, maintenance, and expansion of commercial export markets for agricultural commodities," according to a June 1994 United States Department of Agriculture fact sheet on the program.

Dole, while not an extremely public supporter of MPP specifically, has taken many steps to assure that it remains intact. In November of 1985 he introduced a revised version of the Farm Bill that included the $975 million to fund what would later be renamed the Market Promotion Program.[51] Dole has voted down attempts to eliminate the MPP program every time they have cropped up between 1992–1995.[52] During Agriculture Secretary Dan Glickman's 1995 confirmation hearings, Dole commended Glickman for supporting MPP by saying, "He's [Glickman] consistently taking a stand to make U.S. agriculture trade more competitive, and he has supported ... the Market Promotion Program."[53]

MPP has been broadly criticized for mismanagement and wasteful spending. In a May 1995 study, the Cato Institute said programs such as MPP disproportionately favor large corporations with subsidies at the expense of small farmers. The General Accounting Office, in a June 1993 report, said there was "no clear relationship between the amount spent on MPP and changes in the level of U.S. agricultural exports."[54]

THE CHARMAT METHOD

In 1992, Dole intervened in a dispute between Gallo, the Treasury Department, and champagne producers regarding an attempt by Gallo to change its champagne label. Gallo officials, looking to go upscale, sought the permission of the Bureau of Alcohol, Tobacco, and Firearms to remove the words "bulk processing" from their champagne labels because they thought it sounded degrading. They wanted to replace it with the more sophisticated-sounding "Charmat method."[55] But other producers of champagne-like wines argued that because Gallo's champagne was produced in large vats, and not fermented in individual bottles, it shouldn't be allowed to deceive consumers into thinking they were purchasing a higher-quality product.[56]

Dole, then the minority leader, co-wrote a letter to the Treasury Department asking that the Gallo brothers be given their way. In a letter dated February 7, 1992 Dole said most consumers believe that "champagne is champagne, regardless of the production."[57] The Gallos prevailed and in 1993 were able to remove "bulk processing" from their label. Dole had received $97,000 in contributions from the Gallo family between 1989 and 1992.[58]

GALLO AND HEALTH CARE

Senator Dole, seeking to steal the spotlight from President Clinton in 1993, unveiled his own version of a health care proposal. But there was a big difference between the two. Early in the public debate to enact sweeping health care reform legislation, Clinton proposed to fund his proposal with $105 billion in "sin taxes" on cigarettes and alcohol.[59] Dole's plan conspicuously lacked any alcohol or cigarette taxes. (The Gallos must have been reassured, but let's not leave out Phillip Morris, RJR/Nabisco, and U.S. Tobacco, who collectively gave Dole's various enterprises $13,000, in 1993–1994 and have given $334,250 over his career.)

But before Dole released his own health care proposal in August 1994, he had contemplated sin taxes as a way to fund health care reform. "I'm not interested in sin taxes, but it seems to me we can't say, 'Well, never,' " he said on CNN in August 1993.[60] The idea of the taxes soon evaporated. Between February 1993 and February 1994, when the matter was being debated, the Gallos donated $90,000 to Dole's leadership PAC, Campaign America, and $100,000 to Dole's think tank, the Better America Foundation.

The Archer Daniels Midland Company

Archer Daniels Midland touts itself as the "supermarket to the world." This behemoth, based in Decatur, Illinois, has its fingers in nearly every agribusiness pie. In the corporation's 1994 annual report, chief executive Dwayne Andreas noted that ADM had 165 operating plants, 300 grain elevators, 2,000 barges, 10,000 railroad cars, 100 cargo ships, and 15,000 trucks. Its net sales in fiscal year 1994 exceeded $11 billion and its profits topped $1 billion.[61] A 1995 *Fortune* 500 list ranked the major milling and soybean processor the ninety-second largest in the nation.[62]

The company battled with a spate of bad publicity in the summer of 1995 when the Justice Department, using an ADM informant, made public its undercover investigation into allegations of price-fixing for sweeteners and food additives.[63]

But ADM's influence doesn't stop with agricultural issues. Andreas and ADM, playing it safe, are among the largest contributors to both parties in national political campaigns using their corporate PAC, individual donations, the ADM Foundation, and the Andreas Foundation. In the three-year period between 1991 and 1994, ADM and the Andreas family contributed more than $1 million to the Republican and Democratic national committees, with Republicans netting more than $900,000 of the stash.[64] In 1994, ADM alone gave approximately $2.5 million to various congressional candidates.[65]

Andreas has befriended virtually every president since Nixon. His generosity to all of them is notorious. His $25,000 check to CREEP wound up in the bank account of one of the Watergate burglars.[66] As a result he was investigated but ultimately cleared, by the Senate Watergate Committee. One of Andreas's well-known and closest political allies has been Senator Bob Dole. Dole often tries to downplay the association, arguing that he supports ADM because he is a farm state senator, but the relationship between the two goes much deeper than Dole's roots in Kansas.

Since 1979, ADM has given Dole's senate and presidential campaigns, as well as his leadership PAC and think tank more than $200,000 in contributions, making ADM Dole's fourth-largest patron. That sum does not include the $275,000 Andreas and ADM have given to the Dole Foundation, the senator's charity for the disabled.[67] And Andreas didn't forget Elizabeth Dole. When she took over the reins of the Red Cross, the Andreas Foundation donated $500,000.[68] In response to questions from the Center for Public Integrity regarding campaign donations, Andreas said the money given to Dole through himself and ADM is donated because farm groups have asked him to raise money for the senator. "I have never discussed campaign contributions with Dole—only with his Kansas friends who are farm-oriented," Andreas wrote in an August 1995 letter. Despite saying that he does visit with Dole up to three times a year, Andreas added that, "I only know about Dole's policies what I read in the news and do not discuss it with him."

ADM has also been generous with trips, honoraria, and in-kind contributions. Between January 1983 and March 1995, Dole took thirty-five trips on ADM corporate aircraft, for which ADM was reimbursed $75,283. *Newsweek* (April 1995) reported that Dole reimbursed the company for the equivalent of a first-class fare at "less than 25 percent of the cost of operating a private jet." In 1992, Dole's leadership PAC, Campaign America, reimbursed ADM $20,477 for a single— and the costliest—excursion.[69] During 1993-1994 alone, Dole took an average of a trip a month on ADM aircraft.

THE FLORIDA CONDO

The most intriguing tale of the Dole-Andreas relationship is a Bal Harbour, Florida, oceanfront condominium in the "Sea View" complex that Elizabeth Dole bought from Andreas in 1982. According to the *Wall Street Journal*, Elizabeth Dole and her brother John Hanford "paid $150,000 cash for a three-room, ocean-front apartment at the Sea View in a transaction handled by the hotel's management." Dole, however, didn't begin payments on the apartment until seven months after the purchase occurred, and the property was actually valued at $190,000.[70] Sea View's manager agreed "with a suggestion that if the Sea View corporation were liquidated, the stock held by Mrs. Dole and her brother—a little more than 3 percent—might be valued at more than $300,000."[71] In 1995 Dole's campaign press secretary wrote:

It was not known at the time to Elizabeth, her brother, or Senator Dole that the proceeds of the sale were credited to Dwayne Andreas. Of course, the Doles knew that Mr. Andreas owned a unit in the same building, but his actual ownership interest on this particular unit was unknown to them.

In any event, Elizabeth and her brother paid the fair market "going rate" for the unit. Their purchase price was consistent with the pur-

chase prices of other comparable Sea View units during the same
time period. . . .

Though Senator Dole has disputed any direct involvement
in the purchase of the condominium, documents from Sea
View's executive offices show that in 1982, the three-room
hotel suite was transferred to "Senator and Mrs. Robert
Dole."[72] Both Doles were listed as Sea View stockholders on
the 1986–1987 list of stockholders. And the Dole family
claimed $4,404 in rent from the condo on their joint 1986
income tax return. For his part, Andreas said that "thirty-
three rooms had changed hands for less than the price the
Dole family paid" for the condo.[73]

Ethics experts generally agree it is questionable for a lawmaker or their spouse to purchase real estate from the chairman of a company with business pending before Congress.
Nevertheless, the Senate Ethics Committee has never formally
investigated the Dole–Sea View matter.

The most oft-mentioned return favor to ADM is Dole's advocacy for ethanol. As of May 1995, ADM produced more
than 60 percent of the country's ethanol, an alcohol distilled
from corn and added to gasoline to produce gasohol.[74] Dole's
support of ethanol has been strong and consistent. In November 1989, he held up a steel import bill until his colleagues
would agree to extend the ethanol excise tax credit to the
year 2000. An industry analyst estimated that in 1987 alone,
ADM would garner $150 million from the federal govern-
ment's ethanol program.[75] In 1995 the Department of Energy
estimated that ADM had the capacity to produce 898 million
gallons of ethanol, which would yield the blenders of gasohol
using ADM ethanol a maximum $475 million in tax benefits.
Without the subsidy, there would be no market.[76] But Dole
has done much more to help Andreas and ADM.

According to the U.S. Department of Agriculture, ADM
has raked in at least $424,541,178 in subsidies—excluding
subsidies for ethanol and corn sweetener—from the federal
government between fiscal years 1985–1995. Dole is a senior
member of the Senate Agriculture Committee, through which
these programs must pass; he has never opposed them. Programs such as the Export Enhancement Program and the

extremely lucrative grain trade with the former Soviet Union in particular, have received Dole's enthusiastic backing and resulted in ADM pocketing hundreds of millions of dollars in subsidies.

THE EXPORT ENHANCEMENT PROGRAM

The Export Enhancement Program (EEP) began with the 1985 Farm Bill and was aimed at helping U.S. farmers compete with foreign farmers who received subsidies from their governments.

Between fiscal years 1985 and 1995, ADM received more than $134 million from the program. In several of its annual reports, ADM executives have lauded it as a "glimmer of hope" and a "major benefit" to the company.

In Senate floor speeches, in the form of amendments, and in interviews Dole has endorsed EEP. Examples of Dole's support for the program are well documented and include an amendment to "extend and revise agricultural price support and related programs, [and] to provide for agricultural export;"[78] urging incoming Agriculture Secretary Clayton Yeutter in 1989 to support EEP by saying, "I just think one area that we hope you'll [Yeutter] be very aggressive in, that's the Export Enhancement Program . . . We all hope we are going to have an aggressive, knowledgeable person who's going to be our salesman to the world. . . ."[79] pushing President Bush in 1989 to increase aid to the Soviet Union and to boost EEP, telling him, 'if we're going to trade with the Soviet Union, which we are, then we have to be competitive, we have to meet world prices;' "[80] sending a letter in 1992 to then-Agriculture Secretary Edward Madigan, writing, "I am deeply concerned about the lack of agricultural export activity and the seeming reluctance on the part of the Administration to do anything about it;"[81] and writing, along with eight colleagues, to former Agriculture Secretary Mike Espy in 1993, encouraged Espy to expand EEP to include barley exports (a commodity processed by ADM) and to release $240 million in Russian grain credits even though Russia had not made mandated payments to U.S. banks.[82]

Dole has supported EEP despite criticism from the General

Accounting Office (GAO) and various congressmen that it is inefficient. The conservative Heritage Foundation and Citizens Against Government Waste have recommended that EEP be eliminated.[83] The yearly $4.2 billion program was placed on the Republican chopping block in the spring of 1995 as talks got underway about how to balance the federal budget.

OTHER ADM SUBSIDIES

Dole has also helped ADM by boosting the federal peanut subsidy program. On November 23, 1985, Dole introduced an amendment to the 1985 Farm Bill which included the peanut price-support program.[84] ADM's 1986 annual report noted that peanut prices were remarkably better than they had been the previous year due to the 1985 Farm Bill.[85]

Another area in which ADM benefitted is in the corn sweetener market, of which ADM holds a 30 percent share.[86] Despite ADM's advertising campaign to the contrary, the much-debated sugar loan program reportedly costs American consumers an estimated $3 billion annually by "stabilizing" the cost of sugar at 22 cents a pound. Corn sweetener producers have worked in alliance with the sugar industry in support of the loan program.[87] Producers of corn sweeteners benefit indirectly—by "shadow pricing" below the cost of sugar—gaining some $548 million annually, according to the General Accounting Office.[88]

According to Common Cause, when the Government Printing Office produced a copy of the 1985 Farm Bill a section which pertained to sugar was omitted. It was a provision which would ease the sugar trade restrictions that had been agreed to by members of the House-Senate conference committee. The sponsors of the provision, Representatives Philip Crane and Bill Frenzel, "incredulous and incensed," demanded to know what had happened.[89] An aide to Crane later reported that the elimination of the provision was ordered by Dole. Though Dole's staff has disputed this, according to Philip Stern's *Still the Best Congress Money Can Buy*, the senior senator's spokesman admitted that "Dole's staff read the substitute (Frenzel-Crane) provision and rejected it."[90]

Dole also helped push through the 1986 tax bill. ADM told

its stockholders in 1988 that its tax rate decreased by 6 percent because of the bill.[91]

Andreas denies that his company ever attempted to influence Dole in any way to favor programs which would be beneficial to ADM. "To my knowledge, neither I nor anyone in ADM has ever lobbied Dole for anything having to do with our business," he wrote in 1995. "Indeed, it would be an eminently foolish thing to do because he depends on farmers and farm organizations for his advice and support, not people like me."

But few of Bob Dole's entanglements with financial backers are more interesting than the case of a consistent, longtime patron from his native state, that of Koch Industries.

Koch Industries

After their father's death, David and Charles Koch took over what had become a prosperous Kansas oil company and renamed it Koch Industries. By the mid-1990s, Koch Industries had grown to become the country's second largest private, family-operated company, with over $20 billion in estimated sales.[92] The brothers are now among the wealthiest men in the world, with an estimated fortune of $4.7 billion.[93]

As the company blossomed, so did the Koch brothers' interest in politics. The Koch family helped found the Cato Institute, a libertarian Washington, D.C. think tank, and has provided over $11 million to the institute between 1986 and 1993.[94] In addition, the brothers provided seed money to Citizens for a Sound Economy, a conservative, nonprofit organization. Between 1986 and 1993, the Koch family gave over $7.9 million to the organization.[95]

David Koch views himself as an "opportunist" who was willing to spend money on causes he believes in: "My overall concept is to minimize the role of government and to maximize the role of the private economy and to maximize personal freedoms ... By supporting all these different organizations I am trying to support different approaches to achieve those objectives. It's almost like an investor investing in a whole variety of companies."[96]

To the Koch brothers, Senator Bob Dole could be considered another one of their investments. The senior senator from Kansas has assisted Koch Industries interests on at least two occasions and has been the recipient of the Kochs' largesse. Since 1979, Koch Industries has given Dole campaigns and causes over $240,000. Dole's leadership PAC, Campaign America, and his presidential and senatorial campaigns have accepted a total of $20,000 from the company. Another $225,000 was given to the Better America Foundation, Dole's conservative think tank, making the Koch contribution the second largest ever to the now-defunct organization.[97] Koch has also given thousands to Dole's charity for the disabled, the Dole Foundation.

Koch's public affairs office did not respond to specific questions, but wrote to the Center for Public Integrity: "As a Kansas-based corporation, our support for a home-state senator and his foundation should be easily understood ... While Koch Industries and its leadership have not developed a strong personal relationship with Senator Dole, we believe his leadership has been and will continue to be important in advancing the well-being of society."[98]

In 1995, David Koch helped bolster Dole's 1996 presidential coffers by co-hosting a private $1,000 per person fundraiser on Dole's seventy-second birthday. The campaign benefitted to the tune of $150,000.[99]

Months earlier, Dole had introduced the Comprehensive Regulatory Reform Act of 1995 (S. 343). When he announced the bill on February 2, 1995, Dole touted it as an "effort to inject common sense into a federal regulatory process that is often too costly, too arcane, and too inflexible."[100]

During the spring of the same year, Koch Industries was facing an estimated $54 million civil lawsuit filed by the Environmental Protection Agency, the U.S. Coast Guard, and the Justice Department. The government charged that Koch Industries had spilled 2.3 million gallons of oil in more than 300 incidents in six states since 1990. It was considered one of the largest cases ever filed against a company accused of noncompliance with the Clean Water Act.

The regulatory reform bill was initially drafted at Dole's personal request by C. Boyden Gray, former Bush White

House counsel and chairman of Citizens for a Sound Economy (CSE). CSE also happens to be the recipient of millions in Koch donations; in fact David Koch had once chaired the organization.[101]

The senator, the nonprofit organization, and the lobbyist are further intertwined. The 1995 brochure issued by Dole's Better America Foundation, identified regulatory reform as one of the issues it wanted to pursue, and in May of that year, gave CSE $50,000.[102] Two months earlier, CSE's Gray gave Dole's presidential campaign a $1,000 donation.[103] Dole even tried to help the organization's efforts by penning a fundraising letter on his personal stationery, saying: "If Americans like you don't get more involved now by helping me and Citizens for a Sound Economy (CSE) in important efforts like this Agenda For Leadership, the special interest groups and big government politicians will beat us down on other key reforms I believe you elected us to make."

Dole took ownership of the sweeping regulatory reform bill and early on in the deliberations, a clause was inserted that would allow companies being sued to challenge the government by finding a conflicting or contradictory rule and to prove that the regulation had not been enforced uniformly.[104] If any companies had gotten leniency in the past on any regulations, then Koch Industries could argue under the new regulatory laws that they couldn't be given a stiffer sentence or larger fines.

"It is an invitation to go out and look for things that have nothing to do with a case," said Phil Metzger, chief policy counsel in the EPA's Office of Water. "If a company really wants to stretch things out, they can, even if it's a straightforward case."[105] A senior attorney with the Natural Resources Defense Council, who agreed that the legislation would affect pending cases, said the insertion of the clause "raises the question of who is trying to get their lawsuit fixed."[106]

The bill stalled in the Senate just before Congress's 1995 summer recess because Dole fell short on the number of votes needed to close off debate. But he said he still expected it to pass before the session ended.[107]

Dole had helped Koch Industries before. In November 1989 a report was issued by the Senate Select Committee on

Indian Affairs that said Koch Industries had been engaging in "sophisticated theft" of $10 million in oil from Indian-owned land in Oklahoma, along with $21 million in other areas. FBI officials conducting the initial probe had hidden themselves in the bushes in the heartland and said they observed Koch officials "cheat the Indians out of their oil."[108]

But Koch Industries was never indicted. Koch got a letter from the Justice Department in March 1992 from the U.S. attorney for the Western District of Oklahoma saying that the probe had been "terminated. No indictments are anticipated."[109]

Kenneth A. Ballen, counsel to the special committee, said the decision of federal officials not to pursue charges stemmed from the Koch family's political connections. In May 1992, Ballen was quoted as telling the *National Journal* that Dole and his staff had intervened on Koch's behalf. The company had retained Dole's friend and ally Robert Strauss, along with two other members of Strauss's high-powered Washington, D.C. law firm, to avoid federal prosecution.[110]

Ballen said he was stunned. "If I were a prosecutor, I no doubt would have indicted the company." Ballen, presently a Washington lawyer, now says he was misquoted by the *National Journal*, but allowed that Dole had not been happy with the probe. "Senator Dole made some statements and tried to imply that Koch was being unfairly prosecuted."[111]

Senator Dole has been there for his top contributors when they needed him. He has come a long way since the folks at Dawson's plunked a cigar box down on the drugstore counter to raise money to mend his shattered arm. He's risen from a boy in a hardworking, often struggling family, to a life of comfort at the Watergate apartment complex and his Florida condo over a remarkable, 45-year political career. Indeed, Bob Dole has overcome many obstacles in his lifetime.

Among the challenges he faces in seeking the Republican nomination for president is the tide of anti-Washington, anti-government sentiment that voters exhibited in the 1992 and 1994 elections. Very few members of Congress during the past quarter century have raised more special interest money for their campaigns than this quintessential

Washington insider. Success in Bob Dole's 1996 presidential effort will be made possible, in large part, by how well he is able to plumb the patrons who have contributed millions of dollars in the past.

BOB DOLE
TOP 10 CAREER PATRONS*

1. Ernest & Julio Gallo Winery, Modesto, California — $381,000
2. MacAndrews & Forbes Holdings, Inc., (Ronald O. Perelman) and subsidiaries, holding company, New York, New York — $277,500
3. Koch Industries, oil, Wichita, Kansas — $245,000
4. Archer Daniels Midland, agribusiness, Decatur, Illinois — $217,800
5. American Citizens for Political Action, Republican/Conservative PAC, Washington, D.C. — $192,580
6. Thomas C. Foley, NTC Group, Inc., holding company, New York, New York — $183,285
7. Torchmark, insurance, Birmingham, Alabama — $166,125
8. Philip Anschutz, The Anschutz Corporation, oil, Denver, Colorado — $162,380
9. Massachusetts Mutual Life Insurance Company, insurance Springfield, Massachusetts — $157,358
10. Fisher Brothers, real estate, New York, New York — $121,500

* Includes all U.S. Senate campaign cycles, 1979 through 1994, as well as all donations to Campaign America, for the same period based upon Federal Election Commission records and Center for Responsive Politics data. Figures also include donations to the Better America Foundation, based upon their donor list. Donations to the Dole Foundation could not be included in the compilation of this list, as it does not disclose its donors.

A look at the top 10 career patrons to Dole's presidential and senatorial campaigns, as well as to Campaign America, and independent expenditures on behalf of the candidate over the past fifteen years from 1979 to 1994, shows that only one of the major players in Dole's campaigns is from Kansas and only two are from Midwestern states.

Bob Dornan

Robert K. Dornan never got to drop any bombs on the enemy. Eager to fight for his country, he dropped out of college in 1953 to join the Air Force. His aim was to become a fighter pilot in the Korean War, but before he could see any action, an armistice was declared. Maybe because of his unfulfilled dream, he always appears ready for combat—he wears an Israeli Defense Forces belt buckle, drives a huge pickup truck, and is even rumored to carry a gun. But in the end, Dornan makes lots of noise and has little impact on the outcome of events.[1]

He would like to make some noise in the 1996 presidential campaign, but Dornan told us he has "a feeling of genuine sadness" about the presidential selection process. "My younger brother's a high school teacher. I've already told him to stop telling every young man and now young woman . . . that anybody can be president of the United States. To stop telling them that because it's not so. Not everybody can be president. You must be a millionaire."[2]

Midway through 1995, Dornan had raised the least money of any top Republican candidate, $177,826, and had a paltry $5,463 in cash on hand.[3] No money means no staff, no polling, no political consultants, no media advertising, no plane tickets to key states.

What's curious is that Bob Dornan, mostly through small contributions, has consistently been one of the best fundraisers in the House of Representatives. In 1976, in his first run for public office, Dornan won election to an open seat

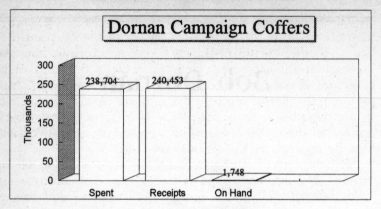

Reporting through September 30, 1995.

Spent figures include all purchases or payments made in connection with or for the purpose of influencing a federal election.
Receipts are anything of value received by a political committee.
On Hand figures include funds held in checking and savings accounts, certificates of deposit, petty cash funds, travelers checks, treasury bills, and other investments valued at cost.

that had traditionally been held by Democrats. His campaign was funded by direct-mail donations and was successful because of Republican direct-mail legend Richard Viguerie. In 1980, he spent more money for his election than any other House candidate in the country. In 1982, redistricting eliminated Dornan's seat, so he took the opportunity to run for the U.S. Senate. He managed to garner only 8 percent of the vote in the Republican primary. Dornan then moved to Orange County, where he ran for Congress and defeated incumbent Democrat Jerry Patterson in 1984.

Despite his fiery reputation as a loose cannon who is rarely taken seriously in Congress, interest groups with both ideological and economic agendas have found him to be a valuable ally. Since he had never been chair or ranking minority member of a committee prior to 1995, however, some have ignored him after his usefulness runs out. The oil industry, for example, gave him more than $29,000 between 1980 and 1984. In 1985, the Reagan administration struck a deal with a number of California representatives to limit offshore drilling. Dornan took up the industry's flag, objecting vociferously, but his efforts were in vain and the regulations remained. He later angered the industry by reversing his stand on offshore drilling when a rig was planned for Santa Monica Bay, which Dornan calls "my swimming pool." Dornan's oil money subsequently dried up. Since 1985, the industry has given him a relatively minuscule average of $2,630 per election.[4]

"The thought of oil rigs in Santa Monica Bay was appalling to me," Dornan told us. "I consider [it] mine and a lot of other people's personal swimming pool, and nobody puts an oil rig in their own swimming pool. But if it's over the horizon, where you cannot see it, and it's unobtrusive, we need energy independence."

While most politicians measure their words, taking care not to use language that might offend or come back to haunt them, Bob Dornan always speaks his mind, no matter how mean-spirited his thoughts might be. In a 1995 episode which earned the censure of his colleagues, Dornan accused President Clinton of "giving aid and comfort to the enemy"[5] during the Vietnam war, using the phrase that forms the legal definition of treason. The House promptly voted to ban Dornan from the floor for a day. He once called then-Representative Tom Downey (D-NY) a "draft-dodging wimp," and seized Downey by the tie on the floor of the House.

His aggressive opposition to abortion has earned him the affection of and $29,072 in contributions from the National Right-to-Life PAC. Dornan counts a bill he sponsored prohibiting abortions on U.S. military bases overseas as one of his proudest legislative achievements.

Dornan is known on Capitol Hill as "B-1 Bob," a moniker he earned through his aggressive support of the B-1 bomber, and his penchant for rhetorical bomb-throwing. So it's no surprise that defense contractors have generously supported the California congressman. McDonnell Douglas, Rockwell, Boeing, and Northrop Grumman have all contributed to Dornan repeatedly, as have a number of smaller contractors. Dornan has sat on the Armed Services Committee since 1985, where he has been an aggressive advocate of higher military spending. Nonetheless, his defense contributions, averaging $10,000 to $20,000 each election cycle, do come close to the contributions accepted by more powerful members of the committee from these same interests; each receives more than $100,000.[6]

Dornan has long been an advocate of the Strategic Defense Initiative (SDI). In 1995, he led efforts in the House to beat back Democratic attempts to cut SDI funding. Not surprisingly, Dornan has received contributions from nine of the top ten SDI contractors.[7] While he held no congressional seat in 1983, it was well known that he would run again in 1984. During that year, Dornan received $11,000 in salary from the American Space Frontier Committee, a pro-SDI group he helped found.[8] When we asked who funded the now-defunct group, Dornan said he could not recall, but, "I would assume contractors who had an interest in SDI." The year 1983 was a busy one during which Dornan made more than $40,000 for acting as an "ambassador" for the Los Angeles-based Institute for Management Resources, approaching companies to hire IMR.[9] The only one he recalls being interested was Martin Marietta, a big SDI contractor that had previously donated $3,750 to Dornan's campaigns.[10]

Dornan is a darling of foreign car dealers. Their interests in Congress lie mostly in trade legislation: They are virulently opposed to tariffs or other restrictions on foreign goods. For his part, Dornan is known in Congress as a free trade advocate. He has been rewarded with $23,000 in contributions from foreign car dealer associations.[11] Nevertheless, he has been willing to sacrifice the principle of free trade if it conflicts with another principle, anti-communism. He opposed granting most favored nation status to China and economic relations with Vietnam.

Dornan is also supported heavily by the construction industry. He received contributions from the Associated General Contractors PAC, from construction companies, and from individual contractors. If these were added together, they would place first on Dornan's top ten list.[12] In the wake of the Persian Gulf War, one construction company allowed Dornan to indulge his penchant for visiting war zones. Dornan was taken on an all-expense-paid trip to Kuwait, courtesy of the Fluor Corporation, the largest construction company in America. In news stories at the time, Dornan talked passionately about Iraqi atrocities, without mentioning the interests of his hosts. Fluor competed for and subsequently received a portion of the estimated $100 billion in contracts.[13]

Dornan has had FEC complaints filed against him, and his campaign was once fined $2,100 for accepting excessive contributions from major donors. No contributor has been more generous to Dornan's quest for the White House than the candidate himself. His presidential committee is in such dire straits that Dornan has made five separate loans to his own campaign, totalling $38,000.[14]

Apparently, Bob Dornan's inability to be taken seriously has followed him into the presidential race. "Since I'm not a millionaire," he said, "my prospects are bleak."

BOB DORNAN
TOP 10 CAREER PATRONS*

1. National Association of Realtors PAC, Chicago, Illinois $31,500
2. American Medical Association, Washington, D.C. $31,500
3. National Rifle Association, Washington, D.C. $31,118
4. Conservative Republican Committee PAC, Washington, D.C. $29,510
5. National Right to Life PAC, Washington, D.C. $29,072
6. Auto Dealers for Free Trade, foreign car dealers, Washington, D.C. $20,500
7. Fund for a Conservative Majority PAC, Washington, D.C. $15,238
8. Citizens for the Republic, Reagan PAC, Washington, D.C. $15,000

9. Northrop-Grumman, defense contractor, San
   Francisco, California $14,864
10. Associated General Contractors PAC,
    Washington, D.C. $11,700

* Based on FEC records and Center for Responsive Politics data. Figures
include congressional campaigns from 1979 through 1994.

Phil Gramm

For Phil Gramm, perhaps more than any candidate in history, the pursuit of the presidency is first a supreme quest for cash. He gave himself a head start by transferring $4.8 million left over from his last Senate campaign into his presidential campaign coffers. Gramm's ability to raise staggering amounts of money, and especially his braggadocio about it, distinguish the Texas Republican from other contenders. Gramm's realization of the need for early fundraising raised the 1996 financial bar to levels so high it helped to drive away potential candidates, including Jack Kemp, Dick Cheney, and Dan Quayle.

The role of money in politics is a prickly topic for most politicians, but in his race for the White House, candidate Gramm seems to have no qualms about spelling out the need for financial backing. He has traversed the country, lecturing repeatedly about "what is entailed in running for president" in 1996, presenting a slick slide show that includes such images as a huge green bag emblazoned with a dollar sign, a bundle of dollar bills, and a stack of gold coins.

The Center for Public Integrity obtained a home-video of the presentation being given to a conservative group in New Hampshire in early 1995. In it Gramm's tone is tough, confident, and matter of fact. He is from Texas, a state second only to California as a source of political money. He has the names and addresses of all 80,000 people who have given to his Senate campaigns and those of all 3.3 million who gave to the National Republican Senatorial Committee when he

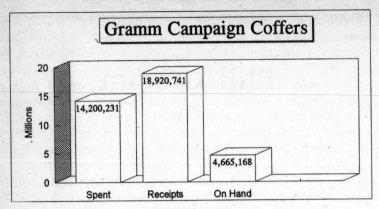

Gramm Campaign Coffers

Reporting through September 30, 1995.

Spent figures include all purchases or payments made in connection with or for the purpose of influencing a federal election.
Receipts are anything of value received by a political committee.
On Hand figures include funds held in checking and savings accounts, certificates of deposit, petty cash funds, travelers checks, treasury bills, and other investments valued at cost.

was chairman. His drawl (actually picked up in his native Georgia) is self-assured and logical as it drives to a conclusion.

Phil Gramm, economist cum politician, reduces the presidential electoral process to a mathematical equation that could be expressed like this: $\$ = P$. "Whenever anybody is trying to throw out exactly what it is going to take to win the Republican nomination and then go on and beat Bill Clinton," he said, pointing to a slide projection of a figure, "that is the magic number: $44.7 million. It is a lot of money."

The slide show is representative of the man himself: brash, generally humorless, analytical, and with a don't-get-in-my-way laser-beam focus. Or as authors Michael Barone and Grant Ujifusa have described Gramm: "[A] bullish aggressiveness, a strong and well-disciplined mind, a gift for the pungent phrase, a folksy southernness which comes from being raised near Fort Benning, Georgia."[1] Respected, but not well-liked by his Senate colleagues, Gramm once told a dinner audience that he does in fact have a heart: "I keep it in a quart jar on my desk."[2]

Phil Gramm is also an elusive, enigmatic figure, full of contradictions and surprises. For a man so consumed by concern over raising substantial sums of campaign money, outside of accepting free construction work on his vacation home, amassing significant personal wealth does not appear to be a principal motivation. He may have flunked three grades as a child, but Gramm rose to become a Ph.D. college economics professor. Today he's known as one of the smartest senators, who "does his homework" and almost always understands the complicated legislative issues frequently before him. He is a Republican politician who started out as a Democrat and has self-deprecatingly referred to his homely looks, saying, "It's called being ugly."[3]

He has made a career of attacking dependence on government, once criticizing welfare recipients by saying, "We're the only nation in the world where all our poor people are fat." Yet he has spent much of his own life—from his birth in a military hospital to his tenure in Congress—on the public payroll. Although he is famous for criticizing government inefficiency and waste, he also boasts unabashedly of his ability to bring home the bacon to the Lone Star state. Gramm has, on occasion, opposed federal projects and money for Texas, and after the federal largesse is awarded over his objections, he has called press conferences to take credit for it. The practice is so frequent that Texas political observers have dubbed the technique "Grammstanding."

"If we should vote next week on whether to begin producing cheese in a factory on the moon, I almost certainly would oppose it," Gramm has said. "On the other hand, if the government decided to institute the policy, it would be my objective to see that a Texas contractor builds this celestial cheese plant, that the milk comes from Texas cows and that the earth distribution center is located in Texas."[4]

The Texas senator—son of an Army sergeant—has always advocated a strong military, and in fact as a child he attended military school, but personally chose to opt out of the draft during the Vietnam War. Gramm is a politician who sometimes sermonizes about "family values" today, despite a divorce in his past and the 1995 revelation that years ago he invested in a "soft porn" movie.

All these incongruities render Phil Gramm somewhat inde-cipherable, regardless of one's party, ideology, or religious background. As Jeff Fisher of the Texas Family Association, a group of religious conservatives, put it, "A lot of people really don't know who he is."[5]

The one constant in Gramm's political agenda from the 1970s to today is his strong, almost unswerving belief that the federal budget must be balanced. As a congressman and a freshman senator, Gramm was a key Capitol Hill ally of the Reagan administration on budget matters. And his name al-most became a household word when he co-authored the Gramm-Rudman-Hollings deficit reduction law.

Other constants in Gramm's political life are his financial supporters. As is common among the candidates in this book—like investors who hold onto a stock which continues to perform—many of those who have given Gramm money have done so over many years. His largest single career spon-sor has been the National Rifle Association, funneling $440,200 to Gramm since 1979, more money than to any other politician in the U.S. during that period. He has unfail-ingly reciprocated and remained publicly loyal to the NRA even after the group's popularity reached new lows in the wake of the Oklahoma City bombing.

The National Rifle Association (NRA)[6]

The alliance goes back at least to 1984 when Representative Phil Gramm, a recent convert to the Republican party, ran for Senate. The NRA established its own Gramm for Senate office in Texas and spent $337,752 on behalf of Gramm's successful campaign.

Since winning his Senate seat, Gramm has not disappointed the NRA. He has introduced, sponsored, or voted with the NRA interests on eighteen key bills concerning gun issues over the past decade. Gramm has solicited contributions for the NRA on the organization's own stationery. In 1987, for example, Gramm wrote a letter telling potential contributors that if they donated $1,000 they would become members of the "Madison Eagles," an exclusive group of contributors.

He explained that becoming a member would provide an
"opportunity to develop a special relationship with civic leaders from around the United States, and celebrities as well
as Senators and Congressmen who are active supporters of
our cause."[7]

In 1987 and 1989, Gramm co-chaired the Annual Charleton
Heston International Celebrity Shoot, attracting celebrities
such as O. J. Simpson, Arnold Schwarzenegger, and Roy Rog-
ers. The money raised at these events went to the "NRA's
Institute for Legislative Action . . . dedicated to preserving the
Second Amendment in the legislatures and on Capitol Hill."

The NRA's support for Gramm's presidential ambitions became apparent at the 1992 Republican national convention
in Houston where the NRA sponsored a "Red, White, and
Boots" gala fundraiser for Gramm. After party-goers contributed $75 per person ($500 for VIPs), they drank beer and
watched a film about Gramm's life entitled "Phil Gramm: A
New Leader for a New America," narrated by Heston.

The NRA's organization and 3.5 million members are
important to Gramm's 1996 presidential hopes, and just how
entwined the NRA and Gramm are became clear in 1995.
Following the Oklahoma City bombing and increased media
coverage of "hate" and militia groups in the U.S., the NRA
took a big hit from both former President George Bush and
President Bill Clinton. The NRA's executive vice president,
Wayne LaPierre, had referred to government officials as
"jack-booted thugs." Bush actually resigned from the NRA,
stating that the group's inflammatory rhetoric "deeply of-
fends my own sense of decency and honor."

By contrast, in February 1995, several NRA leaders, including LaPierre, attended a $1,000-a-plate Dallas dinner for
Gramm, an event that raised $4.1 million for his campaign.
Just days after Bush resigned, Gramm spoke at the national
NRA convention in Phoenix, and there was not a word of
criticism for the organization. He said, "We haven't had a
dedicated, committed hunter in the White House since Theodore Roosevelt. I tell you, it's been too long." Gramm also
thanked the NRA for its activist role in funding Republican
candidates in the House and Senate in 1994. The NRA political action committee was the biggest in the country in the

1993–1994 election cycle, giving out $3.4 million in contributions and independent expenditures, according to the Center for Responsive Politics.

In the crucial 1996 Iowa and New Hampshire presidential contests, the NRA will unofficially greet voters on behalf of Phil Gramm. The chairman of his campaign in Iowa is Kayne Robinson, a duck-hunting buddy and a member of the national executive board of the NRA. In New Hampshire, several prominent conservatives and gun activists support Gramm, including Al Rubega, the head of Gun Owners of New Hampshire; former governor Meldrim Thompson, a longtime NRA supporter who pens a column for the state's largest newspaper, the *Manchester Union Leader*; and Senator Robert Smith, yet another NRA supporter.

The NRA is not alone among large groups with special interests that give to Gramm. The American Medical Association comes in as Gramm's second-largest supporter.

The American Medical Association (AMA)

Gramm began to cultivate a financial relationship with Texas doctors in his very first run for elective office in 1976, when he purchased a mailing list with their names and addresses. In his crucial 1984 Senate race, the American Medical Association transfused his campaign with $117,767 in contributions and independent expenditures. Gramm has since shown a caring bedside manner.

As a congressman in the late 1970s, Gramm helped stymie President Jimmy Carter's efforts to contain health care costs, and in 1994 he helped to kill health care reform legislation in the Senate. Campaigning in New Hampshire in 1995, Gramm boasted, "When Republican pollsters told us it would be suicide to resist I stood up and said, 'The Clinton health care plan is going to pass over my cold, dead political body.' "[8] According to the liberal activist group Citizen Action, between 1979 and June 1994, Gramm raised $1.2 million from the health care and insurance industries.[9]

Gramm's 1984 and 1990 Senate races were well-funded, with a total of $21.8 million. In 1984, federal authorities had questions about how some of the money was raised, but when they asked to see his campaign records Gramm refused to make them available, forcing the government to go to court. After five years of legal wrangling, the Federal Election Commission obtained the records and discovered, among other infractions, 127 illegal corporate contributions totalling just $9,708. Gramm's campaign committee was fined $30,000.

His national reputation as a fabulous fundraiser was really established in the 1990s, when he did something highly unusual by Senate standards—he sought and was elected by a slim margin to a *second* consecutive term as chairman of the National Republican Senatorial Committee. Most senators are ecstatic to give up the grubby job of asking for money nationwide, but not Gramm, who astutely understood the importance of the position to his presidential aspirations. He did two things as chairman that were unprecedented. First, Gramm and his fellow committee members and staff raised $139,176,652 over the four years ending in 1994, $8 million more than the previous four years. Gramm boasts that this money helped Republicans gain majority control of the Senate. Second, Gramm took the invaluable, extensive NRSC mailing list with him for use in his presidential campaign. Other Republican senators privately grouse that this was outright theft.

The Savings and Loan Scandal

More public questions have been raised about Gramm's ethical judgment in accepting $53,586 worth of work and materials from a dubious Texas savings and loan operator and builder. In 1987, a Texas investor and Gramm contributor named Jerry Stiles—involved with three failed thrifts that cost taxpayers an estimated $200 million—paid a contractor and his workers to fly up from Texas and finish building Gramm's two-story vacation home on the Chesapeake Bay. More than $50,000 in construction work was performed, but not billed to Gramm by Stiles, nor paid for by Gramm to this day.

Several months later, Stiles met with Senate banking committee member Gramm in his office, seeking "oversight" assistance with S&L regulators. Gramm has always denied any wrongdoing and told the *New York Times* that he met with Stiles "as an economist, rather than as a senator."[10] Stiles, however, did not visit Gramm's Senate office to get an economics lesson. "The purpose of the meeting with Phil," Stiles said, "was the system is nothing but political. The regulatory industry is nothing but political."[1] The economist-senator later sent letters on his U.S. Senate stationery to federal regulators on Stiles's behalf. The Senate Ethics Committee—not renowned for its stringent standards or aggressive enforcement—did not criticize the Stiles-Gramm interaction, nor did it require Gramm to pay Stiles for the unbilled work, determining that it was not a "gift" but a contractual cost overrun in an informal business situation in which there was no contract. This is one of the rare episodes where Gramm has personally benefitted financially from his actions as a U.S. senator. Gramm declined to be interviewed or respond to written questions submitted by the Center for Public Integrity.

In the meantime, Stiles could probably use the money for the work on Gramm's Chesapeake home. At this writing he is federal penitentiary inmate #04651-078, incarcerated in El Paso, Texas. Following his 1994 conviction for conspiracy, bank bribery, and other federal offenses, he was ordered to pay up to $2.5 million in fines and sentenced to a maximum of fifty-five years in prison.

Gramm's home-away-from-home builder, longtime campaign contributor, and convicted savings and loan operator declined to talk to the Center for Public Integrity. Jerry Stiles contributed thousands of dollars to candidate Phil Gramm, he charged the senator only half of the actual cost of completing his vacation home, and he sought and received Gramm's assistance with federal regulators. Now that Phil Gramm is running for president, maybe Jerry Stiles's last, and most important favor to Gramm, could be his public silence.

What is curious about Gramm's involvement with the S&L industry, though it is not widely known, is that he was one of the first members of the Senate to grasp the seriousness of the S&L crisis. It was shortly after Gramm was elected to the Senate in 1984, well before American taxpayers understood the full magnitude of the debacle and its ultimate cost of between $300 and $500 billion due to fraud and mismanagement.

Edwin J. Gray, then chairman of the Federal Home Bank Board, was a lone Cassandra in the early 1980s who warned of the severe crisis and advocated stricter regulation. A former journalist and political appointee who had been Governor Ronald Reagan's press secretary, Gray found himself in the role of federal regulatory authority over an industry that had successfully achieved substantial deregulation. Expecting another malleable, innocuous caretaker chairman, the politically connected thrift industry and its Washington lawyers and lobbyists soon began to view Gray with suspicion and alarm. He began testifying before Congress and delivering speeches nationwide about the impending disaster, beseeching Congress to act. In Texas and California, states where some of the worst thrift management and rapacious fraud occurred, S&L executives openly called Gray a "Nazi." And the atmosphere in Washington was such that it was Gray, rather than thrift executives, who became the outcast.

In both houses of Congress the savings and loan institutions had donated considerable sums of money to Republican *and* Democratic campaigns. Gray's attempts to bring the federally insured industry under control were met with hostility. In the House, only members like Jim Leach (R-IA) and Henry Gonzales (D-TX) were supportive.

Against this backdrop appeared a most unlikely ally, a freshman member of the Senate Banking Committee from, of all places, Texas. Texas has the unpleasant distinction of topping the list of states with the most S&L failures with sixty-five. The state was second only to California in terms of the value of assets held by failed thrifts: California's thrifts had $18.358 billion in assets compared with Texas's $18.279 billion.[12]

The last place in the United States Gray *ever* thought he would find an ally in Congress was with a senator from the state of Texas, where so many thrift institutions went under after years of political coziness between S&L operators and beneficiaries of their contributions in the Texas congressional delegation. "Phil Gramm was the only Senator who helped us," Gray told the Center for Public Integrity. "He really understood . . . he loaned members of his staff to us."[13] But Gramm did not trumpet his cooperation with Gray. In the mid-1980s, he was also courting favor with a powerful group of Texas thrift operators known as the "High Flyers," a group of interconnected thrifts involved in "a pattern of takeover, rapid growth, and 'insane' loans designed to create the illusion that the thrift was running a huge profit."[14] Gramm, along with other Texas members of Congress, "hobbled" reform legislation "with 'forbearance' amendments that made it nearly impossible for regulators to seize bankrupt thrifts."[15] Forbearance meant that thrifts with extremely low net worth ratios would be allowed to continue to operate. "These provisions were the brainchild of Texas Representative Steve Bartlett and Texas Senator Phil Gramm," reported S&L author James Ring Adams.[16] "The splendidly named Competitive Equality Banking Act of 1987," wrote Martin Mayer in *The Greatest Ever Bank Robbery*, "passed by a Democratic Congress and signed by President Ronald Reagan long after everyone who was paying attention knew the dam had broken, specifically managed 'forbearance' for the benefit of insolvent thrift institutions that were losing more money every day."[17]

Members of Gray's staff found it more than a little strange that Gramm recommended Durward Curlee to the Federal Home Loan Bank Board, to fill what Lone Star state S&L executives considered to be the "Texas seat." The effort went largely unnoticed, with industry magazines carrying only little blurbs. Gramm and Curlee had known each other since the early 1970s when Curlee, then the executive director of the Texas Savings and Loan League, had gotten Gramm to speak at a meeting of S&L managers. Then as now, Gramm was not lacking fire or conviction while expounding on the virtues of the free market, the incompetence of the federal government, or the wastefulness and dubious wisdom of the tax system. The speech was a hit.

"It just got people roaring," Curlee recalled. "It was such a good talk."[18]

In the mid-1980s, Curlee was the designated spokesman for the "High Flyers." William Black, Gray's deputy, said these institutions made up the biggest failures on the FSLIC's books and, on average, were insolvent "by the end of the 1984— well before the steep 1986 drop in oil prices."[19]

FEC records indicate that Phil Gramm received more campaign donations from the S&L industry than all but seven U.S. senators. By 1990, Gramm had reportedly received $86,098 from the thrift operators.[20]

Many High Flyers contributed to Phil Gramm. Among them, Jarret Woods and his wife gave $5,000, Don Dixon gave $1,000, Gene Phillips and his wife gave $4,000 and Durward Curlee gave $1,500, according to FEC records. The Texas Savings and Loan League, Curlee's former employer, gave $5,000 in PAC money to Gramm.

Don Dixon ran Vernon Savings and Loan, which was headquartered in Dallas. Its failure cost taxpayers $1.3 billion.[21] Jarret Woods owned Western Savings Association, the failure of which cost taxpayers $1.4 billion.[22] Gene Phillips owned Southmark Corporation, which owned San Jacinto S&L. Southmark filed for bankruptcy in June 1989, the sixth largest bankruptcy in U.S. history.[23] One account of the incident claimed that Southmark would have total losses "almost certainly exceeding $4 billion."[24] Dixon and many of the others ended up in prison.

As it turned out, the Curlee nomination foundered. After a period of financial reversal, Curlee is now involved with a small insurance concern in Austin. The answering machine at his home greets callers, asking that they leave their message slowly. "I'm not nearly as fast as I used to be," it says.

That also may be true for some of Gramm's other friends with old S&L ties, but it hasn't stopped them from supporting the senior senator from Texas. Bum Bright, a former owner of the Dallas Cowboys whom George Bush once described as "the political godfather" of Phil Gramm, is a key Gramm fundraiser for the 1996 presidential bid.[25] Bright's Bright Banc failed in 1989 at a taxpayer cost of $1.4 billion. Bright also directed First Republic Bank, which collapsed in 1988 at a cost of $3.6 billion to taxpayers. Bright is another supporter who has been around since Gramm's first campaign. Gene Phillips, one of the High Flyers, was a sponsor listed in the program for the Gramm presidential announcement kickoff dinner.

The Gramm Power Couple, Helping Each Other

Gramm has also been criticized for mixing government business and campaign politics by using his Senate office staff to work on campaigns. Richard Whittle, of the *Dallas Morning News*, interviewed nine former Gramm Senate staff aides and obtained hundreds of pages of Gramm's confidential schedules, memos, and other internal papers, which were the basis of two detailed, lengthy articles about Gramm's use of his taxpayer-funded staff to facilitate his 1989–1990 reelection efforts. In a January 1990 memo, Gramm's top Senate staff aide, Ruth Cymber, wrote, "We have made the transition from a Senate-oriented staff to a campaign-oriented staff." Nearly three-fourths of Gramm's Senate staffers in Texas were utilized to "create, publicize, or analyze media events in the state, and he traveled to hundreds of those appearances at Senate expense."[26]

At least two different aides to Senator Gramm have written memos about how Gramm's wife, Wendy, a second-generation Korean American, should be utilized for his reelection bid. Cymber wrote, "The Asians are our natural constituents, philosophically and because of Wendy. This should be an easy sell; we need to continue to activate them, especially financially." Separately, Gramm's state director Jeb Hensarling, his former student at Texas A&M wrote, "Wendy should be scheduled into electronic media markets where outreach to women, minorities, and young professionals is viable . . . Finally, Wendy should be scheduled with the senator on at least several occasions each year so that they may be seen together in large public forums that hopefully garner electronic media. This would help soften the senator's image."[27]

Gramm's Senate staff controlled her activities and schedules in Texas. That is particularly interesting in light of the powerful position she held in Washington as chairwoman of the Commodity Futures Trading Commission. As the nation's leading regulator of futures contracts for all agricultural commodities, Wendy Gramm was under tight ethical constraints as to the degree and nature of her personal daily interaction with agribusiness interests. The sensitivity of her situation, however, apparently eluded Hensarling, who suggested that Wendy Gramm "should be scheduled into various private meetings with ag leadership types and general business types, in hopes of strengthening the senator's financial base, as well as his agricultural constituency."[28]

In other words, the chairwoman of the powerful federal regulatory agency overseeing agriculture commodities futures trading would be helping her U.S. senator husband raise campaign funds from the corporations and individuals she regulated. And in fact, during the 1990 campaign, Phil Gramm raised more money from agricultural interests than any other senator, including nine members of the Senate Agriculture Committee running that year, raking in $484,959.[29]

In 1989, the Gramm campaign paid for most of Wendy Gramm's sojourns to Texas, even when she traveled on CFTC business. Hensarling wrote, "If our campaign pays, we certainly avoid any legal conflicts, but if the funding source is discovered, it would certainly in some sense taint what she is doing. Certainly all parties would be prepared to answer the questions of why Senator Phil Gramm's campaign is paying for Wendy Gramm to do "official CFTC business" in Texas." To enhance the credibility of the enterprise, Gramm's Senate and campaign aides decided which speaking engagements Wendy Gramm should commit to and prepared her Texas schedule, but the actual logistical arrangements were left for her CFTC staff to make.[30]

Wendy Lee Gramm, in her mid-forties when her husband campaigned for his second Senate term, had held several high-profile jobs during the Reagan and Bush administrations. Reagan once called her "my favorite economist."[31] In December of 1987, Wendy Gramm, whom the New York Times then called "one of the Reagan Administration's most vigorous deregulators,"[32] was chosen by the president to head the Commodities Futures Trading Commission, or CFTC.

The CFTC oversees federal regulation of the nation's fourteen commodities and futures exchanges. At those exchanges, contracts to buy and sell a seemingly endless variety of commodities are traded: oil and gas, soybeans, cattle, pork bellies, corn, precious metals, cocoa, lumber, cranberries, and sugar, to name but a few. The regulatory duties of the CFTC are aimed largely at ensuring fairness and stability at the nation's commodities exchanges.

One week after Bill Clinton won the presidential election it became clear that Wendy Gramm would be leaving the politically appointed CFTC post. On November 16, 1992, nine energy companies wrote to the commission seeking to exempt energy derivative contracts, a business valued at $5 trillion a year, from federal regulation.

Historically, there had been no government regulation of the energy contract market. But a recent lawsuit filed by an investor who felt he had been bilked had started talk of whether the energy contracts fell within the jurisdiction of existing regulatory venues.

In response to the energy companies' request, Wendy Gramm set in motion the process that led to those energy derivative contracts, and other exotic financial transactions, being exempted from regulation. She ordered commission staff members to begin an elaborate process of rule-making to allow for the exemption, a move consistent with her free-market, laissez-faire philosophy. What is interesting is that the companies involved had more than a passing familiarity with her husband.

A Center for Public Integrity investigation shows that of the nine companies that requested the exemption, seven had donated to Phil Gramm campaigns through PACs, company officers, or employees. And of the sixteen companies, brokerages, and associations that wrote letters of support for the request, eight had given money to Gramm campaigns.

Cumulatively, Gramm's campaigns had received $157,250 from the people who were asking his wife to exempt energy derivatives and the other transactions from regulation.

Over his career, Mobil has given Gramm $15,500, Phillips Petroleum Company has given $8,050, and Exxon has given $25,250, according to the Center's examination of Gramm's financial disclosure records. Some of the other Gramm donors requesting the exemption were BP Oil Company, Coastal Corporation, Conoco, Phillips Petroleum Company, J.P. Morgan, and Chase Manhattan. The New York Mercantile Exchange, which also requested the exemption, co-hosted a hospitality room in the Houston Astrodome during the 1992 Republican Convention for people who had given $2,000 to the "Gramm '96 Committee."[33]

The name of one company in particular might have caught Wendy Gramm's attention: Enron. It was the only company that signed the original request and two of the supporting letters sent later. It's a fairly large company, based in Houston. Of all the companies that wrote to the CFTC seeking the exemption, Enron was the biggest donor to Gramm campaigns, giving $34,100 over the years.

After taking actions that led to the exemptions from regulation, Wendy Gramm resigned on January 20, 1993, the day Clinton was inaugurated. Five weeks later, she was named to Enron's board of directors. The part-time position pays her $22,000, plus $1,250 for each meeting she attends. In April 1993 the commodities commission voted 2 to 1 against regulating the business. Two seats on the board were vacant at the time; the remaining commissioners, all Bush appointees, were seen as ideologically aligned with Wendy Gramm.

In its 1992 annual report, Enron calls itself the "manager of the largest portfolio of fixed-price and natural-gas derivative contracts in the world." The company also has roughly $4.5 billion in interest-rate swaps, another exotic transaction that Wendy Gramm helped to exempt from deregulation while she was at the CFTC.[34] Enron Chairman Kenneth Lay and his wife are now regional chairs of the Gramm presidential campaign.[35]

IBP

Enron is not the only company regulated by the CFTC that Wendy Gramm became associated with after leaving the commission. She also joined the board of IBP, the Dakota City, Nebraska–based meat-packing giant with a long history of labor and safety problems. So did Gramm for President Finance Chairman Alec Courtelis. The two sat on the company's compensation committee. The beef and pork products

IBP makes are commodities traded in the markets regulated by the CFTC. In an arrangement like many who sit on boards, Wendy annually receives $20,000 and an additional $900 for each meeting she attends. An IBP worker, paid the base wage of $8.97 an hour, working forty hours a week, all fifty-two weeks of the year, would make a gross income of $18,657.60[36] In 1993, a federal court in Washington ruled the IBP had to pay retroactive overtime payments to 24,000 workers at eleven of its factories in six states.[37]

In 1987, the Occupational Safety and Health Administration sought a $3.1 million-dollar fine against IBP for exposing workers to repetitive stress injuries and a $2.6 million fine for failing to report illnesses. The charges were dropped in 1988 in exchange for the company creating a three-year research program to reduce such injuries.[38] The fines were reduced to $975,000 as part of the deal.[39]

Senator Gramm has "joined other GOP senators in voting to cut OSHA's funding by 50 percent over seven years," the *Wall Street Journal* reported. "The mandate from last November's [1994] election, the senator says, is clear: 'Stop the taxing, stop the spending, and stop the regulating.' "[40]

IBP in turn has helped Gramm in his presidential run. The company's PAC has contributed $5,000, the limit, to Gramm's campaign. From 1991–1994, the PAC contributed $31,000 to the National Republican Senatorial Committee.[41] Gramm was the committee's chairman at the time.

In 1995, IBP lent an early helping hand to the campaign. The company distributed a memo urging its workers to attend a "straw poll" in Ames, Iowa. The *Wall Street Journal*, quoted the memo: ". . . IBP is encouraging its management employees to attend and participate in this grand event. Tickets and bus transportation will be provided by the Phil Gramm for President Committee." Gramm said he knew nothing of IBP's activities.[42] He had imported enough people to tie the front-running Bob Dole in the straw poll and pundits, always looking for a "horse race," said the showing had given Gramm a much-needed boost.

In his 1990 Senate campaign, candidate Gramm used his wife's position on the CFTC as a means to reach out to the agricultural community for money and votes. But the campaign also pulled in money from other industries the trading of whose commodities were overseen by the CFTC and Wendy Gramm. Commercial banks gave $264,121; the oil and gas industry—a staple for any Texas politician—gave $715,874; and investment interests gave $179,185.[43]

During Wendy Gramm's tenure with the commodities commission, Phil Gramm accepted $38,500 in commodity honoraria, according to his annual financial disclosure records. Among the groups he spoke to between 1988 and 1992 are the American Gas Association, the Enron Corporation, the Interstate Natural Gas Association of America, Occidental Chemical Corporation, the Chemical Manufacturers Association, the National Lumber and Building Material Dealers Association, the National Forest Products Association, and the Petroleum Manufacturers Association.[44]

At the same time she was heading the commodities commission, he was on the Senate Banking committee. That meant that Phil Gramm, too, had regulatory jurisdiction and oversight regarding commodities. On July 24, 1990, Phil Gramm voted to kill an amendment that would have lowered the sugar price support program loan rate from eighteen cents a pound to sixteen cents a pound. That was a potential conflict of interest because Gramm's disclosures show that at the time the couple owned between $15,000 and $50,000 worth of stock in a sugar company named Castle and Cooke.

All in all, the Gramms make for quite a powerful and influential pair.

"Ready Money"

Gramm's national positioning for the presidential race was particularly apparent following his reelection to the Senate in 1990, when he was elected chairman of the National Republican Senatorial Committee. His tenure was hugely successful, and true to form, Gramm had no compunction bragging about it. "In total we raised $121 million from 3.3 million donors, more money from more people than any committee in history. Which is a big reason we have a Republican majority in the Senate," he boasted on the stump in early 1995.

On February 23, 1995, at a huge fundraising dinner at the Dallas Convention Center, Phil Gramm set the stage for his campaign and his candidacy. In large cursive letters, the dinner program read "Senator Phil Gramm Official Announcement Dinner." About 2,800 Republicans attended the event, which raised $4.1 million in a single night—more money than a federal office candidate had ever raised in a single event.[45]

The program began as the "Vocal Majority" singing group and the Texas Boys Choir sang "America the Beautiful," followed by the invocation delivered by Dr. Don Benton of Lover's Lane United Methodist Church. After the national anthem was played, dinner was served. It was followed by speeches from Senators Paul Coverdell (R-GA), John McCain (R-AZ), Kay Bailey Hutchinson (R-TX), and Texas Governor George W. Bush.

Sitting at the head table were steadfast Gramm supporters Mrs. Ray L. Hunt, Mrs. T. Boone Pickens, Mr. and Mrs. Sam Wyly and Charles Wyly, owners of Sterling Software. Also dining that evening with Gramm were the regional co-chairs of the gala, the chairman of Enron, Kenneth Lay and his wife, co-chair Mrs. H.L. Hunt of the legendary oil fortune, and senior officials of the NRA. They listened as Gramm delivered his speech, "Bringing Back the American Dream."

Senator Phillip William Gramm stood at the podium, looked out at the crowd of loyal, wealthy patrons, and said, "I have the most reliable friend you can have in politics: Ready money."

PHIL GRAMM
TOP 10 CAREER PATRONS*

1. National Rifle Association, Fairfax, Virginia $440,200
2. American Medical Association, Washington, D.C. $140,467
3. Conservative National Committee, Washington, D.C. $103,259
4. Boone Pickens/Mesa Petroleum, Dallas, Texas $73,408
5. First City Bancorporation, bank holding company, Houston, Texas $66,925
6. Bass Enterprises, oil and real estate, Fort Worth, Texas $62,199
7. Hunt Corporation, oil and gas, Dallas, Texas $60,500
8. Baker and Botts, law firm, Houston, Texas $54,475
9. Trammell Crow, construction, Dallas, Texas $52,125
10. H.B. Zachry Co., construction, San Antonio, Texas $51,972

*Includes all PAC and individual contributions for House and Senate races from 1978 to 1994, as well as independent and communications expenditures from 1980 to 1994, from available records. Includes contributions to Leadership for America, Gramm's PAC. Based on FEC records and Center for Responsive Politics data. Totals include PAC donations as well as employee donations for businesses.

Alan Keyes

C andidates hardly ever receive salaries from their campaigns. When they do, the pay is not usually very high. When Alan Keyes was asked about the fact that he was taking a salary of $8,463 a month from his unsuccessful U.S. Senate campaign in 1992, his response was, "I am a successful person. You want me to come work for you, you have got to pay me a certain minimum. That's where I'm established in life. If I don't breathe, eat, and live comfortably I won't be able to function."[1]

Keyes faces a daunting task in seeking the 1996 Republican presidential nomination. He has practically no name recognition or campaign organization and has little fundraising ability. Unable to win state office, the national media have largely ignored his candidacy, and relatively few people seem to take his campaign seriously. Keyes declined to be interviewed for this book.

After getting his Ph.D. in government from Harvard, Keyes joined the foreign service. He attracted the attention of U.N. Ambassador Jeane Kirkpatrick, and soon found himself elevated to the post of America's representative to the U.N.'s Economic and Social Council. The position carried with it the title of ambassador. To this day, his aides refer to him as "Ambassador Keyes."

Keyes served at the U.N. from 1983 until 1985, when he became Assistant Secretary of State for International Organizations. After leaving the State Department, Keyes spent a short time in residence at the American Enterprise Institute

(AEI), a Washington think tank. He was already being mentioned as a possible Republican candidate.

In 1988, a fortuitous series of circumstances led Keyes to run in Maryland for the U.S. Senate. In June, the Republican nominee abruptly pulled out of the race and Jeane Kirkpatrick, Keyes's former boss at the U.N., recommended him to Maryland Republican party officials. Neither of the state's two Republican members of Congress, Helen Bentley and Connie Morella, was interested in challenging incumbent Senator Paul Sarbanes. The door was left open for Keyes, who handily won the party's nomination at a special convention.

In the general election, however, Keyes was no match for Sarbanes. He managed to raise only $662,000, an unimpressive sum for a U.S. Senate race, and less than half of what Sarbanes spent.[2] His message of moralistic conservatism didn't play particularly well in Maryland, a state where Democrats outnumber Republicans by more than two to one. In the end, he garnered 38 percent of the vote.[3]

When he ran again in 1992, on this occasion against incum-

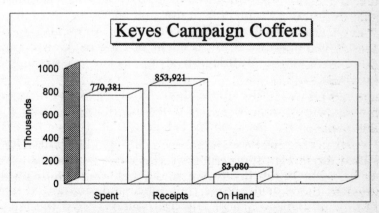

Reporting through September 30, 1995.

Spent figures include all purchases or payments made in connection with or for the purpose of influencing a federal election.
Receipts are anything of value received by a political committee.
On Hand figures include funds held in checking and savings accounts, certificates of deposit, petty cash funds, travelers checks, treasury bills, and other investments valued at cost.

bent Senator Barbara Mikulski, observers gave him even less of a chance than he had the first time. His campaign was especially hurt by the revelation that he drew a salary. On election day, Keyes could only muster 29 percent of the vote.

Keyes, who is black, defended the 1988 Bush presidential campaign's use of the infamous "Willie Horton" ad, calling the furor it caused "disingenuous."[4] He has called Jesse Jackson "a shill for the usual establishment agenda."[5] He is clearly willing to identify racist motives in others, even his own party. In an article he wrote after his first Senate defeat, he charged the media with both liberal bias and racism, saying they had portrayed his candidacy as tokenism and not as a serious campaign.[6] In 1992, he accused the Republican party of abandoning him because of his race. "I do not believe there is a sincere commitment on the part of the Republican Party leadership," he said, "to reach out to the black community."[7]

After losing in 1988, Keyes established the Campaign for Maryland's Future. The PAC's ostensible aim was to support Republican candidates in Maryland. It soon became apparent, however, that the group served to support only one candidate: Alan Keyes. In fact, in 1992, it donated $5,000 to Keyes, then became his official campaign committee. Keyes also spent time between his races as president of Citizens Against Government Waste, a Washington group seeking to streamline government programs.

The National Rifle Association (NRA) is Keyes's largest donor, mostly because of an independent expenditure for communications, made on his behalf in 1992. During his first run in 1988, Maryland passed a significant gun-control law, which Keyes vigorously opposed. To avoid the appearance that his opposition to the law was a result of their financial support, Keyes held a press conference and announced that he was refusing to accept any contributions from the NRA. In Keyes's 1992 race, however, the NRA came through for him. They gave him $7,306 in direct donations and spent $14,903 on communications, making the group far and away Keyes's top giver.[8]

No other PAC has made significant contributions to Keyes. The National Right to Life PAC did reward his ardent pro-life position with an $8,530 independent expenditure in 1992, but no other interests have made similar infusions. The reason is clear: When PACs make donations, they assume something will be done in return and Keyes has simply not been in a position to do it for them.

A look at Keyes's individual campaign donors does not reveal any well-known "fat cats" or scions of traditional American wealth. His most notable contributors have been foreign policy experts like Jeane Kirkpatrick, former National Security Council official Constantine Menges, and conservative intellectual Irving Kristol. Keyes has connections in the Republican intelligencia, but the economic elite has been largely unsupportive.

While he may not have accumulated the holdings of some of the other presidential candidates, Keyes is a wealthy man, earning well into six figures. He owns a house in suburban Maryland which he purchased in 1989 for $490,000.[9] He had a radio show in Baltimore, which has since gone off the air. As of this writing, Keyes had yet to file (despite repeated requests) the required material disclosure form with the FEC, so it is unclear how much he is worth. During his 1992 Senate race, however, he said publicly that his 1991 income was almost $300,000.[10] Keyes is not drawing a salary from his presidential campaign.

Keyes portrays his campaign as a crusade to restore traditional values to America. Many see it as a tactic to champion the anti-abortion cause. His campaign is considered quixotic even by some who know him well. Upon hearing that he planned to run for president, his 1992 Senate campaign manager, Susan Saum-Wicklein, said incredulously, "He's doing what?"[11] The former chairman of the Maryland Republican Party said, "I think this shows that in the United States of America, anyone can run for president."[12]

Keyes, with characteristic immodesty, describes himself as one of the country's best public speakers, but has had little success persuading people to open their checkbooks. In fact, bad financial luck seems to follow him. In July of 1995, he revealed that his campaign had discovered certain "discrepancies" in his exploratory committee, namely that $58,000 had inexplicably disappeared. The finance director quit and refused to turn over his files.[13] For an anemic campaign that an FEC report indicated had only $38,005 in the bank at the time, such a loss was crippling.

Keyes, undaunted, kept campaigning, firm in his conviction that he should be president.

ALAN KEYES
TOP 10 CAREER PATRONS*

1.	National Rifle Association, Washington, D.C.	$22,209
2.	Gilder Gagnon employees/spouses, investment firm, New York	$10,000
3.	National Right to Life PAC, Washington, D.C.	$8,905
4.	Campaign America, Senator Dole PAC, Washington, D.C.	$6,000
5.	Mr. and Mrs. Charles Helmuth, insurance broker, Chevy Chase, Maryland	$6,000
6.	Campaign for Maryland's Future, PAC set up by Keyes, Baltimore, Maryland	$5,000
7.	Fund for America's Future, President Bush PAC, Washington, D.C.	$5,000
8.	Hooper Family, Newton, Pennsylvania	$5,000
9.	Gonzales Family, framing company owners, Springfield, Virginia	$5,000
10.	Hinz Family, Mission Hills, California	$4,000

* Based on FEC records and Center for Responsive Politics data. National Rifle Association and National Right to Life PAC include independent expenditure campaigns. All contributions are from 1988 and 1992 Senate races.

Richard Lugar

The fact that Indiana Senator Richard Lugar is not generally considered to have a real chance of winning the 1996 Republican nomination for president doubtless says more about the process than the candidate. Lugar, like many of the other candidates, has all the traditional qualifications of a serious contender, but is widely perceived as lacking enough money, charisma, and the high profile necessary to make the first tier. Lugar is the quiet and scholarly candidate at a time when even bombast is considered low key.

Lugar has been on the cusp of higher office before. On three occasions, Lugar's name appeared on the vice presidential short lists of Presidents Nixon, Reagan, and Bush, but each time his colleagues were tapped for the position. Bush's 1988 selection of Dan Quayle, the junior senator from Indiana, was particularly embarrassing for Lugar, who had held office much longer than his younger and less experienced cohort. Yet Lugar voiced no public animosity over the choice. *Time*'s Margaret Carlson described the event by saying, "He survived that indignity with grace."[1]

Lugar was born in 1932 in Indianapolis. Just after attending Ohio's Denison University in 1954, he became a Rhodes scholar, got married, and then enlisted in the Navy to serve as an intelligence officer. But after working at the Pentagon for a little over three years, Lugar made the trek back to Indiana in 1960—back to his family-owned farm and food

machinery firm, Thomas L. Green and Co., which was
founded in 1893 by his grandfather.

Lugar first got the itch to plunge into public affairs at
the age of thirty-two, and promptly won a seat on the Indianapolis school board. It took him only three years to become the city's mayor, an office he then held for seven
years. His novel approach to local governance—through a
combination of initiatives including the merging of city and
county governments called the Unigov system—and his call
for fewer federally funded programs for city governments
earned accolades from President Nixon. The president
dubbed Lugar his favorite mayor in America. In 1973,
Lugar made Nixon's list of potential vice presidents after
Spiro Agnew resigned the office.

The Nixon association proved disastrous when Lugar made
a run for the U.S. Senate in 1974—the year of Watergate and
Nixon's resignation. He lost a fairly close race to incumbent
Democratic Senator Birch Bayh. Within two years, however,
Mayor Lugar overcame his lone electoral defeat to beat the
other Democratic incumbent senator, Vance Hartke. Though
his next Senate race in 1982 was tight, the following two saw
Lugar winning by landslides. He is the only senator from Indiana to win four terms in Washington.

In the Senate, Lugar has established himself as a foreign
policy expert. He became a trusted voice for the Reagan administration in the early 1980s, convincing the White House
to press Philippine leader Ferdinand Marcos to step down
after Lugar said he observed Marcos's theft of the election
against Corazon Aquino in 1986. Aquino later said that if it
had not been for Lugar, "There would be no Philippine–U.S.
relations to speak of by now."[3] A few years later Lugar became
an advocate of imposing sanctions against South Africa for its
apartheid system of government. President George Bush also
heard from Lugar on international matters when the Indiana
senator took the lead in pressing for a strong U.S. response
to Iraq's invasion of Kuwait in 1990. Lugar's knowledge of
foreign affairs landed him on the Senate Foreign Relations
Committee, where he served as chairman in 1985–1986, when
the Democrats regained the majority.

*   *   *

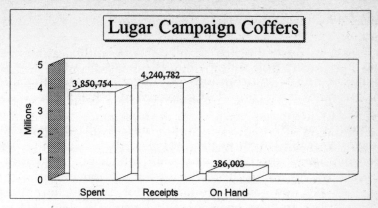

Lugar Campaign Coffers

3,850,754

4,240,782

386,003

Spent   Receipts   On Hand

Millions

Reporting through September 30, 1995.

Spent figures include all purchases or payments made in connection with or for the purpose of influencing a federal election.
Receipts are anything of value received by a political committee.
On Hand figures include funds held in checking and savings accounts, certificates of deposit, petty cash funds, travelers checks, treasury bills, and other investments valued at cost.

On the agricultural front, Lugar has been a prevailing voice on farm issues, working very closely with former Senate Agriculture Committee Chairman Patrick Leahy (D-VT). Lugar took over the job in 1995. But his service on the committee has been unusual in that he has consistently tried to reduce the amount of direct and indirect subsidies that farms and agricultural companies receive from the government, arguing that market forces would be a good thing for the farm industry. Though Lugar still owns an Indiana farm that received more than $40,000 in federal subsidies between 1989 and 1995, and he received more than $50,000 from agribusiness PACs between 1988 and 1992, he advocated the reduction of the program, a move that would cut into his own profits.[4]

Despite his association with agricultural matters, only two of his top ten donors over the past fifteen years are related to agribusiness. Half are PACs based in Washington, D.C. One of the more intriguing financial backers is the only one from his home state, the Eli Lilly Company of Indianapolis.

Eli Lilly

The Eli Lilly Company and its employees have been Lugar's most generous donor since 1979. The pharmaceutical manufacturer's contributions to Lugar's senatorial campaigns and leadership PACs exceeded $82,000 between 1979 and 1994.

Started in 1876 by Colonel Eli Lilly, a pharmacist who fought with the Union in the Civil War, the drug maker has become one of the nation's most influential pharmaceutical companies. Known in the 1920s for the introduction of insulin, Lilly has now gained prominence for its top-selling drug Prozac.[5] The Indiana company and Lugar have had a close relationship dating back to Lugar's years as Indianapolis mayor. The relationship is so close, in fact, that there has been a revolving door between Eli Lilly, its charitable foundation the Lilly Endowment, and Lugar's mayoral, senatorial, and presidential campaign staffs. Terry Holt, Lugar's campaign press secretary, explained the practice by saying that "Indiana is fairly intimate."[6] At least four Lilly employees have gone on to work for Lugar in some political capacity. They are members of what the *Indianapolis Business Journal* called the "Lugar Club."[7] One of them is Lilly executive Mitch Daniels, a former political adviser to President Reagan, who in 1995 was selected to manage Lugar's presidential bid. Daniels also served as Lugar's first Senate chief of staff and has been an individual campaign contributor.[8] "Mitch cut his teeth in politics in Lugar's mayor days," Holt told the Center for Public Integrity.

The closeness between the company and the senator, however, encompasses more than merely sharing a common talent pool. During the volatile debates over President Clinton's health care reform proposal, Lilly launched a massive lobbying campaign to torpedo the plan that contained provisions threatening to control the price of pharmaceuticals.[9] Lugar, for his part, vowed to fight the Democratic plan, specifically saying he would not support reform measures that contained price controls on drugs.[10] In mid-August 1994, Lugar, along with fellow Indiana senator Dan Coats (R), appeared at a Washington, D.C. rally thrown by an Indiana group that

hoped to see the health care bill fail. Lugar, who promised
to block the Democratic bill, was presented with "filibuster
survival kits" by the group, complete with throat lozenges and
cottonball earplugs to block out the protests of the
Democrats.[11]

The bill was pronounced dead in November 1994. Eli Lilly's
stock rose three-eighths of a point after the news broke.[12]
During the two years the health care bill was being formu-
lated and debated, the Eli Lilly company, as well as its employees and their spouses, donated more than $42,000 to Lugar's
Senate campaign. Holt said he did not know if Lilly had lobbied Lugar, but that the senator's opposition to the health
care reform legislation had more to do with ideology than
campaign contributions.

Lugar's support for Eli Lilly has come in varied forms
throughout his political life. In March 1992, Lugar voted
against a cost containment measure for drugs, which would
have penalized companies with the loss of tax credits for
their Puerto Rican plants if the drug makers increased their
pharmaceutical prices more than the rate of inflation. Senator David Pryor (D-AR), who proposed the bill, said drug
costs had been increasing at three times the rate of inflation. The bill failed, 61–36.[13] Lilly had a stake in the bill;
at the time it had in excess of $300 million in capital invest-
ments in Puerto Rico and that year had announced a $65
million expansion of its Puerto Rico facility.[14] The Associated Press estimated that Eli Lilly stood to lose tens of thousands of dollars if the tax credits—exempting Lilly from
paying U.S. income tax on profits earned in Puerto Rico—
were scrapped.[15] A trade publication, the *Institutional Invest-
or's Portfolio Letter*, said Eli Lilly would be hurt by Pryor's
legislation.[16]

In 1991, Lugar asked Brazilian President Fernando Collor
de Mello to meet with Eli Lilly President Sydney Taurel to
discuss pending Brazilian patents legislation that American
pharmaceutical companies believed could adversely affect
them. Taurel was head of the Pharmaceutical Manufacturers
Association delegation to Brazil at the time.[17] The Brazilian
legislation never went anywhere because President Collor re-

signed under a cloud of corruption charges before the plan got underway.

In 1986, Lugar made the announcement that Eli Lilly CEO Richard Wood, another Lugar contributor, had been tapped by President Reagan to join the president's Export Council. Of the appointment, made public by Lugar's office, Lugar said in a statement, "Dick Wood and Eli Lilly have been leaders in expanding America and Indiana's export potential."[18] With respect to Lugar's helping Wood get the appointment, Lugar's campaign press secretary, Terry Holt, said, "Lugar, as a senator, has a certain responsibility."

In 1985 Eli Lilly received a special foreign trade sub-zone provision for their Indiana plants, which at the time produced most of Lilly's $350 million in annual exports. The sub-zone designation exempted Eli Lilly from custom duties on items it used in making the exports. Lugar, who again made the announcement along with Senator Quayle said, "The duty benefits of a trade zone also encourage companies to continue manufacturing in this country. This is good news for Lilly.[19]

The Center for Public Integrity contacted the Eli Lilly Company and asked about its relationship with Lugar. The company did not respond. Terry Holt, however, said, "If people have given Lugar money over the years, it's been because of the decisions he made. The idea [that his vote can be bought] is absurd."

Lugar told the Center for Public Integrity he believes that campaign contributions from any one source rarely have any impact on the way a legislator behaves because federal campaign financing laws, which cap donations, dilute the influence of any one company or PAC. "There is a lack of specific indebtedness," Lugar said, citing the contribution limits. He said it is difficult to try to single out and remember those who made large contributions when dealing with millions of dollars. "It is hard to remember precisely the proportion that anyone [gave]," he added.[20]

That may be the case, but during the course of a long career in public office, Lugar has quite clearly recalled at least one other Indiana patron.

The Marott Hotel

When Lugar was a child, he thought Indianapolis's historic Marott Hotel—where famed actress Betty Grable and other well-known personalities used to live—was quite impressive. He got to know it pretty well when his grandmother lived there. "It was a beautiful place," Lugar recalled in a 1995 interview. Over the years, however, the old hotel had fallen on hard times and needed a serious makeover.

In 1982, Indianapolis developer Kenneth Puller decided it was time to restore some of the grandeur of the building and spearheaded a project to convert the hotel into upscale apartments. But in order to finance the renovation, Puller needed a loan from the Department of Housing and Urban Development. That's where his friend Dick Lugar came into the picture.

"I remember Mr. Puller and his wife were contributors to my campaigns," Lugar told the Center for Public Integrity.[21] "And I think they contributed in more than one instance. . . . They were active in the Indiana builders and people who were doing work for the builders." Puller and his wife contributed $6,000 to Lugar between 1981 and 1982 and $3,000 to the Republican Senatorial Committee when Lugar ran it in 1983 and 1984. Between 1979 and 1994, the National Association of Home Builders PAC gave Lugar $29,500, making them his number four top career patron.

Lugar's aides, with the senator's approval, lobbied HUD officials in Washington, D.C. to approve the loan, despite the fact that the Indianapolis HUD branch had initially rejected the project.[22] Lugar told the Center for Public Integrity that he had sent a letter to HUD on Puller's behalf. In a letter to a Kentucky newspaper, Lugar explained, "A member of my Senate staff worked with the city of Indianapolis and with HUD to convince the latter to take a longer term view and to support the project. These staff conversations occurred by telephone at a relatively low level."[23] At the time, Lugar was chairman of the Senate Housing and Urban Affairs Committee. Two weeks after the Indiana office rejected the Puller loan, a Lugar supporter and campaign contributor, Martha Lamkin, was appointed to take over the Indianapolis HUD office. She and her husband gave $2,455 between 1979 and 1994. Lamkin told *Newsday* that she was instructed by the regional HUD officers to approve the loan immediately.

Puller was successful in securing a nearly $13 million HUD loan. But by early 1989, despite the fact that most of the apartments in the renovated Marott Hotel were occupied, he was forced into default on the loan after higher-than-expected construction costs rendered Puller unable to pay back the debt. HUD wound up buying back the mortgage, costing taxpayers millions. The hotel was sold at auction in January 1994 for $2.5 million.[24]

Lugar has admitted his involvement in the matter, but says he does not regret helping to revive the hotel. "I'm still delighted the Marott Hotel was resurrected," he told the Center for Public Integrity. During a press conference in the days immediately following news of his efforts in *Newsday*, Lugar said, "I think that my intervention was appropriate, and I would say, at no time, did I visit with the secretary of HUD or other higher officials with regard to this."[25]

Lugar also helped Puller in the early 1980s when the senator wrote to HUD officials asking that Puller be admitted into a new HUD program called "co-insurance." The program replaced HUD staff with private entities who would receive fees for processing loans for housing projects "by selling securities backed by the Government National Mortgage Association," according to *Newsday*. If the private lenders defaulted, the government would assume 80 percent of the cost. Puller's company was the first to participate in the program, where he eventually developed $400 million worth of HUD-backed projects, with the potential for Puller to earn tens of millions of dollars. However, in 1989, HUD indefinitely suspended Puller's contract.[26]

Lugar told the Center for Public Integrity that he helped another campaign contributor, J. Irwin Miller, the chairman of Cummins Engine Co., and other citizens of Columbus, Indiana, obtain HUD financing for a development project there. Lugar actually visited then-Secretary of HUD, Samuel Pierce, to discuss the matter.[27] Miller, whom Lugar described as "one of the patron saints of the country," has donated $4,850 to Lugar's Senate campaigns.

Despite Lugar's entanglements with Eli Lilly and developer Kenneth Puller, he has generally been regarded as a "clean" member of Congress, one who is not overtly interested in the fast-paced race for cash, and who is more concerned with policy questions. But it is Lugar's involvement with the politics of money that have spawned the relatively sparse negative publicity Lugar has received throughout his career. Even though he failed to land a VP spot on various GOP tickets, Lugar was not deterred from getting further involved in the highly competitive arena of partisan politics, particularly the monetary aspect of it. In 1979 and 1980, Lugar got a firsthand feel for a national political race when he managed the short-lived presidential campaign of his friend, then-Senate Republican leader Howard Baker. Though Baker's effort was unsuccessful, he later rewarded Lugar by handing him the reins of the National Republican Senatorial Committee (NRSC), which Lugar held between 1983 and 1984, and later the Republican Majority Fund, Baker's one-time leadership PAC that became Lugar's in 1987. Though the PAC has not raised any money since 1990, Lugar did raise $515,846 for the Republican Majority Fund between 1987 and 1990, as well as $81.6 million for the NRSC in his two-year tenure as its chair.

A 1989 Common Cause study showed that of all the senators receiving honoraria between 1983 and 1987, Lugar kept the most—$238,076—and came in second for the most raised with $399,135.[28] Other Common Cause studies showed that Lugar several times ranked among the top senators for most honoraria received.[29] Most of that money came from agricultural interests and financial institutions.

Lugar has also fared well in fundraising for his senatorial campaigns, raising more than $9.5 million between 1979 and 1994.[30]

To become the nation's chief executive, Lugar will have to do much better than that to catch up with the money leaders in the 1996 presidential race. "I can't say we have been hobbled by a lack of money," Lugar said in the summer of 1995. ". . . We're going to be competitive."

RICHARD LUGAR
TOP 10 CAREER PATRONS*

1. Eli Lilly company and employees, Lilly Endowment, pharmaceuticals, Indianapolis, Indiana $82,693
2. Contractors of America, Washington, D.C. $48,500
3. Chicago Mercantile Exchange, commodity investment, Chicago, Illinois $30,000
4. National Association of Home Builders, Washington, D.C. $29,500
5. American Bankers Association, Washington, D.C. $28,500
6. Harris Corporation, electronics/defense, Melbourne, Florida $27,000
7. Insurance Agents of America, Washington, D.C. $24,500
8. National Association of Realtors, Chicago, Illinois $24,500
9. Chicago Board of Trade, Chicago, Illinois $21,750
10. American Medical Association, Washington, D.C. $21,000

* Includes contributions to Lugar's Senate campaigns between 1979 and 1994, as well as independent expenditures made on behalf of the candidate. Based on the FEC records and Center for Responsive Politics data.

Arlen Specter

Perhaps no current presidential candidate is more adept at turning lemons into lemonade than Republican Arlen Specter. Electorally, he has failed more often than any other major candidate in the 1996 field, but he believes that shows voters he is "battle-tested." "I lost three elections in the seventies and a fourth in the sixties. I've had tougher elections than anyone else running for president," Specter told us in an interview.[1]

He is the only presidential candidate who has undergone life-threatening surgery in the past five years, for the removal of a nonmalignant brain tumor in June 1993, and seems strangely invigorated by the experience; he has increased his workload by plunging headlong into national presidential politics and travel. An unapologetic career politician in an era of anti-incumbency and overall distrust of politicians, Specter also is the only presidential candidate whose spouse is an elected official: Joan Specter is a member of the Philadelphia City Council.

Specter is probably best remembered for alienating millions of American women, traditionally his supporters, during the 1991 Clarence Thomas Supreme Court confirmation hearings when he grilled Anita Hill. In 1995, he was one of Senator Bob Packwood's most loyal defenders against numerous charges of sexual harassment, although he voted to televise hearings on the matter. Oddly, his 1996 presidential campaign strategy depends on appealing directly to women voters.

Jewish and pro-choice in a political party that has largely moved to stand for Christian family values, conservatism, and staunch opposition to abortion, Arlen Specter has boldly launched a frontal assault on the Christian Coalition. He casts himself as the party's voice of moderation opposed to a "radical social agenda." As he said in his announcement speech, "We need tolerance and simple humanity. When [executive director of the Christian Coalition] Ralph Reed says a pro-choice Republican isn't qualified to be our president, I say the Republican party will not be blackmailed. I and millions of other pro-choice Republicans will not be disenfranchised."[2] As an elected official, his positions defy pigeonholing. Indeed, when Arlen Specter walks onto the floor of the United States Senate as the senior senator from Pennsylvania, sometimes no one, including his own staff, knows which way he will vote. During the Bush years, the White House viewed him as a "dangerous wild card," and in 1991, he supported his party and president legislatively less than 40 percent of the time.[3] Despite his decades-long public image as a tough prosecutor and crime buster, the National Rifle Association has been his largest single supporter since 1979, and Specter has voted the NRA positions consistently—against banning assault weapons, against a ban on interstate handgun sales, and against a fourteen-day registration period for handgun purchases.

Specter grew up in Russell, Kansas—also Bob Dole's hometown. Given his immigrant father's painful memories of religious persecution in Russia and his own isolation as the only Jew in a gentile society (at school students were led daily in a prayer with "Jesus Christ in it"), it is not difficult to understand why Specter is so defiantly critical of the religious-right wing of the Republican party. "It was an isolating factor. It affected me in a number of ways," Specter said. "One way was to really let me know I was Jewish, and to bring out a pride in being Jewish. That was what I was, and I was proud of it. It sort of told me who I was."[4]

Specter began his career in public service in the early 1960s as an assistant district attorney of Philadelphia, winning highly publicized labor racketeering convictions. In 1964, he was appointed assistant counsel to the Warren Commission, which

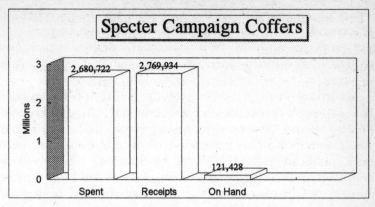

Reporting through September 30, 1995.

Spent figures include all purchases or payments made in connection with or for the purpose of influencing a federal election.
Receipts are anything of value received by a political committee.
On Hand figures include funds held in checking and savings accounts, certificates of deposit, petty cash funds, travelers checks, treasury bills, and other investments valued at cost.

was formed by President Lyndon Johnson to investigate the assassination of John F. Kennedy. Specter helped to devise the official Warren Commission "single-bullet" theory, saying there was a lone gunman, Lee Harvey Oswald. More than two decades later he found himself criticized for his involvement in the movie *JFK.*

Until 1965 he had been a registered Democrat, but in the year of his political conversion Republican Specter was elected in his first political office, district attorney of Philadelphia, the first Republican elected to that post in eighteen years.[5] In 1967, he unsuccessfully challenged incumbent mayor, James Tate. Specter was elected again in 1969 as district attorney, with Tom Gola as comptroller. They ran an excellent campaign with the slogan, "They are young, they are tough, and nobody owns them."[6]

Near the end of his term, however, Specter's image was tarnished when investigative reporters Donald L. Barlett and James B. Steele of the *Philadelphia Inquirer* wrote a series of articles on the crisis within the criminal justice system in Philadelphia that questioned the success of the D.A.'s office. "It is a system where the district attorney cries out in public for stiff penalties while his assistants quietly negotiate pleas and recommend short sentences or probation," the authors wrote.

According to Barlett and Steele, in 1971, Specter's staff of 158 attorneys prosecuted 12,456 criminal cases in Philadelphia's Common Pleas Court. The seven-month journalistic investigation found that for major violent crimes, a third of all indictments were later dropped by Specter's office. The *Inquirer* found that "while assembling one of the largest prosecutor's staffs in the country . . . Specter also had posted one of the poorest conviction rates in the nation. In fact, it may very well be the worst."[8]

In 1973, Specter failed in his third attempt to be elected district attorney of Philadelphia. He practiced law in Philadelphia until 1976, when he entered a GOP primary fight for retiring Senator Hugh Scott's seat, and was defeated by then-Congressman John Heinz. In 1978, Specter ran for governor of Pennsylvania, but lost in a Republican primary to Richard Thornburgh.

Arlen Specter was forty-eight years old, and a four-time political loser. It looked as though his once-promising career as an elected official might be over. But Specter did not quit.

He decided to try for statewide office one more time when Republican Senator Richard S. Schweiker announced he would not seek reelection in 1980. Specter won that year, the same year of the Reagan presidential landslide in which the Senate went Republican. Specter's hard work and perseverance had paid off. "The guy is tenacious," Democratic consultant Saul Shorr told the *Washington Post.* "He believes in himself."[9]

In 1986, he was reelected to his second term in the Senate in a decisive win. According to Federal Election Commission records, the National Rifle Association spent $111,757 on behalf of Specter's 1986 reelection campaign. It was the second largest amount of money spent by the NRA that year and it remains one of the largest totals on record by the gun lobby. Indeed, the NRA's cumulative support for Specter over his

Washington career, $134,829, makes that powerful special interest Specter's largest career patron.

Nearly all of the 1986 NRA money consisted of independent political expenditures made on Specter's behalf, on advertising and hunting parties. Specter denied having knowledge of those expenditures until after the elections were over. "I genuinely didn't know about it," Specter said of the NRA expenditures. "They made substantial expenditures on my behalf. I was sitting over at a Republican meeting, I was looking over [Senator] Don Nickle's (R-OK) shoulder one day [when I] saw the independent expenditure, about two years later."

Asked to explain his various votes on gun issues, Specter said, "I know that gun control does not keep guns out of the hands of criminals. I also know that tough sentencing does." He is aware, of course, that Pennsylvania has the nation's second largest NRA membership, after California. "It's a fair constituent concern in Pennsylvania when you have about four million sportsmen in the state, and you have the Second Amendment right to bear arms," the senator said. He insisted that NRA contributions do not influence his voting record in any way.

As he began his second Senate term, Specter received national exposure for taking a stand more in line with his moderate reputation. In 1987 he opposed the Supreme Court nomination of Robert H. Bork. Despite receiving almost 75,000 pieces of mail, 50,000 phone calls, and even personal requests from the administration, Specter refused to support the Reagan nominee. "The problem I had," Specter said, "is how you deal with a man of powerful intellect who disagrees so fundamentally with the underlying philosophy of so much of constitutional law."[10] Specter's questioning and opposition to Bork was a significant factor in the failure of his nomination.

His nonconformity enraged conservative Republicans. Specter "is seen by many in the Senate as a loner, an arrogant and abrasive man who does not deal in the currency of clubby collegiality that often gets the job done in Congress and who has a penchant for shallow publicity," according to one account.[11]

Specter got his chance to make amends to his party colleagues in October 1991, during the riveting televised Judiciary Committee confirmation hearings of Clarence Thomas, who was nominated by President George Bush to the Supreme Court. The testimony surrounding whether Thomas had sexually harassed Anita Hill was lurid and unpredictable by any standard, replete with stories about movies with titles such as *Long Dong Silver* and anecdotes about pubic hair on Coke cans.

Against this bizarre backdrop, Arlen Specter suddenly became a pivotal presence. The Bush White House and the Thomas nomination's leading supporters, Senators John Danforth (R-MO) and Orrin Hatch (R-UT), had decided that there were two shrewd advantages to having former prosecutor Specter lead the Republican questioning of Hill. First, he was indisputably the most experienced and qualified GOP member of the panel to ask piercing questions. And second, Specter had been publicly dubious about Thomas's judicial experience and qualifications. As journalists Jane Mayer and Jill Abramson have reported, the pro-Thomas camp correctly predicted that engaging Specter's considerable ego would also enlist his involvement and support for Thomas. Not only did Specter grill Anita Hill, he even accused her of perjury, a charge he later regretted making. According to then-Senate Judiciary Committee Chairman Joe Biden (D-DE), "As soon as [Specter] saw himself as the star prosecutor, he couldn't resist. They knew his personality better than he did."[12] "It was quite a learning experience for me, and I think a learning experience for the country," Specter reflected.

In a period of just days, he had alienated one of his core constituencies. Women's groups that had long viewed Specter as a supporter and friend, were stunned and angry. Over his career, he had endorsed the Equal Rights Amendment and the Civil Rights Act of 1991, by which women got the right to sue for discrimination in the workplace. He promoted research on women's health and federal aid for women and children. "I was a leader on breast cancer research long before it became a *cause celebre nationale*, long before the Hill-Thomas story," Specter said.[13]

Specter's 1992 reelection campaign opened with a primary challenge from Republican Stephen Friend, a staunch anti-abortion advocate. Specter won the primary handily, but in the "Year of the Woman" Specter barely beat Democrat Lynn Yeakel, winning by only three percentage points, though he outspent her two to one.[14]

Specter's campaign expenditures increased from $1,488,588 in 1980 to $6,451,649 in 1986 to $9,744,696 in 1992. He was among the top six Senate recipients of campaign money in 1991–1992 from lawyers and lobbying firms. Specter, who received $911,005, in individual and PAC contributions from lawyers and lobbying firms, is a member of the Judiciary Committee. Specter also received substantial support from the insurance industry, $265,203; from health professionals, $294,135; and from the makers of pharmaceuticals and health products, $108,326.[15]

Why have these interests taken such a generous personal interest in Arlen Specter? One reason is that the committee on which he serves, and the Congress generally, has been a battleground between forces competing over efforts to change the legal system on liability cases. Trial lawyers have had a direct financial stake in keeping tort reform off the table, because limiting civil litigation means limiting the number of cases that can be brought, and limiting the awards and the legal fees they can earn. The nation's wealthiest corporations, insurance companies and doctors who are the targets of lawsuits, want to limit their legal and financial exposure. In 1995, after roughly a decade of intense, expensive lobbying, tort reform legislation to limit liability was passed by Congress. Specter voted against the bill.

Although Specter insisted, "I believe there should be tort reform because there is a lot of frivolous litigation," in 1995 and in other years he has frequently supported the position of the trial lawyers. His son Shanin is a trial lawyer in Philadelphia, and a member of the Philadelphia Trial Lawyers Association.

As a member of the Defense Appropriations Subcommittee, Specter attracted $204,899 from the defense industry in PAC and individual contributions for his 1992 campaign, ranking him second among Senate recipients of defense money that year.[16] Specter was a strong supporter of the Persian Gulf war resolution and has generally supported most Pentagon programs. In 1991, the Bush administration announced it would close the Philadelphia Naval Shipyard, which employed 7,000 workers and was among eighty-one installations selected to be closed or scaled back that year. Specter filed a case against the navy which he eventually argued personally before the U.S. Supreme Court. He lost.

Specter's senior position on both the Appropriations Committee panel, which deals with Medicare and Medicaid, and the Veterans' Affairs Committee, with jurisdiction over the VA's mail-order "Rx" program, made him a favorite of the health industry donors. In 1992, Specter was the top recipient of health industry contributions, $364,403, in the Senate.[17] The group Citizen Action calculated that health industry PACs and "large donors" have given Specter $33,900 since 1993, and $990,121 since 1979.[18]

That same year, Specter ranked second among members of Congress as a recipient of contributions from the cable TV industry. According to FEC records, the Rigas family, which owns Adelphia Communications in Pennsylvania, contributed $13,000 to Specter for his 1992 reelection campaign. Since 1983, Specter has voted in favor of cable deregulation, then in favor of re-regulation, and in 1995 he voted in favor of the telecommunications bill, which was supported by cable TV interests.

Some of Specter's constituent representation has resulted in some sweet deals. In the 1980s, Joan Specter, the senator's wife, was the owner of a bakery, "Joan Specter's Desserts," which supplied pies to the Senate. The Senate bought $100 worth of large pies from her every week.[19] "When I came to the Senate, I gave pies to everyone here, and the Senate bought her pies for a relatively short time. She's been out of the business for a long time now," Specter told us.

A bake sale is not in the offing, but Specter's campaign is not nearly as well funded as the Dole, Gramm, Alexander, or Clinton efforts. "It's a lot harder to raise money for president if you are a pro-choice Republican," he said.

"People don't think you can win." But Specter believes he has enough money to mount a credible candidacy. "I think America's always been governed from the center, wants to be governed from the center," he told us. "This year I believe there is a chance to win because it's a wide-open field."

Quixotic or brilliantly perceptive, Specter does not seem the slightest bit daunted by the formidable prospect of sailing against the very strong winds of his own party. He has gained a distinctive perspective from having had a brain tumor. "There's a new insight into life when you lie in a hospital bed the night before they're going to use a saw to open up your skull after a doctor's told you you have three to six weeks to live," Specter said. "And it's reinforced my view of activism and independence."[20]

ARLEN SPECTER
TOP 10 CAREER PATRONS*

1. NRA Political Victory Fund, Washington, D.C. $134,829
2. Realtors PAC, Chicago, Illinois $31,200
3. Marshall PAC, Attorneys and Law Firms,
   Philadelphia, Pennsylvania $27,750
4. Desert Caucus, Pro-Israel, Tucson, Arizona $22,500
5. American Bankers Association BankPAC,
   Washington, D.C. $22,500
6. National Association of Life Underwriters
   PAC, Washington, D.C. $21,500
7. Smith-Kline Beecham Corporation PAC,
   Philadelphia, Pennsylvania $21,300
8. Westinghouse Electric Corporation Employees
   Political Participation Program, Pittsburgh,
   Pennsylvania $21,000
9. Rockwell International Corporation,
   Pittsburgh, Pennsylvania $21,000

10. Action Committee for Rural Electrification,
       Washington, D.C. $21,000

* Includes all U.S. Senate campaign cycles, 1979 through 1994, as well as independent expenditures made on the senator's behalf through his career. Based on Federal Election Commission records and Center for Responsive Politics data.

Pete Wilson

Pete Wilson's official campaign for the 1996 Republican presidential nomination lasted a month. The reason, one so unusual for him, was a lack of funds. As a state legislator, mayor, senator, and governor, he has held elective office continuously for nearly three decades, longer than any other major 1996 presidential candidate except Bob Dole. But over the past quarter century, no politician in America has raised more cash for his campaigns than Pete Wilson, the chief executive of California. That he holds this distinction over Dole, Republican leader of the United States Senate for more than a decade and presidential candidate in 1980 and 1988, is remarkable. From his second reelection triumph as mayor of San Diego in 1978, to two U.S. Senate and three gubernatorial campaigns, Wilson has raised and spent more than $80 million. Interestingly, this Republican's most generous career patron has been a union of government employees. In the state that already has the most prisons in America and is spending billions of taxpayer dollars to build many more, Pete Wilson's campaigns, directly and indirectly, have received $1.57 million from the California Correctional Peace Officers Association, which represents thousands of state-employed prison guards and other correctional employees. Wilson declined to be interviewed by the Center for Public Integrity, and did not respond to the written questions we submitted.

Wilson has always been scrappy, hard-working, and tenacious. Though he weighed only 155 pounds, he insistently tried out for his college football team. He passed the California bar exam on his determined fourth effort. Politically he has confounded his critics and political observers many times, winning elections no one thought he could ever win.

Underneath the tough ex-Marine exterior is a leatherneck-shrewd politician who is acutely attuned and responsive to shifts in popular sentiment. He knows how to calibrate his message quickly to connect to the broadest numbers of eligible voters. As San Diego mayor he was known for his environmentalism and opposition to the conservative tax-cutting ballot initiative known as Proposition 13. As senator and governor he has been firmly pro-choice on abortion and as a presidential candidate he played on white America's racial insecurities on such sensitive issues as immigration and affirmative action. He is described as a "centrist" or a "chameleon," depending on who is doing the describing. A Republican who has raised taxes and supports gay rights and AIDS research, he is willing to defy convention and break campaign promises: he ran for governor in 1990 just two years after winning reelection to the U.S. Senate, and then sought the 1996 Republican nomination after he promised California voters in 1994 that if reelected governor, he would not run for president. Bill Clinton made the same promise to the voters of Arkansas in 1990 before running for the White House in 1992. Breaking the promise hurt Wilson's fundraising efforts and contributed to the campaign lowering its target from $20 million in 1995 to $12 million, Wilson's press secretary said. Some of his most loyal California contributors were not happy that Wilson was willing to give up the governorship despite his argument that he could do more for California as president. That reality caught up with Wilson on September 29, 1995, when he announced he would drop out of the 1996 race.

"To go on would be to run up an unacceptable debt," Wilson told a rally in Sacramento. "As much as your hearts and mine tell me to fight on, my conscience tells me that to do so would be unfair to all of us." Wilson added that his supporters' hopes "simply are not and will not be matched by the necessary campaign funds to take this message to the people who need to hear it."

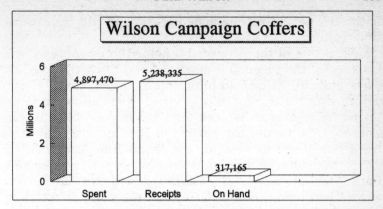

Wilson Campaign Coffers

Reporting through September 30, 1995.

Spent figures include all purchases or payments made in connection with or for the purpose of influencing a federal election.
Receipts are anything of value received by a political committee.
On Hand figures include funds held in checking and savings accounts, certificates of deposit, petty cash funds, travelers checks, treasury bills, and other investments valued at cost.

Wilson was a loyal advance man for Richard Nixon during one of the lowest points in Nixon's political career. In 1962, the former vice president, having narrowly lost the presidency to John F. Kennedy two years earlier, suffered a frustrating political defeat in his native California, losing to Edmund G. "Pat" Brown in the gubernatorial election. Longtime Nixon aide and friend, Herb Klein, then editor of the *San Diego Union*, was with Nixon and Haldeman the morning after the humiliating loss. Just moments after an embittered Nixon made his famous comment to the press—"You won't have Dick Nixon to kick around anymore"—he left the hotel for a waiting car. Wilson's assignment, according to Klein, was to make sure that Nixon "got into the car" without incident.

Revenge was sweet for Wilson when, thirty-two years later, he defeated Kathleen Brown—daughter of the man who had defeated Nixon in 1962, Pat Brown—in a come-from-behind victory. In a deathbed interview with his former White House speechwriter and *New York Times* columnist William Safire, Richard Nixon predicted, "If Pete Wilson survives in California in '94, he will be nominated in '96 and will be a strong candidate."[1]

Klein is one of the people who helped to convince Wilson to move to San Diego and enter politics. "I thought he was a very attractive person to bring into politics . . . very bright, very attractive, with a lot of principles." Klein and others "arranged for him to go to work for a law firm," which he did. Klein told the Center for Public Integrity that "several of us urged him to go to work for the Republican Associates," a group that conducted political research and helped identify future political candidates.[2] Wilson followed their advice and became part-time executive director of the group of southern California Republican businessmen.

Wilson first ran in 1966 for a seat in the California Assembly representing San Diego. Before running, he talked with Nixon, and as Wilson later recalled at Nixon's 1994 funeral, "In classic Nixon fashion he gave me a cool look and his first question was: "Pete, do you think you can win? Because if you do, you've got to try or you'll never forgive yourself!'"[3]

Wilson took the plunge, was successful at the polls, and served two terms in the California legislature. Subsequently, he was elected mayor of San Diego in 1971, and went on to serve eleven years in that position. His only political defeat occurred in 1978, when he placed a dismal fourth in a GOP gubernatorial primary, garnering just 9 percent of the votes. In 1982, he was elected to the United States Senate, defeating Jerry Brown, and he was reelected in 1988. The announcement that Republican Governor George Deukmejian would not be seeking reelection in 1990 gave Wilson a chance at the gubernatorial seat. California GOP powers that be—worried about the upcoming redistricting of the state legislature—implored him to run. Wilson agreed, and defeated former San Francisco mayor Dianne Feinstein. He had a difficult term, during which he was forced to support a major tax increase among other politically thorny issues. By 1994 he seemed vulnerable against gubernatorial challenger Kathleen Brown. But Wilson ran an excellent, focused campaign with a coherent theme, stressing such differences with his opponent as his longtime support for the death penalty, and his support for a ballot initiative called Proposition 187, a measure to halt government services to illegal immigrants. Wilson won, 55–41 percent.[4]

During the 1994 campaign, Wilson unequivocally said he would not run for president in 1996, and that if elected he would faithfully execute his duties as governor for the full, four-year term. Within months of beginning his second term, he made it clear he was running for the 1996 Republican presidential nomination. Wilson told CNN's Larry King, "I can do so much more as president for California than I can as governor."[5] What is clear is that Wilson has already done a lot for certain California interests.

Money Meets Power

Politician Wilson has developed a unique, convenient, "one-stop shopping" approach to the money chase: fundraising events at which wealthy donors have ponied up cash for an opportunity to talk not only with the governor, but also with the accompanying state government regulators of particular industries. It is not often that *quid* so readily meets *quo*. Indeed, it is service with a smile.

One such social mingling of regulators and representatives from the powerful waste industry occurred at a May 11, 1993, fundraiser held by Wilson. The $5,000-per-couple affair was attended by thirty industry representatives from the major garbage firms, Wilson and his senior administrators. Also present were four of the six members of the California Integrated Waste Management Board, the state agency responsible for regulation of the waste industry.[6]

It was a perfect opportunity for the waste industry's large political contributors. For the modest price of $5,000 they spent a night socializing with a majority of the state waste board, in front of which they had landfill deals and other business pending. When the event was criticized, Dan Schnur, Wilson's communications director, told the *Sacramento Bee* that "the decision of our fund-raiser to invite regulators was clearly a mistake."[7] Despite the fact that Wilson himself was in attendance, Schnur also asserted that the fundraiser, Brad

Zerbe, acted to invite the members without the "knowledge or approval" of the rest of the administration.[8]

But that is not the only such commingling of contributors and regulators. The California Ski Industry Association got a real lift when it hosted a fundraising lunch for Wilson that raised $23,900. Nine resort representatives dined with Wilson, who brought along the director of the Highway Patrol, the director of Caltrans, the secretary of resources and the secretary of trade and commerce.[9] The ski resorts had convenient access to the very people who decide whether to keep the roads open in the snow, promote tourism, and deal with water and air quality issues.

Despite numerous examples of official acts that specifically benefitted his campaign benefactors, Wilson maintains that he cannot be influenced. In 1990, he told the *Los Angeles Times*, "There is no *quid pro quo* in any decision. You do not [help a supporter] for campaign contributions. You do it only because it . . . benefits the public."[10]

However broadly or narrowly one chooses to define "the public," Wilson does have one trademark core belief to which he has been steadfast and faithful throughout his political career. All politicians like to say they are "tough on crime." Wilson has been saying it and meaning it for just about thirty years. He has been a consistent supporter of the death penalty, and as a senator even sponsored legislation to impose the death penalty for the murder of a law enforcement officer attempting to apprehend drug offenders.[11] Wilson was a vocal supporter of, and as governor signed, the "three strikes and you're out" legislation into law in March 1994. The law requires substantially longer prison sentences for second- and third-time convicted felons.[12]

Most politicians who talk about crime have never been victimized by it, directly or indirectly through family members. Wilson's mother, Margaret Callahan, was the daughter of Irish immigrants. Her father, Mike Callahan, Pete Wilson's grandfather, was a Chicago cop killed in the line of duty. One night in 1908, thirty-year-old Callahan happened upon three members of a gang of cocaine dealers and robbers, when one of them pulled out a gun and shot him in the stomach. He died the next day.[13]

Wilson has acknowledged that his grandfather's murder made an impact on his thinking about crime issues. "I am obviously aware that my mother grew up without a father because a thug on the streets of Chicago gunned down my grandfather." Wilson's widowed grandmother took a job cleaning hotel rooms to support herself and her young daughter Margaret, then eighteen months old.[14]

So it is no secret among law enforcement officials in California that Wilson is sympathetic to what they do. In 1990, then-Senator Wilson spoke to Los Angeles Police Academy graduates and mentioned his slain grandfather, adding proudly that "he also got the man who got him." When Wilson finished, the then-chief of the LAPD, Daryl F. Gates, "welcomed him as a member of the brotherhood and sisterhood of law enforcement, saying that once a cop—or a family of a cop—always a cop."[15] Today, the framed police badge, No. 2842, of Detective Mike Callahan, sits on a bookshelf in Governor Pete Wilson's Sacramento office.[16]

Police officers are campaign contributors with special interest agendas like anyone else. In a 1990 gubernatorial campaign debate, Wilson criticized his opponent, Dianne Feinstein, for accepting $150,000 in campaign funds from the Highway Patrol Officers. Wilson said in the debate that he was "truly shocked that [Feinstein] would be so blind to such a gross conflict of interest."[17]

California Correctional Peace Officers Association

His shock over Feinstein's conflict-of-interest blindness is ironic given Wilson's own relationship with the California Correctional Peace Officers Association (CCPOA). The state union of more than 25,000 prison guards, medical technicians, and parole officers has spent at least $1.57 million to keep Governor Pete Wilson in power. Of the roughly $80 million Wilson has raised for his various campaigns since 1978, his single most generous benefactor has been the CCPOA, which only began supporting Wilson in 1990. That year, the organization spent nearly $1 million in an advertising campaign on gubernatorial candidate Wilson's behalf.[18]

In the 1994 race, this same organization of state employees spent more than $500,000 in support of his campaign.

The prison workers union is headed by a man named Don Novey, a colorful former prison guard who wears a fedora and a mustache. He has built CCPOA into a powerhouse political force with a $9.5 million annual budget and a $3 million state headquarters in Sacramento. Since 1980 prison guard salaries have doubled, and union membership has burgeoned from 2,000 to 25,500 members, and counting.[19] CCPOA spends half a million dollars a year on public relations. When the Center for Public Integrity contacted their offices, we were admonished against using the term "prison guard." Novey and his union prefer the term "correctional officers." When asked about the large sums of money lavished upon Pete Wilson and several members of the state legislature, Novey complained to reporters in California, "I've never seen the media attack the California Medical Association, ARCO, the California Trial Lawyers Association, when they're doing the big spend. But once the little blue-collar worker gets up to the plate, everyone gets antsy."[20]

California has the largest prison system in the nation with 131,590 inmates in thirty prisons. With the "three strikes" law on the books it is estimated that California will need fifteen or more new prisons to house an additional 62,000 or so inmates who will be serving time by the year 2000. And that means thousands more prison guards, and hundreds of thousands of dollars pouring into the union each year in membership dues.[21] In 1993, a year of heavy general budget cuts, Governor Pete Wilson's administration managed to get California prison guards and other correctional officers a raise.[22]

Prison guards receive about $1 billion a year to watch over inmates, who themselves cost the state $25,000 each per year. The average salary for a prison guard is about $60,000 a year including overtime, 25 percent more than that of California school teachers.[23] The 1995–1996 budget of the Department of Corrections is $3.4 billion.[24]

In an interview with the Center for Public Integrity, CCPOA president Novey acknowledged that Wilson "has been able to maintain solid public safety programs. And it's been beneficial to us, yes . . . We've been very fortuitous. We've been very lucky, that's all it is."[25]

When asked what would have happened to Pete Wilson if the CCPOA had not pumped $1.57 million in contributions and independent expenditures into his 1990 and 1994 gubernatorial campaigns, Novey said matter of factly, "He would have lost." In 1994, Novey and the CCPOA submitted a "Magic 13" question survey to Governor Wilson, which he successfully answered in order to receive the organization's endorsement. Many of the questions related to membership concerns, such as "binding arbitration" in the resolution of disputes, and a particular type of "retirement system for CPO's [Correctional Peace Officers]."[26]

"Everybody said, 'Hell, all you are is a bunch of prison guards,' but they weren't cognizant that we had close to a million dollars set aside to support what candidate we thought would have been best," Novey related. Although the CCPOA was not involved formally in the Wilson presidential effort, Novey said, "I'll probably be personally." The CCPOA formed a federal political action committee in mid-1995 and "we might have to look at [an] independent expenditure."

Wilson's closeness to the California Correctional Peace Officers Association has not gone unnoticed. According to Democratic California state senator Tom Hayden: "By giving Wilson a million dollars in 1990, they [CCPOA] guaranteed a good position at the bargaining table." He called CCPOA's contract with the state after the 1990 election a "sweetheart deal" and a "total conflict of interest . . . If that's not a crime, it ought to be."[27]

In the 1990s, funding for California state four-year colleges has been decreasing steadily, while the funding for prisons has risen. Wilson has said that his hands are tied on the issue of education spending, because the available state funds have to be put toward housing the increasing number of inmates who are being locked up each year.[28]

Insurance

The insurance industry and Pete Wilson have both benefitted substantially over the years from their relationship. Collectively, insurance interests have underwritten Wilson campaigns since the 1970s, spending more than $2.8 million.[29] From the industry's perspective, the close relationship with Wilson has been an excellent policy. For example, the Agents and Brokers Legislative Council bragged in a late 1994 newsletter that they had "successfully obtained the governor's signature on every sponsored legislative proposal put forth in 1994."[30] The group's president even explained that campaign contributions were one reason the group had so much success with the governor.[31] Wilson has supported such insurance industry-backed issues as tort reform, worker's compensation reform, and opposed consumer ballot initiatives such as Proposition 103 designed to roll back auto insurance premiums even after they have been approved by California voters.

Fruitful Interests

Another relationship that has been fruitful for all involved is Wilson's relationship with agribusiness interests. Take the case of Sun-Diamond Growers, which began sponsoring Wilson in 1982, during his first run for the U.S. Senate. Richard Douglas, senior vice president of Sun-Diamond, told the *Los Angeles Times* why his group was supporting Wilson in 1994. "Pete has had a personal relationship with the leadership of Sun-Diamond for over a decade. We want to see him remain at the helm of the ship."[32]

To help keep Wilson afloat as a political officeholder, Sun-Diamond Growers has invested $254,250 in his campaigns. In the same interview Douglas explained, "Certainly your phone calls are going to get answered quicker than the calls from someone who didn't toil in the vineyards to bring in the harvest."[33]

While in Washington as a twice-elected senator from California, Wilson received at least $2.3 million from political action committees. Agriculture-related PACs were responsible for $236,000 of that money and aerospace and defense contractors kicked in $129,000 altogether.[34] Wilson held positions on both the Senate Agriculture Committee and Armed Services Committee.

One example of how the agribusiness industry has reaped the seeds it sowed with Wilson is evident in his opposition to fruit industry regulation by federal health officials. The California fruit industry knew all too well from its studies that if you take the red cherry out of fruit cocktail, people stop buying it. So in the 1980s, when the Food and Drug Administration (FDA) was deciding on whether to ban the potentially cancer-causing red dye No. 3 used to color fruit, California growers leaned on Wilson to help prevent the ban from taking effect. Wilson responded in both 1984 and 1988 by asking the FDA to rethink the decision, arguing that many scientists believe that the dye causes no harm to people. His suggestion was to allow the food industry itself to finance and conduct a study into the dye's effects.[35]

The delay worked, but the battle was not won. Although the FDA held off on the ban in order to study the data that Wilson had cited, the federal health agency ultimately concluded that the dye that produced cancerous tumors in laboratory rats does pose a risk to humans and should be banned.

The ban went into effect in January of 1990. When Wilson was asked about his support of the potentially cancer-causing dye, he claimed that he had never heard of red dye No. 3 and said his staff used the office's automatic pen to replicate his signature on letters to the FDA without his authorization.[36]

Another agriculture interest associated with Wilson has been Sunkist Growers, Inc. The *Los Angeles Times* reported that while a senator, Wilson "urged the Federal Trade Commission in February 1986 not to seek a $5 million civil penalty against Sunkist Growers, Inc. for allegedly attempting to monopolize several citrus markets."[37] The company and the FTC agreed on September 18, 1986, to a $375,000 settlement. Wilson's "urging" came in the form of a letter to the FTC, which the newspaper obtained by filing a request under the Freedom of Information Act. The FTC had filed a complaint against Sunkist and contended the company had "illegally cornered" the marketing and distribution of lemons and oranges in Canada and the United States. The Federal Trade Commission had ordered the sale of Sunkist's Yuma, Arizona, citrus processing plant by February 1983, but Sunkist faced a sizable fine for not selling the plant until August 1984.[38]

Sunkist vice president William Quarles told the Center for Public Integrity, "There was never, to my knowledge, any intervention by Pete Wilson."[39] Quarles added that Sunkist had supported Wilson because of his stance on agriculture issues and that its contributions were in line with what other agribusiness interests had made. Dale Cunningham, Sunkist's general counsel, said of the FTC's actions, "I don't remember them saying they were seeking $5 million."[40]

Sunkist made $12,000 in campaign contributions to Wilson prior to February 1986 and $60,450 since that time.[41]

But you don't raise more money for your own campaigns than any other politician in America by relying upon the largesse of just one industry sector; many other industries have substantially supported Wilson. On occasion Wilson has aided his patrons by helping to legislate new business for them. Take the case of Ron Cedillos, a supporter who hosted a fundraiser for Wilson's 1990 gubernatorial campaign that netted $140,000.[42] Cedillos also happened to run a firm that tests fasteners, such as heavy duty bolts, which were found to be at fault in many industrial accidents in the construction and aerospace industries. The same year Cedillos sponsored Wilson's fundraiser, Wilson got a telephone call from the supporter urging him to strengthen a bill before the Senate, which aimed to ensure the quality of these fasteners. Wilson then delayed the bill, pushing for stronger measures, such as an amendment requiring that fasteners be tested by outside firms.[43]

Over the years, numerous special interests have acquired access to Pete Wilson in creative ways beyond the traditional campaign contribution. For example, between 1982 and 1988, then-Senator Wilson also accepted $211,358, mostly in speech honoraria.[44] Today the practice is illegal. He gave away only slightly more than $8,000 of that money to charity, returning only $3,000 to one company, Monex International Ltd. The precious metals dealer based in Newport Beach, California, was alleged by a Senate investigation to be competing unfairly. Wilson was criticized for his relationship with Monex and for trying to prevent legislation that would shut down the company. Monex stayed open. "Wilson later accepted

$6,000 for his Senate and gubernatorial campaigns and $1,426 in expenses for a weekend trip to a Florida resort," the *Los Angeles Times* reported.[45]

Beyond contributions and honoraria, in the name of saving taxpayer money, Wilson has set up special, private interest funding of public business.

Tripping with the Governor

When Wilson wanted to take a privately funded trip to Asia to promote business and economic development in California, his staff found a loophole that would permit him to go despite state law limiting gifts to public officials to $270 a year. All private contributions underwriting the trip were given through the Trade and Commerce Agency, the state group responsible for promoting international trade. According to the Fair Political Practices Commission, California's version of the FEC, this move was legal since the donors did not specify how the money was to be used.[46]

So the seventeen-day trip of late 1993, which included eleven state officials, was largely paid for by twenty special interest groups contributing a total of $107,000.[47]

The presence of an additional seven officials present on the trip were paid for with taxpayer dollars. Twenty representatives of private businesses accompanied Wilson at their own expense.

The Atlantic Richfield Company (ARCO), contributors of $7,500 to the trip fund and Wilson's second largest career patron with $358,605, sent its senior vice president. The Los Angeles–based oil company ARCO and others present on the trip had a perfect situation: They traveled to a potentially huge market for their business with the governor of their state, someone able to connect them to the top Asian officials in international trade. Gaining vital access to these competitive markets had the potential of bringing in millions of dollars worth of business, though ARCO said no deals came out of the trip. Representatives from Sunkist and Sun-Diamond Growers were among the others on the group roster.

"We went to great lengths to set up a system that allowed

for the trip to be paid for privately," Dan Schnur, Wilson's communications director at the time, explained.[48] Wilson and his staff hold that they did California a great service by relieving the taxpayers of the burden of paying for the pricey excursion. No one seems to have addressed the fact that the state's chief executive was out of state, out of country, promoting the business of a few wealthy constituents at the exclusion of others.

Gimme Shelter

Pete Wilson does not own a residence anywhere in California. As governor and during part of the time he was mayor of San Diego, he lives rent and maintenance free in apartments paid for by wealthy friends or companies with interests before the government. In another move ostensibly designed to save the taxpayers' money, the Wilsons' living expenses are paid for by the California Governor's Foundation. Established in 1991, this tax-exempt foundation originally paid only for maintenance on the governor's home in Sacramento. The California Governor's Foundation received more than critical attention when the Wilsons asked its chairman to pick up the tab for a condominium in Century City (Los Angeles), to the tune of $4,000 per month for rent alone. The Wilsons realized that they were spending large amounts of time in Los Angeles and wanted to rent a condominium instead of bearing the cost and inconvenience of regular hotel stays. So as a charitable contribution to the state, the foundation approved the lease and the Wilsons had their home away from home at no personal cost. In 1993 alone, the foundation spent $115,024 on the two Wilson homes.[49] Wilson is not required to claim the rent payment as income on his personal taxes, nor does he have to include the free housing in his annual statement of economic interest.

Some of Wilson's leading campaign contributors—Pacific Gas and Electric, Southern California Edison, and Bank of America, to name just three—have taken an interest in the Wilsons' comfort and well being by making tax-deductible donations to the California Governor's Foundation. Through

August 1994 the foundation had collected over $504,234 in all. Wilson's inaugural committee had given $352,903 toward that total and his campaign account had kicked over another $22,376.[50] Meanwhile, Wilson's Sacramento residence is owned by another similar foundation, the California Residence Foundation, set up under former Governor Deukmejian to establish a permanent residence for future governors.

California Democrats have protested Wilson's living arrangements, formally asking the state Fair Political Practices Commission (FPPC) to determine if California laws controlling gifts to state officials have been violated. The Democrats alleged that the Century City condo was a corporate gift and should be ruled a violation of the state's yearly limit on the amount spent on such gifts. The FPPC decided that no laws had been violated.

It was not the first time Wilson had to defend his acceptance of free housing. In 1982, after separating from his first wife, there were questions raised about the San Diego Hillcrest apartments he occupied that were paid for by friends of Wilson. Good government groups in California wanted Wilson's use of the apartments to be listed as political contributions and disclosed.[51] Despite a $36,625 salary as San Diego mayor, Wilson claimed not to have enough money for rent.[52]

The board of the California Governor's Foundation is a close-knit group, financially and politically connected to Wilson and the University of California Board of Regents, an important and prestigious board appointed by the governor. The foundation includes some of Wilson's big contributors such as Ward Connerly, a Sacramento developer and Wilson U.C. Regents appointee; Bob White, former Wilson chief of staff; and Bill Hauck, a former aide and close political adviser. All three quit the board soon after it was decided that the foundation would lease the Century City condo for Wilson. The reasoning: they thought it would be better to have a board of outsiders rather than insiders.[53] Even without these "inside" board members, it strains credulity to assert that the remaining board members are outsiders.

The chairman of the Governor's Foundation, John G. Davies, is the regent who has the strongest connections to Wilson. A campaign contributor and fundraiser who donated

$11,500 to Wilson's 1990 gubernatorial campaign and afterward was appointed by Wilson to the prestigious University of California Board of Regents, Davies attended law school with Wilson and is one of his closest friends. Davies was the trustee for Wilson's blind trust and for years acted as Wilson's personal attorney, handling Wilson's divorce from his first wife, Betty, in 1991. Davies also orchestrated Wilson's living rent-free for nineteen months in the San Diego Hillcrest apartment in the early 1980s.[54] Phone calls to Davies by the Center for Public Integrity were not returned.

After graduating from law school together, Davies helped Wilson get a job in his father's law firm. In 1964, Davies co-founded a group that groomed candidates for office called the Republican Associates, which also employed Wilson. When Wilson ran for the state assembly in 1966, this group was behind him all the way. Wilson, as mayor of San Diego, appointed Davies to a position on the San Diego Commission, which Davies later chaired. While simultaneously working in a law firm specializing in real estate, commission chairman Davies "loyally implemented Wilson's land-planning goals."[55] Later, during Wilson's years in the Senate, he relied on Davies to help him find candidates for federal judgeships.[56]

This California Governor's Foundation chairman, Wilson appointee to the U.C. Board of Regents, and longtime friend and contributor held another significant role: He is the former trustee of the Wilson Blind Trust, who left the position in 1994. The trust was set up to manage Wilson's money to avoid any charges of impropriety in policy decisions should they appear to benefit his personal finances.[57]

Pete Wilson is an experienced public official, a dogged campaigner, and a media-savvy candidate from the media state with the most electoral votes. He's the eighty-plus million-dollar man. By the middle of 1995, he lagged behind the other candidates in raising the financial resources to amplify his ideas and his message to the electorate. In part because he could not speak due to throat surgery, he had a slow start. His inability to reinvent himself as a conservative combined with longtime contributors' disaffection over his broken promise to serve a full term as governor defeated his fledgling 1996 campaign.

PETE WILSON
TOP 10 CAREER PATRONS*

1. California Correctional Peace Officers
   Association, Sacramento, California $1,576,717
2. Atlantic Richfield (ARCO), oil, Los Angeles,
   California $358,605
3. Hewlett Packard, electronics, Palo Alto,
   California $341,500
4. E&J Gallo Winery, Modesto, California $314,671
5. Sam Bamieh, developer, San Mateo,
   California $289,000
6. Irvine Company/Donald Bren, real estate,
   Newport Beach, California $288,589
7. Association of California Insurance Co's
   PAC, Woodland Hills, California $285,625
8. A.G. Spanos, construction, Stockton,
   California $263,626
9. Sun-Diamond Growers, agriculture,
   Alameda/Stockton, California $254,250
10. A. J. Perenchio, Hollywood executive, Los
    Angeles, California $213,500

* Based on FEC records and the Center for Responsive Politics, California
Fair Political Practices Commission, and California Secretary of State. Includes the 1982 and 1988 Senate and 1990 and 1994 gubernatorial
campaigns.

Wild Cards

In the summer of 1995, the American public was clearly dissatisfied with the country's political system. That is, if you believed the polls that came out around the weekend of August 11 when Ross Perot, billionaire and 1992 independent candidate for the presidency, held a little gathering in Dallas. Thousands of Perot's followers, who comprised the grassroots organization United We Stand America, went to the Dallas Convention Center to listen to speeches from dozens of politicians and experts. The event, at the direction of the movement's leader, turned into what some wags in Washington who did not attend were calling a "panderthon."

Every major Republican presidential candidate was in Dallas. The president sent his longtime friend and White House counselor, Mack McLarty. Even Jesse Jackson, who had not yet ruled out a run for the White House, showed up. On August 12 his image was plastered on the front pages of newspapers standing next to, embracing, or shaking hands with Perot. Newt Gingrich spoke on opening night.

All these politicians had traveled to Texas ostensibly to educate voters, and to talk about how to fix the nation's problems. What they really went to do, Republican and Democrat alike, was to tell those congregated that their party had done more than the other to implement independent ideas and wishes. Even the president said so from Washington. They had all seen, and were responding to, the polls.

Three major polls conducted just before the Dallas meeting showed that anywhere from a low of 43 percent to a

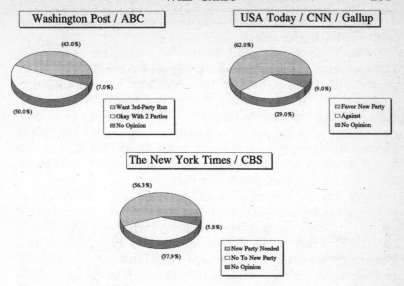

Washington Post / ABC

(43.0%)

(7.0%)

(50.0%)

☐ Want 3rd-Party Run
☐ Okay With 2 Parties
▨ No Opinion

USA Today / CNN / Gallup

(62.0%)

(9.0%)

(29.0%)

☐ Favor New Party
☐ Against
▨ No Opinion

The New York Times / CBS

(56.3%)

(5.8%)

(37.9%)

▨ New Party Needed
☐ No To New Party
▨ No Opinion

high of 62 percent of those surveyed wanted more choices in the presidential race. The *USA Today*/CNN/Gallup Poll showed 62 percent of respondents were for the creation of a new political party, up from 58 percent in 1992.[1] A *New York Times*/CBS poll showed 56.3 percent said the country needed a new party.[2] A *Washington Post*/ABC News poll had 43 percent supporting the notion of a third-party candidate if Clinton and Dole were the nominees of the major parties.[3]

In the presidential election of 1992, 273 candidates ran for president.[4] As the 1996 race began, any number of potential candidates tested the waters. Former Republican U.S. Senator Lowell Weicker, who had become governor of his home state of Connecticut as an independent, commissioned a study on what it would take to get him on the ballot in fifty states. Arthur Fletcher, the seventy-year-old who was the head of the U.S. Civil Rights Commission under Presidents Ford, Reagan, and Bush, was running in an effort to keep affirmative action on the Republican agenda in 1996. Megabucks magazine publisher and New Jersey Republican Steve Forbes was considering using $25 million of his own money to get the GOP nomination, pushing a flat tax plan that could save him millions of dollars in taxes.

Democratic Senator Bill Bradley was another prospective Garden State candidate from a different turnpike exit. "Disgusted with [the] politics of both parties," he announced in August 1995 that he would not seek a fourth Senate term but would remain in "public life." His statement prompted speculation that he would rebound and shoot for the White House. By summer's end, Perot announced that United We Stand America would attempt to form a national third party, calling itself the Independence Party.

All of this created more than the usual uncertainty on the political landscape. Analysts were making calculations based on any number of possible scenarios. What if Colin Powell entered the race as an independent? As a Republican? As a Democrat? Who would win head-to-head-to-head in a Clinton vs. Dole vs. Perot race? How badly would a Jesse Jackson third-party run hurt Clinton? What about Newt? The emphasis remained on answering the question, "Who would win?" Much of the point was lost on the pundits and on the politicians. In the summer of 1995, of the prominent politicians still considering whether to run, all were of the established political order, even Perot.

Bill Bradley

When Bill Bradley announced on August 16, 1995 that he would not seek reelection to the Senate, he said he was tired of the politics of both parties. The *Wall Street Journal* called him "the most admirable Senator of this era."[1] He made a point of saying he would not challenge President Clinton for the Democratic nomination in 1996, but speculation arose that Bradley would make an independent run. While Bill Bradley is generally regarded as one of the most intelligent and frequently eloquent members of the Senate, he has hardly been independent.

Bradley, a Rhodes scholar, was elected to the Senate from

New Jersey in his first run for office in 1982. In the preceding decade he played basketball for the New York Knicks and earned the nickname "Dollar Bill" for his clutch play. That moniker is not easily discarded. Bradley runs the race for money better than most. In 1990, his last election year, he received more money than any other Senate candidate from securities firms, pharmaceutical manufacturers, lawyers and lobbyists, entertainment companies, general contractors, publishers, insurance companies, and realtors. Although he declined to be interviewed, in a letter to the Center for Public Integrity, Senator Bradley wrote, "I received more money from these sectors in 1990 than other candidates because I raised more money for 1990 than most candidates, and because the bulk of my contributions came from New Jersey and New York, the financial center of the country."

The Center for Responsive Politics, which monitors contributions to public officials, called Bradley "the king of bundled contributions."[2] Bundling describes donations given to a candidate by multiple employees of a single company. Although Bradley's PAC contributions are not particularly notable, the bundled contributions he has received are staggering. In fact, Bradley received fifteen of the twenty-eight largest bundled contributions made to senators in 1990. No other senator was even close.[3] Nine bundles were from securities firms.

The $71,800 that Shearson Lehman Hutton gave to Bradley was the largest donation to a Senate candidate that year. The way Shearson did it made a mockery of campaign contribution limits. On June 16, 1989, thirty different employees made contributions of $500 to $1,000 to Bradley's campaign. One week later, thirty-two more Shearson employees made similar donations. Shearson was later bought by American Express. The combined donations of American Express–Shearson Lehman Hutton over Bradley's career total $132,550—$112,350 of which comes from the company's employees.

Bradley reaped similar one-day bonanzas from other securities firms. On November 16, 1983, fifteen Salomon Brothers employees gave to Bradley. In his next campaign, thirty-six Salomon employees gave on June 4, 1990. Twenty-seven Smith Barney employees gave identical $500 contributions to Bradley on February 23, 1990. In two days in October of 1986, twenty-six employees of Prudential-Bache Securities donated to Bradley, most giving the maximum allowable $1,000. On August 21, 1990, Bradley received donations from forty-four Prudential-Bache employees.[4]

Prudential-Bache's donations attracted the attention of the FEC. In 1994, it was revealed that the securities firm had violated campaign laws by instructing its employees and vendors to donate to Bradley and other candidates. The contributions to Bradley amounted to $140,000. In the largest fine ever levied by the FEC, Prudential agreed to pay a penalty of $550,000.[5] Bradley immediately announced that he would return Prudential's money. Bradley, however, kept the bundles he received from his other Wall Street patrons. The following chart shows Bradley's career contributions from selected securities firms.[6]

From his seat on the Senate Finance Committee, where he was the third ranking Democrat, Bradley wielded an enormous amount of influence over tax law. In fact, in 1990 no other member of the Finance Committee got more money from financial interests than Bradley.[7] He has been friendly to Wall Street. *Investment Dealers' Digest* ranks him among "Wall Street's strongest advocates."[8] In 1992, Bradley was one of only eight Democrats who joined with Republicans to oppose an urban aid bill raising taxes on securities firms.[9]

Bradley's sentiments were already known to Wall Street in 1990. The 1986 Tax Reform Act, which came about largely due to efforts Bradley had initiated years before, dramatically lowered tax rates on the wealthy while eliminating a number of loopholes some used to avoid paying taxes altogether. In the end, the act served mostly to benefit the wealthy.[10] In fairness to Bradley, by the time the bill passed, it contained many provisions he had not intended. Nonetheless, the fact that he moved a tax reform bill through a Republican Senate during Ronald Reagan's second term is worthy of note. Bradley wrote to us that the 1986 tax reform bill "is one of my proudest achievements in the Senate ... 6 million working poor people stopped paying income taxes at all as a result of this bill."

Bradley has also been receptive to pharmaceutical companies, a prominent New Jersey industry. In 1990, no other Senate candidate got more money from drug companies than Bradley.[11] He has helped them primarily by fighting to protect an obscure provision of the Internal Revenue code known as Section 936. Originally intended as a measure to promote jobs in Puerto Rico, Section 936 allows companies to avoid paying taxes on profits generated in the commonwealth. Pharmaceutical companies have exploited the measure by conducting their extensive research and development of drugs on the mainland, moving the relatively inexpensive manufacturing to Puerto Rico, then claiming all profits relating to the drugs as tax free. According to the General Accounting Office, the tax benefits they receive amount to more than double the wages they pay. In short, the American people pay drug manufacturers more than $70,000 per year for every job they create in Puerto Rico.[12] Section 936 tax benefits to these companies total over $1 billion per year.[13]

When the tax code was being revised in 1986, the drug companies realized their sweetheart deal in Puerto Rico might be in jeopardy. In a letter to Bradley, the CEOs of nine drug companies made a thinly veiled threat to move their operations to foreign countries if Section 936 was repealed, and wrote, "We would welcome the opportunity of apprising the senior senator from New Jersey, the nation's medicine chest, of our position on the issue."[14] According to Bradley, he doesn't remember the missive, nor would it have mattered. "The pharmaceutical industry is one of the largest employers in New Jersey (50,000 jobs) and I didn't need a letter from the companies to know the importance of the industry to my state and my constituents." Section 936 survived the 1986 Tax Reform Act. In response to our question, "Do you believe money buys access to power?" Bradley wrote, "The assumption that the only reason anyone donates to a political campaign is to 'buy access to power' is insulting to those who participate in politics." That said, Bradley acknowledges that the perception "is undeniable" that "large amounts of money needed to run major campaigns in this country have a corrosive effect on the political system."

When he announced he would not run for reelection in

1996, Bradley said he would go out and listen to the people before deciding whether to run for president. What is evident from his career is that he already knows money talks.

Newt Gingrich

In June of 1995, Newt Gingrich visited New Hampshire. The speaker of the House of Representatives had gone to the Granite State to see a moose. Of course, as it was only seven months before the crucial New Hampshire primary, the news media portrayed the trip as an opportunity to test the waters of a 1996 presidential bid. While there, Gingrich appeared with President Clinton before a group of senior citizens.

One of them asked if the two *de facto* leaders of the major political parties were willing to appoint an independent commission to make unamendable recommendations to clean up the game of politics. Both Gingrich and Clinton said they would. The crowd applauded. Little happened.

That was no surprise really. In fact, one of the things that most clearly distinguishes Newt Gingrich (and Bill Clinton) is just how early and often in his political career he has claimed himself a reform crusader. In announcing his first race for Congress in 1974, he assured voters, "I have no desire to curry favor with lobbyists or accumulate power for my own sake. I will not play the game of special interest politics."[1]

In 1978, Gingrich won a seat in Congress and began taking money from special interests. He managed to raise $90,320 from PACs during his freshman year in Congress. During his first year as minority whip, he received $436,987 from PACs. Between 1979 and the end of June 1994, he received more than $400,000 from his top ten PAC contributors alone. During the 1994 election cycle, while Gingrich was proclaiming that he and his "Contract with America," the legislative program House Republicans sought to pass in the 104th Congress, would take power from special interests and give it back to the people, he received $769,480 in PAC contributions.

The money really started pouring in when Gingrich became

minority whip in 1989. In 1988, his reelection campaign received a total of $851,786. The portion from PACs amounted to $260,476. In the 1989–1990 reporting cycle, he received $436,487 from PACs out of a total $1,558,934 in contributions.[2] Gingrich—who once organized a "PAC Appreciation Day" in Atlanta[3]—saw a 67.5 percent jump in PAC money. The money was coming from some of the groups that benefitted most from a lack of reform to the political system.

Gingrich was instrumental in the defeat of the 1994 lobby reform bill in the 103rd Congress. The legislation would have tightened the disclosure requirements for lobbyists, and would also have banned them from providing gifts, free travel, or junkets to legislators.[4]

During the formulation of the bill then-Speaker Tom Foley (D-WA) "asked the Republican leadership what would be acceptable. [Minority Whip] Gingrich offered his support if the Democrats would 'strengthen' the language requiring lobbyists to disclose how much they were spending on 'grassroots organizing.' "[5] Later, he took the floor to speak against that very same measure, characterizing it as an insidious attempt by the government to strangle grassroots political and religious activity. Although the bill passed the House, Gingrich is credited with having mobilized the Christian Coalition and the network of conservative radio talk show hosts against the measure. Democrats in the Senate were unable to break a filibuster against the bill.

Gingrich's contributions from lawyers and lobbyists increased from $43,050 to $73,759 (71.3 percent) between the 1990 and 1992 elections.[6] Gingrich, a master of money and politics, went even further. "[I]n a private meeting with special-interest lobbyists in Washington, Gingrich . . . reminded the audience [that he and his fellow Republicans] had blocked passage of a reform bill that lobbyists had fought bitterly," the *Atlanta Constitution* reported. "In the meeting, Gingrich laid out what he wanted as a reward for his deed: He wanted campaign money for Republican candidates for Congress. . . . 'For anybody not on board now, it's going to be the coldest two years in Washington,' he told the lobbyists."[7]

The National Rifle Association has been on board, giving Gingrich $44,777 over the course of his career. In return, the

Washington Post reported, "Shortly after taking charge of the House . . . Gingrich . . . promised the National Rifle Association in writing that no gun control legislation would move out of committee or on the House floor as long as he is speaker."[8] Speaker Gingrich declined to be interviewed for this book.

Much has been written about Gingrich's ties to GOPAC, the nonprofit group he headed until May of 1995 which did not fully disclose its contributors and which is the subject of a Federal Elections Commission lawsuit and ethics complaints against the speaker. Less is known about the tax-exempt Progress and Freedom Foundation (PFF). PFF has no official connection with Gingrich, but there were ties through GOPAC. Created in 1993 by former GOPAC executive director and close Gingrich adviser Jeff Eisenach, PFF's early existence focused on the production and promotion of Gingrich's televised college course, "Renewing American Civilization," also a subject of ethics complaints.

Organizing and supporting the course required large expenditures and Gingrich "boldly promotes companies that fund the course. He also touts his major political backers."[9] HealthSouth, a $15,000 contributor to the course, was promoted in a lecture on "Health and Wellness" in November of 1993.[10] HealthSouth also contributed more than $30,000 over a decade to Gingrich's campaign committee.[11]

Gingrich extended this practice to his best-selling book, *To Renew America*.[12] Golden Rule Insurance received positive exposure in the class, as well as in the book. Gingrich failed to mention, however, that Golden Rule is the sole sponsor of the PFF's television show, "Progress Report," co-hosted by Gingrich.[13] He also neglected to inform the reader or the student that Golden Rule executives have contributed more than $117,000[14] to PFF during Gingrich's tenure on the program. Golden Rule has also donated $42,510 to Gingrich's campaign committee.[15]

Minority Whip Gingrich was an early and vociferous critic of the 1993 Clinton health plan. Between 1990 and 1992, Gingrich's receipts from the health industry rose 83.8 percent from $62,208 to $114,360.[16] In 1993–1994, his health care take totaled $374,493—top among members of Congress according to the pro-health care reform public interest group Citizen Action.[17]

Gingrich has more recently gone to bat for the pharmaceutical industry. Of the nine pieces of legislation he offered during the 1993–1994 session of Congress, the *Wall Street Journal* reported, "Gingrich introduced three ... to suspend duties on drug ingredients imported by a company that contributed $30,000 to a think tank affiliated with the congressman."[18] The think tank was the Progress and Freedom Foundation.

On July 22, 1994, Gingrich and Republican Cass Ballenger (R-NC) wrote to the FDA on behalf of Solvay Pharmaceuticals, a PFF contributor and the company that Gingrich's legislation would have directly benefitted. PFF's Rick O'Donnell told the Center for Public Integrity, "They were completely mutually exclusive events that just happened to occur coincidentally."[19]

Gingrich has helped telecommunications legislation in the interest of his publisher, Rupert Murdoch, get through Congress, and he has helped an offshore corporation which then subsequently hired his wife.[20] It's anyone's guess how many more times Newt Gingrich would declare a desire to reform the political system if he were to become a presidential candidate. Or how many times "mutually exclusive events" would occur coincidentally.

Jesse Jackson

He is a shadow senator with no government-funded staff, no budget, and no state. From "Meet the Press to "Saturday Night Live," his visual image is ubiquitous. He pops up at strikes, protests, natural disasters, and concerts around the nation. He is one of America's most inspiring and charismatic leaders, yet a man who has never held any public office. Controversy has dogged him at the organizations he has headed.

Jesse Jackson first ran for president of the United States in 1984. He won more than 75 percent of the black vote in the Democratic primaries. As the *Atlantic Monthly* reported in

1987, "He defied the black political establishment . . . He ended up doing what no other black leader has ever done; he ran a national political campaign that activated the black constituency and defined black concerns and aspirations." The Democratic nominee blamed Jackson for his loss to Ronald Reagan. "If he had not been a candidate," Walter Mondale said, "I would have been nominated much earlier, could have put the party together, raised money, and had a more unified campaign—all those things I was denied."[1]

The next time Jackson sought the Democratic presidential nomination, in 1988, he received seven million votes, finishing second to Michael Dukakis. In the course of that impressive effort, he violated numerous campaign finance laws and ultimately paid $150,000 to the Federal Election Commission, the largest such penalty in U.S. history. In his second run, Jesse Jackson was regarded as wiser and more mature.[2] Jackson visited rural communities that were devastated after 650,000 farmers lost their holdings and proposed an income tax hike for the 650,000 richest Americans. He spoke at high schools and pledged to double the national education budget. After eight years of Reaganomics, Jackson wanted to cut 10 percent of all military spending, cancel the Strategic Defensive Initiative (SDI), and freeze nuclear weapons testing. He also called for federally administered health care, an increase in food stamps, and fortifying drug prevention programs by expanding the Coast Guard. No other Democratic candidate suggested such bold measures.[3]

Jackson's campaign budgets have been small in relation to those of other candidates. His largest PAC contributions in 1984 were in the amounts of $5,000 from the National Alliance for Political Action, Postal and Federal employees, and the Grumman PAC. He also received $4,000 from the United Auto Workers (UAW) community action program. But the majority of his patrons lived in rural areas.[4] The same was true in 1988.

Jackson is famous for campaigning with "money" buckets passed around the audience. The yellow one was for donations to the Rainbow Coalition, the red one was for his campaign. Frank Watkins, the political director at the Rainbow Coalition, told the Center for Public Integrity that Jackson's money has always come from unions and from average citizens.[5] Because of this, Jackson's campaign relied heavily on the federal matching funds program. For every donation a candidate receives under $200, the federal government matches it. Jackson received $3,061,394 in matching funds in 1984 and $7,608,016 in 1988.

Since 1988, Jackson's main occupation has been heading the Rainbow Coalition, a 501(c)(6) nonprofit group headquartered in the heart of Washington's central business district. Visitors pass through a marble lobby on their way to the 8,000-square-foot office on the eighth floor.[6] The movement dedicated to racial equality, social justice, and defending the poor has some fifteen individual offices, several conference rooms, a full kitchen, and a large general office area. The most spacious office is that of the Reverend Jesse Louis Jackson.[7]

In self-styled introductory speeches, the Reverend Jackson has been called "defender of the poor and disadvantaged."[8] In 1988, he listed assets of more than $300,000.[9] With every speech and handshake, Jackson recruits more people for the Rainbow's new database, which boasts 470,000 names.[10]

Mike Carter, the group's financial officer, told the Center for Public Integrity that they run an annual deficit between $50,000 and $100,000, spending about $1.5 million in salaries and operations. Carter would not disclose the source of the group's funding, saying, "We'll never tell you that," adding that if he revealed the information, then the confidentiality of donors would be violated.[11] Some of the companies that had earlier associations with Jackson ventures are said to be donors. Kentucky Fried Chicken's assistant manager of corporate relations, Chrystal Johnson, said the company has given to the Rainbow Coalition in the past.[12] Watkins said the movement hopes to apply for foundation grants in the future.[13] Jesse Jackson declined to be interviewed for this book.

Ever since the 1971 founding of Operation PUSH—People United To Serve Humanity—Jackson has sought to support the endeavors of black businesses and increase the number of minority positions in the business world.[14] PUSH operated by threatening companies with boycotts until targeted businesses agreed to increase the number of minority employees, franchise owners, and managerial positions. Through the PUSH International Trade Bureau, Jackson negotiated contracts with Kentucky Fried Chicken, Burger King, Coca-Cola, Anheuser-Busch, and Seven-Up, to name only a few companies.[15]

Questionable financial dealings have plagued PUSH. Once business acquiesced to a "contract" with PUSH, the PUSH International Trade Bureau (ITB) submitted a list of "approved" black entrepreneurs. They included Jackson's half-brother, Noah Robinson, who owned a Coca-Cola bottling franchise, a string of Wendy's restaurants, and other enterprises. Others who benefitted from Jackson's efforts were Byron Lewis, a PUSH supporter and ITB member, who received an $8 million contract for his advertising agency from Burger King; and ITB Board member Owen Funderburg, chairman of the Citizens Trust Bank of Atlanta, who acquired deposits from Burger King and Seven-Eleven. The ITB Corporation was involuntarily dissolved by the State of Illinois in 1991 for failing to file its annual report and pay franchise taxes.[16]

Finally, under the umbrella of PUSH, Jackson created PUSH for Excellence, also known as PUSH Excel. PUSH Excel was designed to promote study skills and self-esteem among inner-city teens. Jackson himself went from school to school and served as a role model for youths. His "I am somebody" speeches rocked school auditoriums. Ernest Green, former U.S. assistant secretary of labor who awarded $2 million to Push Excel, was listed on Jackson's "approved" list of black entrepreneurs and received contracts from Coca-Cola, Seven-Eleven, and Heublein for his consulting firm.[17]

Jackson ran Operation PUSH from 1971 to 1983, leaving it with a deficit of close to $2 million. More than $325,000 was owed to banks, individuals, and businesses such as Federal Express. The federal government accused Push Excel of misusing $1.2 million of the $4.9 million it received in grants.[18] In 1988, after lengthy negotiations, Push Excel agreed to repay $550,000 to federal agencies. But in 1991, the *Chicago Tribune* reported that PUSH had missed a quarterly payment on the debt, had a deficit of $200,000, and owed $50,000 in federal taxes.[19] PUSH would not release its annual financial statement and IRS "990" forms—which show financial information and some activities—to the Center for Public Integrity, although it is required by law to do so.

The White House is just a few blocks from Jackson's Washington office, but has been unattainable. Jackson did not run in 1992. He has crafted a public life that he loves and even if he never becomes commander-in-chief, he will continue to influence Democratic presidential politics. By dint of a strong personality and strong message, Jesse Jackson could easily remain America's permanent politician without a portfolio.

Ross Perot

Henry Ross Perot perceives himself as a great American hero and says it is his personal mission to ensure that anyone can achieve the "American Dream." From his persistent search for missing MIA/POWs in Vietnam to the 1993 NAFTA debates, Perot has cast himself in the role of America's savior, using his vast fortune to do so. Running for president in 1992, the Texas billionaire spent $65 million of his own money.[1] He has said he would do it again, grudgingly, only if Clinton and Congress failed to meet the needs of the country.[2] "I've got to honestly believe that's the only reason I would want to go serve a hitch in hell, and that's, you know, the kindest word you could put on it in terms of being in public life."[3]

Perot has a unique perspective about public life. He has been a Washington player dating back to the Nixon White House.[4] In many cases, Perot's own business dealings have been the special interests that influenced his Washington game. Despite his populist rhetoric against Washington in 1992, Ross Perot has long been a part of the money and politics mercenary culture that exists today. In 1974, the same year of the Watergate-inspired reforms, Perot contributed $90,000 to each of the major political parties. Between 1979 and 1991, he contributed $51,000 to the Republican Party.[5] Perot has sailed on the presidential yacht, eaten dinner at the White House, and lobbied both the president and Congress. As *Time* magazine reported, "He has backslapped and arm-twisted with the best of them."[6]

Perot didn't always have a lot of money. In 1956, he married Margot Birmingham and became a salesman for IBM. As the now-famous story goes, in 1962 he borrowed $1,000 from Margot to start a one-man data processing company, Electronic Data Systems.[7] Six years later, Perot was a multimillionaire.

EDS's first big contract was with the federal government. In 1965, when the United States began providing Medicare and Medicaid, EDS marketed a computerized system for paying the claims.[8] Perot's profits soared for the first time that year. The Nixon White House furthered the company's success by securing Perot another $62,500 contract, without competitive bidding, even though Perot's price was $10,000 over the spending limit. Nixon also helped Perot escape accusations by the Social Security Administration that EDS had overcharged for processing Medicare claims.[9]

Perot was equally generous to Nixon. In 1968, he paid the salaries of ten EDS employees while they worked on Nixon's campaign. A year later, he spent $1 million on newspaper ads and a thirty-minute TV program to generate support for the president's Vietnam policy. In 1972, Perot gave $200,000 to Richard Nixon's reelection campaign.[10]

Nixon is not the only politician with whom Perot has worked in an attempt to benefit his interests. In 1975, Perot almost succeeded in rigging the federal tax bill to get himself a $15 million tax break. He contributed more than $27,000 to twelve members of the House Ways and Means Committee responsible for the bill.[11] Perot would have reportedly received "an unheard-of capital-loss carry back." While twenty of the thirty-eight committee members voted for the measure, it was removed on the House floor. Still, it was "a coup most lobbyists only dream about."[12]

This episode was revisited in 1993 during Perot's NAFTA debate with Al Gore on CNN. Perot lobbied intensely against NAFTA. The vice president accused Perot of lobbying Congress for favorable tax legislation, and Perot responded with, "You're lying." But the *Wall Street Journal* editor who broke the story in 1975 said on NBC's "Today" Show after the

NAFTA debate that he remembered Perot had "hired every lobbyist in town he could get, including a former IRS commissioner."[13]

Perot found himself in the midst of another kind of controversy in 1984, when he sold EDS, the company he had founded on the largesse of a federal contract, to General Motors for $2.5 billion. He continued to serve on the corporation's board of directors until GM forced Perot's removal in 1986. Perot struck a deal with GM that in exchange for a $700 million buyout, he would leave the company and agree not to compete for profits with EDS for three years. By 1992, Ross Perot was estimated to be the thirteenth wealthiest man in America with a net worth of around $3 billion.[14]

Perot returned to the Washington scene in stunning fashion in 1992 with his presidential run. Perot's campaign committee, Perot '92, managed to get his name on the ballot in all fifty states—no small accomplishment given the propensity of the major parties to monopolize the process. According to Herb Asher, a political science professor at Ohio State University, Perot drew equally from Clinton and Bush supporters.[15] But many pundits assert that Perot's campaign sufficiently detracted from Bush's supporters to help President Clinton with the election.

After dropping out in July and reentering the race in October, Perot won 19 percent of the vote in the general election, garnering twenty million ballots. He did remarkably well in Maine, winning 30 percent of the vote, and in other states like New Hampshire with 23 percent, 22 percent in Texas, and 21 percent in California.[16]

What is little known about Perot's campaign is that he received more than $190,000 in campaign contributions from individuals.[17] He also violated FEC rules by misreporting twelve contributions totaling more than $10,000. Perot paid a $65,000 penalty for this infraction.

The most enduring tangible outcome of Perot's 1992 campaign was the creation of his political movement, United We Stand America (UWSA). UWSA's agenda usually echoes Perot's campaign: the deficit, term limits, and tax reform. Perot has spent $10 million on the group and his picture appears in every newsletter above his column. The group has had its ups and downs with Perot.

At UWSA's Dallas convention in August 1995, Perot urged his supporters to "get to work" within the system. Surveys had shown that most of his followers thought he could do more *not* running for president. The *Washington Times* reported Perot saying, "[I]f the Republicans and Democrats do 'what ordinary citizens want done in this country,' there will be no need for a third party and no political future for him."[18] Then on September 25, apparently less than satisfied with the performance of the Republicans in Congress and the Democrat in the White House, Perot announced an effort to get a new party, the Independence Party, on the ballot in all fifty states, at the same time saying on CNN's "Larry King Live," "It's nothing to do with me."

Of course, this came from a shrewd, unpredictable man who keeps a copy of a favorite book (for which he wrote the foreword) on a shelf in his office: *Leadership Secrets of Attila The Hun.*[19]

Colin Powell

For much of 1995, the media speculated that Colin Powell, a retired four-star general and former chairman of the Joint Chiefs of Staff (JCS), would run for president. If public opinion polls are any measure, he is well-liked and respected by the American people, who sometimes appear willing to see in the unspecific Powell a reflection of their own views. His politics are difficult to decipher, but his life since he left the military—giving speeches for $60,000 and being asked to sit on corporate boards—suggests that prospective candidate Colin Powell would be a lot more like the other candidates than he is different from them.

During Powell's second tour in Vietnam, he worked with the army's chief of staff for operations and had jurisdiction over the notorious 11th Infantry Brigade. That was the unit responsible for the My Lai massacre, in which American soldiers raped and murdered more than a hundred Vietnamese villagers in March,

1968. Little was known about the massacre until a commission of inquiry was organized in April, 1969. Powell said that when the commission of inquiry approached him that spring, he had responded appropriately, handing over records that displayed unusually large losses of life on the date in question.[1]

But Powell had failed to act at all when a letter describing atrocities similar to the My Lai massacre had crossed his desk in December, 1968, five months before the commission was established. A soldier named Tom Glen had sent a letter to the U.S. high command describing the murder and torture of villagers. Powell, who had arrived in Vietnam in June, roughly ten weeks after My Lai, was ordered to look into the matter on December 9, 1968. Powell's response assumed that the young soldier's claims were false. Powell wrote in a memo, "In direct refutation of this portrayal is the fact that relations between American soldiers and the Vietnamese people are excellent."[2]

Powell left Vietnam with the Legion of Merit medal citation, among other medals, for his ability to "grasp and analyze problems of grave and far-reaching consequence" and "to render flawless decisions."[3]

In the 1980s, Powell found himself uncomfortably close to another international scandal: the Iran-Contra arms-for-hostages affair. Both Powell and Defense Secretary Caspar Weinberger maintained that they opposed the sale of arms to Iran from the beginning. Despite this opposition, Weinberger ordered Powell to arrange for the transfer of 4,508 TOW missiles to the CIA, through which they would be shipped to Iran. Powell purposely arranged for the transfer under the Economy Act, which allows for government agencies to provide goods and services to other agencies so long as they are reimbursed. As the scandal unfolded, both Powell and Weinberger testified that they had no knowledge of a shipment of arms to Iran.[4] Powell was never indicted and independent counsel Lawrence Walsh told the Center for Public Integrity that Powell did not perjure himself.[5]

In 1987, President Reagan appointed Powell to be his seventh National Security Adviser, largely because he believed that Powell was the best man to rebuild the National Security Council so disgraced by Iran-Contra.[6] It came as no surprise when President Bush named Powell as chairman of the JCS in 1989. Bush felt Powell had proven his gift for negotiation by repairing rifts between the Defense and the State Departments.[7] And Powell was respected in both administrations for his ability to settle personal conflicts in a disinterested manner.[8]

Powell made headlines as chairman of the JCS for his "Base-Force" plan. Every three years, the JCS chairman must reevaluate the roles and missions of the armed services. In 1989, he realized that the end of the Cold War required a reduction of Pentagon resources, and he wanted to effect the changes before civilian policymakers got involved. Powell's plan was to establish the minimum number of troops and weapons needed to fight two small regional conflicts simultaneously. With the passing of the Soviet Union, that's where the threats would be, Powell argued.[9] The plan was approved, but Powell got flak from military budget reformers who thought he could have further reduced the budget.

Lawrence Korb, former assistant secretary of defense for manpower, reserve affairs, installations, and logistics in the Reagan administration, told the Center for Public Integrity that Powell inflated the budget by exaggerating the perceived threat of conflicts in countries like Iran and North Korea.[10]

Jon Meacham, of the *Washington Monthly,* reported that "Powell helped preserve an essentially Cold War budget with no Cold War foe to fight." Regardless of the outcome of the Base Force debate, half of the 1989 military budget still applied to containment of the Soviet Union.[11] On the other hand, even his critics, such as Korb, concede that the JCS chairman's principal priority, institutionally, has always been to safeguard the military budget.

Powell's performance as JCS chairman during the Persian Gulf War, which he initially opposed, solidified his star power with the American public.[12] When support for Desert Storm waned one week into the war, Powell laid out the Allied plan with the words, "Our strategy for going after this army is very, very simple. First we are going to cut it off, and then we are going to kill it."[13] He has since been heralded as one of the war's heroes. He is also known for the ease with which he dealt with the press. Powell has said that one lesson he took from his days in the Nixon White House was the "importance of public relations and media control."[14]

Powell has been doing an excellent job of safeguarding his own personal family budget and income since leaving the Pentagon. He and his wife Alma live in a home worth $1.3 million in McLean, Virginia.[15] His decision to sell his memoirs, *My American Journey,* earned him a $6.5 million advance—the most money for a book ever paid to an ex-government official except for Powell's old boss, Ronald Reagan, who received $7 million for his biography and a collection of speeches.[16] Powell's spokesman said in the summer of 1995 that Powell was too busy with the book to be interviewed by the Center for Public Integrity.[17]

While he remains popular, Powell's positions are relatively unknown and closely kept. He is staunchly pro-family and proud of his close relationship with his three children. He opposes gays in the military, women in combat, and the flag burning amendment. He is pro-choice on abortion and a supporter of Medicare. On race, he has said that he is against programs that give advantages to people who no longer need them, but in the same breath he has proclaimed that institutional racism thrives in America.[18] Powell has made it clear that he supports affirmative action.

The challenge of unlocking the puzzle that is Colin Powell helps to explain, in part, the great and expensive curiosity thousands of Americans have in hearing the general speak nationwide. An account of what happened at one of these events is somewhat insightful about Powell.

In November of 1994, he journeyed to Greencastle, Indiana, and spoke to a packed audience at DePauw University, a small but relatively wealthy school with less than 3,000 undergraduate students. In answering a question about his future plans, Powell said, "I have no political ambitions at this time."[19]

At the end, someone in the audience asked Powell for an autograph, and in an orderly, almost military fashion, he asked how many people would like an autograph. Dozens of hands went up. He directed them to form a single-file line on the left side of the auditorium, and began signing away. He was asked to sign a "Colin Powell for President" picture poster, and he wrote "Republican, Democrat or ? " before signing his name.

Concluding Thoughts

The Czech writer Vaclav Havel, in his essay "The Power of the Powerless," writes of a greengrocer who, for most of his days, went along with a totalitarian system of government in order to "get along in life." One day, Havel recounts, "something in our greengrocer snaps" and he stops living a lie. "He rejects the ritual and breaks the rules of the game. He discovers once more his suppressed identity and dignity. He gives his freedom a concrete significance. Rejecting the manipulation, Havel's hero begins to *"live within the truth"* . . . he has shattered the world of appearances. . . . He has broken through the exalted facade of the system and exposed the real, base foundations of power."[1]

This book has attempted to expose the real foundations of power in the 1996 presidential election and in the U.S. national political process, in the hopes that everyday citizens in this country will stop living the lie of quadrennial campaign pap, vacuous rhetoric, advertising, and who's-ahead? analysis.

The synergy of the investigative profiles in *The Buying of the President* reveals a grim, extraordinarily compromising, political process. There is an entirely legal, corrupt mercenary culture full of nuance and subtlety, in which ultimately all participants in the money chase become tainted. Even the best-intentioned, thoughtful, innately honest candidate can find his schedule booked day and night with fundraising events and exclusive breakfast, lunch, and dinner schmooze sessions with America's wealthiest patrons—and later find himself doing favors for them in return for their campaign contribution largesse.

As we have shown throughout this book, every major announced presidential candidate has become entangled over the course of his public career with multimillion-dollar interests instrumental to his electoral success. None of these candidates or the would-be "wild card" contenders are "reformers" outside of the established political order.

It is contrary to human nature to admit being beholden to anyone. Politicians, of course, do not like to discuss who has underwritten their candidacies, and seldom do. But that lack of responsiveness by our representatives, the people who work for us, should no longer be acceptable. A democracy without accountability is hardly a democracy at all. The people must be able to ask questions of their elected representatives and be heard. Our political discourse today desperately requires more straightforward candor and openness. Our chosen leaders can cloud or ignore potentially unflattering questions, because we tolerate and, therefore, allow it. Instead of using campaign finance income disclosure filings to measure stature and support as a *viable* candidate, the public and the news media should ask not only where the money comes from, but exactly what it buys. Instead of referring reporters to the Federal Election Commission or saying "we'll get back to you," politicians should be put on the spot, now, "live" and in person, and asked tough-but-fair questions about their campaign cash and what they have done to receive it over the years. Instead of being spoon-fed the candidates' policy positions or being subjected to superficial news and advertising soundbites, it's time the voter discovered a different kind of scorecard—not just the candidates' positions on issues but "follow the money" information illuminating why they may happen to hold such positions. That was the precise intent of *The Buying of the President*.

We have provided specific information about specific candidates for this specific presidential election, in an attempt to better inform voters as they select the next president of the United States. Beyond that we hope this book has opened some eyes about how this country actually chooses its national leader. In 1992, $1.47 billion was contributed to candidates for federal office, only a paltry amount of which came from "ordinary citizens." The Center for Responsive Politics has computed that less than one percent of the population gave 77 percent of all campaign contributions to congressional races that year![2] Simply stated, the wealthiest interests bankroll and, in effect, help to preselect the specific major candidates months and months *before* a single vote is cast anywhere. We are thus allowing our government *of the people, by the people, and for the people* to be led by someone initially chosen by only some of the people—narrow, vested interests with a direct financial stake in specific government policies and decisions. *We, the people* have become a mere afterthought of those whom we have put in office, a prop in our own play.

As passive participants watching and thereby allowing our elected officials to assume and maintain power in a money-dependent manner, we detach ourselves as citizens from the process because it all seems overwhelming, impermeable, and inaccessible to a mere individual. The candidates too frequently speak in soothing, irrelevant bromides, and unless you are a wealthy donor, they are difficult to talk to directly before or after the election. We either go to the polls mumbling about our limited choices, or we don't bother to vote at all. The distrust and disenchantment about politics in America today are not particularly mysterious.

James Madison wrote in *The Federalist Papers (No. 51)* that "if men were angels, no government would be necessary." As citizens we generally understand that government is essential as a public arbiter between competing financial and other interests. For government to play such a significant, mediative, consensus-building role, however, the people must have confidence and trust in their public officials and their official decisions. Are our leaders protecting and serving the broad public interest, acting for the common good of the nation?

A positive response to that question is, to put it kindly, difficult to summon for a great many Americans today. But the gnawing reality for too many of us is that simply "voting them out" never seems to change all that much because they are all products of the same system. In 1992, the American people turned out an incumbent Republican president. In 1994, they rejected the Democratic-controlled Congress. In

1995, public opinion polls indicated that the American people trust their government *less* than during the Watergate scandal in 1972–1974.[3] No fewer than 93 percent of Americans believe that "government wastes too much of our money," but interestingly, there is no consensus whatsoever about how this happens in Washington, which interests benefit, and how to reform it.[4] Incumbent politicians understand that the rage is unfocused and unharnessed, enabling them to remain substantively unresponsive. Some of that rage was throttled in 1995 when the Supreme Court ruled that "throw-all-the-bums-out" term limit initiatives are unconstitutional. Change never begat change: The Republican "reform" Congress led by Speaker Newt Gingrich and his "Contract with America," and the Democratic administration of Bill Clinton, whose campaign slogan was "Putting People First," both postured then punted on political reform proposals to reduce the role of money in campaigns and drastically curb the influence of lobbyists in Washington. It didn't take long for the newcomers to feel at home in Washington. The seventy-three freshmen "reform" Republicans elected in 1994, who had pledged to clean up Washington, took in $11 million toward their *reelection* from special interests in their first six months in office.[5]

Against such a sordid backdrop, there is no reason to believe that the 1992 and 1994 popular anger and frustration have subsided in the least in 1996. The problem, though, is that the electorate is disconnected not only from Washington, but from any palpable hope and solution for cleaning up the political process. Volumes have been written and hundreds of ideas espoused about how to reform the campaign finance system, from reducing the role of private money completely through public financing, to removing all regulation and returning to the cash-in-suitcases days that led up to Watergate. There is no national consensus, however, about what should be done, which is not surprising since there also has been no national "bully pulpit" education or leadership on this issue. To top it all off, any national solution must be approved by incumbent beneficiaries of the current, corrosive money politics system, which is tantamount to asking the foxes to lock themselves out of the henhouse.

So what, then, can we really do? Through *The Buying of the President* and other information, you should recognize the truth and hold public officials to a higher standard of conduct and accountability about the role of money in politics today. If candidates promised during the campaign to "clean up Washington," find out specifically if or how they have attempted to accomplish that "on the job." Remember to look closely behind mere public posturing; just how active and aggressively responsive to the popular will have they been as your public servants? And how closely are their public actions and positions related to the agendas of their career patrons? Follow the money.

Regardless of the absence of leadership and national consensus, the mechanism by which to change things does, and has always, existed. Never particularly easy to use, it ultimately allows citizens to affirm or deny who shall represent their interests, through everything from various party primaries and caucuses to the general election and beyond that, and to directly change the system through state ballot initiatives or even constitutional amendments. The mechanism has been corroded and corrupted, but the citizens of this nation are still ultimately responsible for the quality of our government. For Havel, who became the president of his country, that American reality gave him hope while he was a political prisoner. We have come to take it for granted. The political process has lost its identity and dignity. That should not stand as the example of American democracy to the world.

Author's Note

In the six years since founding the Center for Public Integrity, we have written eighteen investigative studies about public service and ethics-related issues.[1] But none of our past projects compares in terms of sheer size and volume to this ambitious undertaking. Producing *The Buying of the President* involved six reporters, sixteen researchers, and 103 undergraduate and graduate student database researchers working for more than a year. Entire books and thousands of major news media stories have been written about the individual 1996 White House contenders, but before this book no one had ever systematically examined the financial relationships and entanglements of America's presidential candidates.

In the Center for Public Integrity's tradition of exhaustive, methodical research, after studying virtually all major secondary sources about the 1996 announced and potential major presidential candidates, we "followed the money," collecting and analyzing thousands of Federal Election Commission contributions, independent expenditures and audit records going back to the mid-1970s.

We were generously, tirelessly assisted by Ellen Miller and the Center for Responsive Politics, whose computerized analysis of money and politics in this country is without equal. We are grateful for their friendship and collaboration. Kent Cooper and the rest of the fine public servants who staff the public records room of the Federal Election Commission graciously answered dozens of questions over a period of months.

It should be noted that campaign records are too often incomplete, making compilations about employer affiliations and family ties difficult. The candidate chapters and "Top Ten Career Patrons" lists relied on this limited information (the latter feature is included only for major announced 1996 candidates). Candidates Alexander, Clinton, and former candidate Wilson presented an additional challenge because of state campaign finance information kept in Nashville, Little Rock, and Sacramento, but those important data were also obtained. We studied legislative voting records and gathered financial disclosure, mortgage documents, and other materials to better understand the candidates' backgrounds.

The financial net worth analysis in the Introduction may be the first time anyone has ever attempted to look at the presidential candidates in this manner. Financial disclosure records for members of Congress are unavailable to the public after five years, so we had to obtain them through other means; to place information in appropriate context, we studied U.S. census income and other data over the past decade or so.

After the "paper," or the secondary source and public records phase of the research, we conducted hundreds of interviews. All of this prodigious effort produced the most thorough investigation of the presidential candidates and their backgrounds ever undertaken before the primaries. Over a period of more than six months, we called and wrote to each presidential candidate, seeking an interview or, failing that, the answers to specific questions. The least responsive candidates and campaigns were Alexander, Clinton, Gramm, and Keyes, who even declined to respond to written questions.

There are three individuals whose work on this project deserves special mention: Center Managing Director Alejandro Benes, who really does believe the *only* true doctrine in life is that "good pitching beats good hitting every time and vice versa" and whose wit, management genius, and editorial talents were magnificent; Center veteran Margaret Ebrahim and newcomer Meredith O'Brien, who both provided leadership to this endeavor.

Special thanks to our literary agent, Nina Graybill; our editor at Avon Books, Lisa Considine; and Marc Miller, our lawyer. We are especially grateful to the funders of this project: the Arca Foundation, Carnegie Corporation of New York and C.C. Dockery, as well as major, general Center supporters, including the Deer Creek Foundation, the Hafif Family Foundation, the Rockefeller Family Fund, the John D. and Catherine T. MacArthur Foundation, and the Town Creek Foundation.

The project was helped by the participation of students at the School of Communications at The American University: Angela Baggetta, Jeremy Birch, Kathleen Cooper, Meredith Dewey, Kerry Anne DiGrazia, Paola Farer, Andrea Gilman, Cheryl Hudson, Kristin Hussey, George Janes, Ola Kinnander, Michelle Leff, Adam Luysterborghs, Jennifer McMillian, Catherine McNamara, Erin Murphy, Megan Pincus, Steffanie Rivers, Christopher Swope, and Kathleen Tobin. We thank them and hope the experience was valuable.

The College of Journalism at the University of Maryland also collaborated with us on the book, particularly in database research. We thank instructors Daniel Barkin, Jody Brannon, and Michael Dorsher and their students Rabiah Abdullah, Chris Anderson, Daniel Brown, Christine Chou, Jennifer Ciotola, Courtney Clelan, Stephen Corbett, Doreen Craig, Corey Dade, Jason Da Ponte, Usheen Davar, Rachel Davis, Melissa Doherty, Nicole Ellison, Randall Evans, Matthew Fanning, Jessica Farquhar, Jared Featherstone, Anthony Fiteni, Jacquelyn Flowers, Christina Frasch, Renee Giroux, Nina Glazer, Maria Godoy, Andrew Goglia, Christine Green, Neal Greene, Judy Grunberger, Danielle Guido, Stephanie Holmes, Andrew Hong, Melody Hultgren, Neill Jakobe, Dawn Jeffries, Gregg Kanner, Kawana Lloyd, Maria LoPiccolo, Jennifer Lord, Christie Machiran, Jeffrey Matheny, Katrina McGarry, Jennifer McMenamin, Catherine Meketa, Florence Menson, Nicole Messina, Carey Migliaccio, Kate Milani, Benjamin Miller, Cara Newman, Hilary Newton, Deborah Nieman, Maricka Oglesby, Augusta Olsen, Jennifer Peterson, Sean Phelan, Timothy Pohlig, Richard Porcaro, Eric Relkin, Julie Reynolds, Shaneen Robertson, Jason Rockel, Jeffrey Rossi, Paul Rosynsky, Emily Salmon, Jeremy Settle, Lauren Shyman, Farid Siahatgar, Andrea Silberman, Vandana Sinha, Ginger Swiston, Michael

Tavss, Charles Thorne, Salima Usman, Christopher Vaccari, Jennifer Weissman, Angela West, Matthew Winkler, Ji Who Yoon.

We amassed far more data than this book could contain, and there are several specific databases available only through the Center's web site at *http://www.essential.org/CPI*. These include Commerce Secretary Ron Brown's global excursions with the captains of industry, replete with dates, campaign contributions, and other information; all of Bill Clinton's campaign donors since 1984; Lamar Alexander's 1978 and 1982 gubernatorial contributors; financial disclosure data about all of the major candidates, etc. This organization has made a major commitment through 1996 to keep voters fully informed about the candidates and the process by which our democracy selects its national leader, via the web site and databases, via our periodic newsletter, *The Public i*, and via articles and studies we write.

Finally, on a more personal note, I want to thank the Center's Board of Directors, especially Charles Piller, who like Alejandro Benes was present at its creation, and the Advisory Board members for their unwavering support and encouragement. I am indebted to Bill Moyers and John Moyers of the Schumann Foundation for their trenchant insights and encouragement. I also want to express my sincere gratitude to three Delaware political science professors who more than twenty years ago first opened my eyes to politics as it is, not as we wish it would be: Jim Soles, Jim Oliver, and John Deiner.

And no one has been more steadfast in sharing my dream of the Center for Public Integrity, an organization that uniquely combines political science and in-depth journalism in a new genre, than my family: my parents, Charles and Dorothy Lewis; my sister and brother-in-law, Mary Lewis and Randy Fisher; my daughter, Cassandra Bunting Lewis; and my wife, Pamela Gilbert.

Charles Lewis
September 14, 1995
Washington, D.C.

Endnotes

Introduction

1. Theodore H. White, *The Making of the President, 1960* (New York: Atheneum House, 1961), p. 13.

2. Stan Huckaby, *Analysis of the Financial Requirements for the 1996 Presidential Primary Process* (Huckaby and Associates, Inc., 1995).

3. E. J. Dionne, Jr., *Why Americans Hate Politics* (New York: Simon and Schuster, 1991), p. 323.

4. Herbert E. Alexander, *Financing Politics: Money, Elections & Political Reform* (Washington: CQ Press, 1992), Fourth Edition, p. 18.

5. Ibid., p. 21.

6. John Herbers, "Bill to Reform Campaign Funds Signed by Ford Despite Doubts," *New York Times,* October 16, 1974.

7. Chuck Alston, "Big Money Slips Back Into Government," *Congressional Quarterly Weekly Report,* March 7, 1992, p. 590.

8. Ibid.; Alexander, *Financing Politics,* p. 105.

9. Jill Abramson and Thomas Petzinger, Jr., "Deja Vu: Big Political Donors Find Ways Around Watergate Reforms," *Wall Street Journal,* June 11, 1992, pp. 1, 12.

10. Ibid., p. 1.

11. Ibid.

12. Interview with Jack Kemp, April 20, 1995.

13. Ibid.

14. Ibid.

15. Ruth Marcus, "Before the Campaign Trail, the Money Chase," *Washington Post,* March 5, 1995, p. A6.

16. Interview with Ted Welch, March 23, 1995.

17. Steven W. Colford, "On the Electronic Campaign Trail: Gov. Alexander

Beams Political Marketing Into The New-Media Age," *Advertising Age*, August 29, 1994, p. 14.

18. Includes contributions from 1979 to 1994 to his Senate and presidential campaigns, his leadership PAC, and the nonprofit organization he chaired, the Better America Foundation.

19. Center for Responsive Politics, as cited in Marcus, "Before the Campaign Trail," p. A6.

20. Louise Overacker, *Money in Elections* (New York: Macmillan, 1932), p. 71n.

21. Carl Sandburg, *Abraham Lincoln: The Prairie Years* (New York: Harcourt, Brace and World, 1926), Vol. 2, p. 344.

22. Philip H. Burch, Jr., *Elites in American History* (New York: Holmes and Meier Publishers, Inc., 1980), pp. 6–7.

23. James MacGregor Burns, *The Lion and the Fox* (Harcourt Brace Jovanovich, Inc., 1956), pp. 120, 168.

24. Louise Overacker, "Campaign Funds in the Presidential Election of 1936," *American Political Science Review*, p. 487.

25. In the analyses of the net worth of each of the candidates, all available sources of financial disclosure information were used. These include FEC records, House and Senate records, Executive branch disclosures and records made available by the candidates as well as some turned up from other sources for the years 1984 and 1994. The Clinton calculation is based on 1983 data because 1984 was unavailable.

26. Jeff Gerth and Stephen Engelberg, "Documents Show Clintons Got Vast Benefit From Their Partner in Whitewater Deal," *New York Times*, July 16, 1995, p. 18.

27. Brooks Jackson, *Honest Graft* (New York: Alfred Knopf, 1988), p. 167.

Party Animals

1. Arthur M. Schlesinger, Jr., *The Cycles of American History* (Boston: Houghton Mifflin Company, 1986), p. 258.

2. Joel H. Silbey, "The Rise and Fall of American Political Parties, 1790–1990," in Maisel, ed., *The Parties Respond* (Boulder: Westview Press, 1990), p. 4.

3. Joyce Gelb, Marian Lief Palley, *Tradition and Change in American Party Politics* (New York: Thomas Y. Crowell Co., 1975), p. 3.

4. Schlesinger, *The Cycles of American History*, p. 260.

5. Robert Kuttner, "Ass Backward: A Bestiary of Democratic Money Men," *The New Republic*, April 22, 1985, p. 18.

6. Robert Kuttner, *The Life of the Party* (New York: Viking Penguin, 1987), p. 55.

7. Ibid., pp. 55 and 56.

8. William Greider, *Who Will Tell the People: The Betrayal of American Democracy* (New York: Simon and Schuster, 1992), p. 91.

9. Ibid., p. 253.

10. Ibid., p. 253.

11. Ibid., p. 258.

12. Louise Overacker, *Money in Elections* (New York: MacMillan Company, 1932), pp. 374–375.

13. Charles Babcock, "$100,000 Political Donations on the Rise Again," *Washington Post*, September 30, 1991, p. A1.

14. *Private Parties: Political Party Leadership in Washington's Mercenary Culture* (Washington, D.C.: the Center for Public Integrity, September 1992), p. 1.

15. Ibid., p. 2.

16. Ibid., p. 3.

17. Lynn Sweet, "The President's Price List: Party Selling Perk Package," *Chicago Sun-Times*, June 30, 1995, p. 1. Graphic taken from the *Washington Times*.

18. Paul Bedard, "$100,000 Buys Meal with Clinton; DNC accused of selling office," *Washington Times*, July 6, 1995, p. A1.

19. Paul Bedard, "GOP sells access—for less," *Washington Times*, July 19, 1995, p. A4.

20. Ibid.

21. Sheila Kaplan, "For Corporate Givers: Political Party Time," *Legal Times*, May 4, 1992, p. 1; "Lobby Talk: Lobbies Plan Parties for the Party," Ibid., August 17, 1992, p. 5; "Smoking Up the GOP in Houston," Ibid., August 24, 1992, p. 1.

22. The Center for Public Integrity, *Private Parties*, p. 14.

23. Ibid., p. 14.

Bill Clinton

1. Meredith L. Oakley, *On the Make: The Rise of Bill Clinton* (Washington: Regnery Publishing, 1994), pp. 522–524.

2. Associated Press, "Clinton OK'd State Lease with S&L in '84, Memo Reveals," *Los Angeles Times*, July 31, 1995, p. A8.

3. John Brummett, *High Wire: The Education of Bill Clinton* (New York: Hyperion, 1994) pp. 240–241.

4. Ibid., p. 139.

5. Douglas Frantz, "How Tyson Became the Chicken King," *New York Times*, August 28, 1994, p. C1.

6. Ibid.

7. Michael Kelly, "The President's Past," *New York Times Magazine*, July 31, 1994, p. 20.

8. Ibid.

9. David Maraniss, *First in His Class* (New York: Simon and Schuster, 1995), p. 359.

10. Kelly, "The President's Past," p. 20.

11. Ibid.

12. Dan McGraw, "The Birdman of Arkansas," *U.S. News & World Report,* July 18, 1994, p. 42.

13. Jeff Gerth, "The 1992 Campaign: Candidate's Record; Clinton Worked to Exempt His Office From Ethics Code," *New York Times,* March 27, 1992, p. 1.

14. Ibid.

15. *Under the Influence: Presidential Candidates and their Campaign Advisers* (Washington D.C.: Center for Public Integrity, 1992). Also see Charles Lewis, "The Rainmakers in Bill's Parade," *The Nation,* December 7, 1992, p. 693.

16. *Private Parties: Political Party Leadership in Washington's Mercenary Culture* (Washington D.C.: Center for Public Integrity, 1992), pp. 38–51.

17. Sheila Kaplan, "Special Interests, Firms Offer Up Loans, Gifts, In-Kind Help," *Legal Times,* January 11, 1993, p. 1.

18. Steve Daley, "Big Money Rears Its Head At 'People's Inaugural,' " *Chicago Tribune,* January 20, 1993, p. 1.

19. Stephen Labaton, "Commerce Nominee Cancels Party Planned by Companies," *New York Times,* January 14, 1993, p. 1.

20. Priscilla Painton, "Guess Who's Paying For Dinner?" *Time,* January 25, 1993, p. 37.

21. Bob Woodward, *The Agenda: Inside the Clinton White House* (New York: Simon and Schuster, 1994), p. 84.

22. Susan Garland, "Romancing the Stone-Faced: How CEOs Were Won Over," *Business Week,* April 5, 1993, p. 54.

23. Peter H. Stone, "Friends, After All," *National Journal,* October 22, 1994, p. 2440.

24. Ibid.

25. Much of this section was previously reported by the Center for Public Integrity in various media, including its newsletter, *The Public i.*

26. The findings are based on the minimum available information. The Commerce Department did not fully disclose pertinent data.

27. M. E. Freeman, "Process to Get on Trade Mission Wasn't Political, Entergy Insists," *Arkansas Democrat-Gazette,* May 20, 1995, p. 3B.

28. Brown testimony before the Senate Governmental Affairs Committee, July 25, 1995.

29. Reported on CNN, May 10, 1994.

30. Mark Memmott, "Mission for business, Commerce chief helps move exports," *USA Today,* March 31, 1994, p. 1B.

31. Joan Duffy, "Blacks fear Shackelford a casino figurehead," *Commercial Appeal*, October 17, 1994, p. 6A.

32. *Washington Representative* (Washington, D.C.: Columbia Books, 1995), p. 202.

33. OPIC Annual Report, 1994, p. 26.

34. Interview with Lottie Shackelford, August 24, 1995.

35. OPIC Annual Report, 1994, p. 5.

36. Ibid., p. 20.

37. Export-Import Bank of the United States Annual Report, 1994, p. 1.

38. Export-Import Bank of the United States Annual Report, 1994, p. 54.

39. Export-Import Bank of the United States Annual Reports, 1993 and 1994.

40. Export-Import Bank Annual Report, 1993.

41. Export-Import Bank Annual Reports, 1993 and 1994.

42. Interview with Christopher Dorval, August 22, 1995.

43. Woodward, *The Agenda*, p. 81; Rebecca Borders and Alejandro Benes, "Goldman Sachs and the White House Connection," *Washington Times*, October 28, 1994, p. A23.

44. Susan Schmidt, "2 Clinton Aides Bring Wall St. Perspective to S&L Task," *Washington Post*, December 24, 1992, p. D7.

45. Audit Report A95-DE-010, RTC's Financial Advisor Contract with Goldman Sachs and Co., June 21, 1995, p. 16. The report called for a management decision on corrective action, but the process had not been exhausted by the time this book went to the printer. Essentially, Goldman Sachs had sixty days to respond to the report after which the RTC takes it up at a resolution committee meeting. A decision was expected in October of 1995.

46. Ibid.

47. The Resolution Trust Corporation, or RTC, was created by the Financial Institutions Reform Recovery and Enforcement Act of 1989, signed on August 9, 1989, to liquidate failed savings and loan institutions. The RTC Completion Act put the RTC out of business on December 31, 1995.

48. Audit Report A95-DE-010, p. 16.

49. Thomas Burnside, "The Great Texas Bank Robbery," *New York Times*, July 23, 1994, p. 19.

50. Jeffrey Birnbaum, "Democratic Party Betting Big on Losing in 1994, Is Now $5 Million in the Hole" *Wall Street Journal*, December 13, 1994.

51. *American Banker Washington Watch*, December 19, 1994, Vol. 4, No. 48, p. 5.

52. Steven Lipin, "Banks Bracing for the Removal of Interstate Barriers," *Wall Street Journal*, March 11, 1994.

53. "McColl of NationsBank Climbed on Clinton Bandwagon Just in Time," *American Banker*, November 9, 1992, p. 10.

54. Jim McTague, "The Unmitigated Gall of NationsBank's McColl," *American Banker,* August 2, 1993, p. 18.

55. In 1991–1992, NationsBank had three PACs: NationsBank Corporation, NationsBank of North Carolina, and NationsBank of Texas.

56. Norbert McCrady, "Branching Will Help Fat Cats Feed Clinton's War Chest," *American Banker,* April 27, 1994, p. 17.

57. US Newswire, August 23, 1994.

58. Interview with Joe Martin, June 29, 1995.

59. Interview with Brad Marshall and Joe Sandler, June 29, 1995.

60. Kenneth Cline, "McColl Plays Starring Role in Long Campaign for Branching," *American Banker,* September 15, 1994, p. 4.

61. Interview with George Stephanopoulos, June 21, 1995.

62. Russell Mitchell and Judith H. Dobrzynski, "Getting Business Aboard the Clinton Bandwagon," *Business Week,* September 28, 1992, p. 51.

63. CNN transcript of Gore's remarks, December 14, 1992, at the Little Rock Economic Summit, in a conversation with Robert Allen, chief executive officer of AT&T.

64. Vice President Albert Gore speech at the National Press Club, December 21, 1993.

65. Ibid.

66. Interview with Greg Simon, August 11, 1995.

67. Doug Halonen, "Congress Wades into Cable-Phone War," *Crain Communication Inc.,* May 22, 1989, p. 3.

68. Sherry Keene-Osborn, "Taking Aim at the King of Cable," *Newsweek,* October 4, 1993, p. 89.

69. John Burgess, "Data Highways . . . Can We Get There From Here," *Washington Post,* May 2, 1993, p. H1.

70. At this writing, final action on the legislation was pending.

71. Mike Mills, "In Hollywood, Bells Are Ringing," *Washington Post,* November 1, 1994, p. D1.

72. Leslie Cauley, "Three Baby Bells Plan Two Ventures, Assisted by Hollywood's Creative Artists," *Wall Street Journal,* October 26, 1994, p. C1.

73. Bernard Weinraub, "The Media Business: A Whole New Script," *New York Times,* August 15, 1995, p. 1A.

74. FEC records and Alan C. Miller and Dwight Morris, "Local Firms Spent Heavily on Campaign Contributions," *Los Angeles Times,* January 10, 1993, p. B3.

75. Center for Responsive Politics.

76. Patrick J. Sloyan, "Rules Exception: Pentagon Quietly Waived Ethnics Standard for Official," *Newsday,* December 4, 1994, p. A18.

77. Ibid.

78. Nick Gilbert and Jennifer Reingold, "The Old Boy," *Financial World,* August 16, 1994, p. 26.

79. Sloyan, "Rules Exception."

80. Ibid.

81. Federal News Service, May 10, 1995, "Remarks by Jeffrey Garten, Undersecretary of Commerce for International Trade at the Export-Import Bank of the United States."

82. *Arms Sales Monitor,* newsletter, April 30, 1994.

83. Deborah Lutterbeck, "How Uncle Sam helps weapons merchants arm the world," *Common Cause Magazine,* June, 1994.

84. *Arms Sales Monitor* newsletter, July 30, 1994.

85. Statement by Brown before the Senate Government Affairs Committee, July 25, 1995, pp. 103–104.

86. Associated Press, "Brazil Suspends Raytheon Deal," *New York Times,* July 5, 1995, p. D4.

87. Agence France Presse, June 1, 1995, "Brazil informs U.S. of 1.4 billion dollar Amazon radar deal with Raytheon."

88. Geoffrey Smith, Amy Borrus, and Bill Hinchberger, "It's Raytheon vs. Thomson," *Business Week,* August 1, 1994, p. 30.

89. Nancy Dunne, "Clinton & Co's sales machine cashes in—'High-level advocacy' pays dividends for U.S." *Financial Times,* February 18, 1994, p. 7.

90. Douglas Frantz, "U.S. Backing Work on Czech Reactors by Westinghouse," *New York Times,* May 22, 1994, p. A1.

91. *The Trading Game: Inside Lobbying for the North American Free Trade Agreement* (Washington, D.C.: Center for Public Integrity, 1993), p. 25.

92. The 1991–92 figure of $4,181,234 included labor donations to the DNC, DCCC, DSCC, the DNC Dinner Committee, and the Association of Democratic Chairs. The 1993–94 figure of $3,681,089 includes labor donations to the DNC, College Democrats, DCCC, and the Democratic Victory Fund, yielding a four-year total of $7,862,323.

93. Lane Kirkland is on the advisory board of the Center for Public Integrity.

94. *Well-Healed: Inside Lobbying for Health Care Reform* (Washington, D.C.: Center for Public Integrity, 1994), p. 70.

95. Louis Uchitelle, "Gore Says Clinton Will Move To Help Striking Workers," *New York Times,* February 21, 1995, p. D1.

96. Thomas C. Hayes, "Profile/Don Tyson; Mr. Chicken goes to Washington," *New York Times,* January 17, 1993, p. 11.

97. Douglas Frantz, "How Tyson Became the Chicken King," *New York Times,* August 28, 1994, p. C1.

98. Richard Behar and Michael Kramer, "Something Smells Fowl," *Time,* October 17, 1994, p. 42.

99. Franz, "How Tyson Became the Chicken King," p. C1.

100. Caroline Baum and Victor Niederhoffer, "Herd Instincts," *National Review,* February 20, 1995, p. 45.

Lamar Alexander

1. United Press International, February 8, 1985, "Republicans Give $75,000 to Alexander 'Travel Fund.' "

2. Peter Maas, *Marie, A True Story* (New York: Random House, 1983), p. 6.

3. Interview with John Siegenthaler, August 15, 1995.

4. National Press Club luncheon speech transcript, April 18, 1995, p. 9.

5. Pat Choate, *Agents of Influence: How Japan's Lobbyists in the United States Manipulate America's Political and Economic System* (New York: Knopf, 1990), p. 138.

6. Ibid., p. 139.

7. Stephanie Epstein, *Buying the American Mind: Japan's Quest for U.S. Ideas in Science, Economic Policy and the Schools* (Washington, D.C.: Center for Public Integrity, 1991), p. 1.

8. Doug Ireland, "The Rich Rise of Lamar Alexander," *The Nation,* April 17, 1995, p. 518.

9. Ibid.

10. Edward T. Pound and Hilary Stout, "Bush Nominee Alexander's Investment Successes Have Made Senate Investigators Very Inquisitive," *Wall Street Journal,* March 5, 1991, p. A18*ff.*

11. Richard Behar, "Partners in Crime," *Forbes,* February 11, 1985, p. 112.

12. Pound and Stout, "Bush Nominee Alexander's Investment Successes," p. A16.

13. Ireland, "The Rich Rise of Lamar Alexander," p. 518.

14. Pound and Stout, "Bush Nominee Alexander's Investment Successes," p. A18.

15. Ruth Marcus, "Ventures During Public Service Multiplied Net Worth by 10," *Washington Post,* February 26, 1995, p. A19; Pound and Stout, "Bush Nominee Alexander's Investment Successes," p. A18.

16. Sheila Wissner, "Alexander Worth Examined: 4 Deals Made $1.9 Million," *Nashville Tennessean,* March 6, 1991, p. 2A.

17. Pound and Stout, "Bush Nominee Alexander's Investment Successes," *Wall Street Journal,* March 5, 1991.

18. Leigh Ann Eagleston, "Lamar Says No Wrongdoing; Inn Called Sentimental," *Nashville Tennessean,* August 11, 1991, p. 2A.

19. Larry Daughtrey and James Pratt, "Planned road 7 miles from Alexanderland," *Nashville Tennessean,* March 2, 1986, p. 1.

20. Larry Daughtrey and James Pratt, "Alexander Halts Road Expansion Plan near Farm," *Nashville Tennessean,* March 3, 1986, p. 1.

21. From the Snodgrass letter as part of the Special Report: *University of Tennessee Review of Contractural Arrangements with Consultants and Use of Blackberry Farm* (State of Tennessee, Comptroller of the Treasury, May 1992).

22. Interview with Lewis Lavine, August 16, 1995.

23. Reed Branson, "Ex-Alexander aides' firm urged UT post," *Commercial Appeal*, May 15, 1992, p. A1.

24. Special Report: *University of Tennessee Review of Contractural Arrangements with Consultants and Use of Blackberry Farm*, pp. 2–3.

25. Ibid., Snodgrass letter, p. 15.

26. *Congressional Record*, Senate, March 14, 1991, p. S3375.

27. Pound and Stout, "Bush Nominee Alexander's Investment Successes," p. A18.

28. Sheila Wissner, "Alexander Worth Examined," p. 2A.

29. Hearing of the Committee on Labor and Human Resources, United States Senate, Andrew L. Alexander of Tennessee, to be Secretary, Department of Education, February 6, 1991, p. 35.

30. Telephone interview with Christopher Whittle, August 11, 1995.

31. John S. Friedman, "Big business goes to school," *The Nation*, February 17, 1992, p. 188.

32. Ibid., p. 190.

33. Associated Press, "Alexander Says he Lost $200,000 on Home Sale to Whittle Executive" *Daily Times*, August 16, 1991, p. 6A.

34. Wissner, "Alexander Worth Examined," p. 1A.

35. David Warsh, "In education, as in politics, 3rd parties pariahs," *Chicago Tribune*, May 31, 1992, p. 7B.

36. Friedman, "Big business goes to school," p. 190.

37. David Morris, "Alexander Used Non-Profit Network to Raise Money, Hone Issues," Associated Press, June 21, 1995.

38. Ibid.

39. James W. Brosnan, "Alexander shares in Marietta bounty," *Commercial Appeal*, March 18, 1995, p. 1A.

40. Ibid; "Lockheed execs get post-deal bonuses," *Marietta Daily Journal*, March 18, 1995, p. A1.

41. James W. Brosnan, " 'Contract lawyer' Alexander watches his step, Job designed to avoid impropriety," *Commercial Appeal*, March 12, 1995.

42. Bruce Ingersoll, "Alexander, Helped by Business Friends, Runs Bid for Presidency With Little Financial Concern," *Wall Street Journal*, April 6, 1995, p. A18.

43. Fax memorandum from Ben Adams to the Center for Public Integrity, August 22, 1995.

44. "Questions Continue: Alexander should open books on his finances," *Nashville Banner*, August 16, 1991.

45. National Press Club Lamar Alexander luncheon speech, April 18, 1995, transcribed by Federal News Service, p. 12–13.

Pat Buchanan

1. John Aloysius Farrell, "Buchanan's two sides: gracious, querulous," *Boston Globe*, January 28, 1992, p. 1.

2. Interview with Pat Buchanan, July 25, 1995.

3. W. Dale Nelson, "Pat Buchanan: He was shaped by his family and religion, a world of clarity and absolutes," *St. Louis Post-Dispatch*, March 6, 1992, p. 1C.

4. Bob Woodward and Carl Bernstein, *The Final Days* (New York: Avon, 1975), p. 65.

5. Theodore H. White, *Breach of Faith: The Fall of Richard Nixon* (New York: Dell, 1973), p. 27.

6. Ruth Marcus, "Unfettered Pundit Joining Race: Buchanan faces task unlike '92 challenge to Bush," *Washington Post*, March 19, 1995, p. A1.

7. Ibid.

8. Anne Groer, "The Commentator and Rejuvenator Pat Buchanan," *Orlando Sentinel Tribune*, February 23, 1992, p. 1A.

9. Marcus, "Unfettered Pundit Joining Race," p. A1.

10. Ibid.

11. Interview with Pat Buchanan, July 25, 1995.

12. Rita Beamish, "Billed as the true conservative: Buchanan declares candidacy," Associated Press, March 21, 1995.

13. Pat Buchanan speech in Manchester, New Hampshire, March 20, 1995.

14. 1995 FEC financial disclosure.

15. Pat Buchanan, in his address to the Republican National Convention, August 17, 1992.

16. Final audit report on Buchanan for President, FEC. Approved October 11, 1994.

17. Brian Hartman, "Spartanburg cash helps fund Buchanan campaign," States News Service, June 26, 1995; FEC records.

18. Joyce Barrett, "Trade stance puts some textile execs in Buchanan's camp," *Women's Wear Daily*, March 6, 1992, p. 18.

Bob Dole

1. ABC News Transcript No. 145–1, April 27, 1994, Dole's eulogy at Nixon's funeral.

2. Richard Ben Cramer, *What It Takes* (New York: Vintage Books, 1993), p. 599.

3. FEC records. These figures do not include the 1976 or 1978 election cycles for the Dole for Senate Committee because those records are not

available. Before 1980, the FEC did not require filings in years during which senatorial candidates did not run for election or reelection.

4. Jake H. Thompson, *Bob Dole: The Republicans' Man For All Seasons* (New York: Donald I. Fine, Inc., 1994), p. 67.

5. Ibid., p. 74.

6. Cramer, *What It Takes,* p. 746.

7. Ibid., p. 747.

8. In Foster's 1995 case, then–Senate Majority Leader Dole, who said he opposed Foster's nomination because he had performed abortions and had not fully disclosed the exact number he had done, was credited by anti-abortion organizations for preventing a formal vote in the Senate. In the second day of the debate, covered by C-SPAN, a Republican senator displayed a doll resembling a fetus as well as large graphic drawings of rare third-trimester abortions, implying that Foster had done late-term abortions; Thompson, *Bob Dole,* p. 79.

9. Bob and Elizabeth Dole, *The Doles: Unlimited Partners* (New York: Simon and Schuster, 1988), pp. 130–131.

10. Interview with David Owen, July 28, 1995.

11. FEC materials, including a July 29, 1980 letter to Senator Dole's 1980 presidential campaign from Robert Brogin, of the FEC.

12. According to his December 14, 1979 letter, Owen arranged for Mrs. Dole's loan to get a 13.5 percent interest rate, well below the prime rate. In the same letter, Owen lamented that he was required by law to charge 1 percent above the rate Mrs. Dole received on the certificate of deposit she used as collateral.

13. Bank statement from the Dole for President account at the First American Bank of Virginia, in McLean, Virginia.

14. FEC documents, including an October 26, 1981 letter from Charles N. Steele, general counsel of the FEC to the Dole campaign. The main reason for the investigation was that any contributions or loans from individuals to campaign committees are subject to a $1,000 limit, which the loan from Elizabeth exceeded. But under federal law, any candidate who receives federal matching funds, which Dole did for his presidential campaign in 1980, is allowed to spend up to $50,000 of his or her own money on the campaign. Dole argued that his wife's money is his money, also. But under Kansas law at the time, property that was only in one spouse's name, or that was bequeathed or given to only one spouse, was not considered community property. To purchase the CD she used as collateral, Mrs. Dole used income from a blind trust as well as part of the money from her father's pension fund, of which she became beneficiary when he died. The original charges by the FEC arose because they said this pension was bequeathed to Mrs. Dole, and that she was named the beneficiary of it before her marriage to Dole, so it was therefore solely her property, making both the CD and the loan her sole property as well. Her lawyers argued that the charges were unconstitutionally biased against the Doles, saying if

they happened to live in a "community property state," there would be no charges. The final recommendation to not pursue the matter further was issued on October 26, 1981.

15. Bill Dalton, Rich Hood, and Andrew C. Miller, "Donations to Dole effort may have been illegal," *Kansas City Star,* January 28, 1988, section A.

16. Ibid.

17. Interview with David Owen, July 28, 1995.

18. "Tax Returns—Conviction for False Tax Returns Affirmed Where Former Politician Disguised Campaign Contributions as Business Expenses," *Daily Report for Executives,* February 3, 1994.

19. Letter from Nelson Warfield to the Center for Public Integrity, August 15, 1995.

20. Dan Morgan and Anne Swardson, "Dole Ally Out After Queries on Trust Role," *Washington Post,* January 15, 1988, p. A1.

21. FEC documents.

22. Thompson, *Bob Dole,* p. 21.

23. Cramer, *What It Takes,* pp. 99–103.

24. Bob and Elizabeth Dole, *The Doles,* p. 45.

25. Thompson, *Bob Dole,* p. 35.

26. Reported on ABC News "Prime Time Live" in April 1995; Senate sources.

27. Thompson, *Bob Dole,* pp. 39–40.

28. Bob and Elizabeth Dole, *The Doles,* pp. 126–127.

29. Thompson, *Bob Dole,* p. 66.

30. Cramer, *What It Takes,* p. 122.

31. Ibid., p. 759.

32. Thompson, *Bob Dole,* pp. 107–108.

33. Bob and Elizabeth Dole, *The Doles,* p. 186.

34. Thompson, *Bob Dole,* pp. 124–126.

35. Morgan and Swardson, "Dole Ally Out," p. A1.

36. Interview with Fred Wertheimer, August 16, 1995.

37. Dole testimony before the Senate Committee on Commerce Communications Subcommittee, March 4, 1971.

38. Ibid.

39. Brooks Jackson, *Honest Graft: Big Money and the American Political Process* (Washington, D.C.: Farragut, 1990), p. 244.

40. *Congressional Record,* April 10, 1989, pp. S3537–3538.

41. Philip M. Stern, *Still The Best Congress Money Can Buy* (Washington, D.C.: Regnery Gateway, 1992), p. 111.

42. Michael Isikoff, Mark Hosenball, and Lucy Shackelford, "Dole's Frequent-Flier Miles," *Newsweek,* April 24, 1995; available FEC records from Campaign America and Senate Public Financial Disclosure Reports.

43. Thompson, *Bob Dole,* p. 134.

44. Interview with Jim Whittinghill, April 28, 1995.

45. Reprinted in *The Capital Eye,* the newsletter of the Center for Responsive Politics, August 15, 1995, from *Washington Post,* June 21, 1995.

46. The Dole Foundation contributions were obtained from the Foundation Center in Washington, D.C., though the Gallo family may have contributed more to the cause prior to 1989. The Dole Foundation does not release exact figures. The Better America Foundation figures came from a press release issued by the organization.

47. Marjorie Williams, "The Fall of the House of Coelho," *Washington Post Magazine,* January 8, 1995, p. 18.

48. Jackson, *Honest Graft,* p. 117.

49. *Hoover Business Report* (New York: Reference Press, October 12, 1994).

50. Figures provided by the Market Promotion Program.

51. *Congressional Record,* November 23, 1985, pp. 33,495–33,498.

52. *Vote Report* from Reed Elsevier Inc., 1992 Senate Vote No. 156, 1993 Senate Vote No. 214, 1994 Senate Vote No. 206, and 1995 Senate Vote 130.

53. Hearing of the Senate Agriculture Committee, Federal News Service, March 21, 1995.

54. "Effectiveness of Market Promotion Program Remains Unclear," report of the General Accounting Office of June 1993.

55. Michael Doyle, "Debate Over Champagne Bubbles to the Surface," *Sacramento Bee,* August 23, 1992, p. 1A.

56. Ibid.

57. Paul Houston, "Two Senators Backing Gallo Got $112,000," *Los Angeles Times,* February 21, 1992, p. 7.

58. Thompson, *Bob Dole,* p. 203.

59. Muriel Dobbin, "Will U.S. Swallow Health Care RX?" *Sacramento Bee,* September 12, 1993, p. 1A.

60. CNN "Newsmaker Sunday" Transcript No. 187, August 29, 1993.

61. Archer-Daniels-Midland Annual Report, 1994.

62. Scott Kilman, Thomas M. Burton, and Richard Gibson, "An Executive Becomes Informant for FBI, Stunning giant ADM," *Wall Street Journal,* July 10, 1995, p. 1.

63. Ibid.

64. FEC data.

65. "End Corporate Welfare," *USA Today,* April 20, 1995, p. 12A.

66. E. J. Kahn Jr., *Supermarket to the World: The Story of Dwayne Andreas* (New York: Time Warner, 1991), pp. 181–184.

67. Frank Greve, "He Gives, He Gets—You Pay," *The Charlotte Observer,* January 23, 1995. Better America Foundation figures are from a press release issued by the organization on June 26, 1995.

68. Ibid.

69. Available FEC records from Campaign America, and Senate Public Financial Disclosure Reports; Isikoff, Hosenball, and Shackelford, "Dole's Frequent-Flier Miles," p. 32.

70. Martin Tolchin and Jeff Gerth, "The Contradictions of Bob Dole," *New York Times Magazine,* November 8, 1987, p. 88.

71. Edward T. Pound, "Minority Leader's Friend, Backer Gains From the Senator's Support for Gasahol," *Wall Street Journal,* September 25, 1987.

72. Letter from the executive offices of Sea View to Dwayne Andreas, June 10, 1987.

73. Faxed response from the "Office of Dwayne Andreas," August 28, 1995.

74. Timothy Noah and Scott Kilman, "Archer, Ethanol Industry Dealt a Blow As Court Blocks EPA Gasoline Order," *Wall Street Journal,* May 1, 1995; Michael J. Weiss, "The High-Octane Ethanol Lobby," *New York Times,* April 1, 1990, p. 19.

75. Pound, "Minority Leader's Friend;" Richard E. Cohen, author of the 1992 book *Washington at Work: Back Rooms and Clean Air,* explained the ethanol program as a tax-credit program: "The new tax credit exempted purchases of ethanol-blended fuels from a share of the federal gasoline tax. As of 1991, the 5.4 cents credit (lowering the 14.5 cents per gallon tax to 9.1 cents) costs the federal government about $600 million annually."

76. Information Resources Inc., 1995; "U.S. Fuel Ethanol Production Capacity," *Biofuels Update,* National Renewable Energy Lab, Winter 1995.

77. Figures are from the Foreign Agriculture Service, Department of Agriculture, compiled at the request of the Center for Public Integrity. The deputy administrator for export credits Mary T. Chambliss, informed that the U.S.D.A. does "not maintain complete information." Also, telephone interviews with Roland Olson, director, Consolidated Farm Service Agency, U.S.D.A., August 1995.

78. *Congressional Record,* November 23, 1985, p. 33,495.

79. Senate Agriculture Committee Confirmation Hearing for Agriculture Secretary-Designate Clayton Yeutter, Federal News Service, February 2, 1989.

80. Tom Raum, "Bush OKs subsidies for wheat" Associated Press, May 3, 1989.

81. Letter to Madigan from Dole, August 3, 1992.

82. Letter to Espy from Dole, March 24, 1993.

83. Ray Archer, "Prime Cuts: 1.5 Trillion Ways to Balance the Federal Budget," *Arizona Republic,* April 24, 1995, p. B4.

84. *Congressional Record,* November 23, 1985, pp. 33,477–33,525.

85. Archer-Daniels-Midland Annual Report, 1986, p. 10.

86. Frank Greve, Knight-Ridder Newspapers, January 22, 1995.

87. Stern, p. 114; and Robert McGough, "Sweet Charity," *Financial World,* April 4, 1989.

88. Center for Responsive Politics, "The Politics of Sugar," May 1995, p. 27.

89. Stern, p. 115.

90. Ibid.

91. Archer-Daniels-Midland Annual Report, 1988, p. 14.

92. Hoover's Handbook Database (Austin, Texas: The Reference Press, Inc., 1994.)

93. Leslie Wayne, "Pulling the Wraps Off Koch Industries," *New York Times,* November 20, 1994, p. C1.

94. "Special Access for Special Interests," (Washington, D.C.: Citizens for Sensible Safeguards, July 1995), p. 24.

95. Figures from 1986 to 1990 from W. John Moore, "Witchita Pipeline," *National Journal,* May 16, 1992, p. 52. Figures from 1991 to 1993 from Citizens for Sensible Safeguards, pp. 25–26.

96. Moore, "Wichita Pipeline," p. 52.

97. FEC and from a Better America Foundation press release, June 26, 1995.

98. Fax from Riff Yeager, Koch Industries, to the Center for Public Integrity, August 30, 1995.

99. Irving Long, "Backroom," *Newsday,* July 26, 1995, p. A21; Jack Nelson, "At 72, Dole has Healthy Respect for Age Issue," *Los Angeles Times,* July 22, 1995, p. 1A.

100. *Congressional Record,* February 2, 1995, p. 2056.

101. David S. Cloud, "Industry, Politics Intertwined in Dole's Regulatory Bill," *Congressional Quarterly,* May 6, 1995, p. 1221.

102. Better America Foundation press release, June 26, 1995.

103. FEC records.

104. Section 708, Affirmative defense, of S. 343 as proposed by Senator Dole: "Notwithstanding any other provision of law, it shall be an affirmative defense in any enforcement action brought by an agency that the regulated person or entity reasonably relied on and is complying with a rule, regulation, adjudication, directive, or order or such agency or any other agency that is incompatible, contradictory, or otherwise cannot be reconciled with the agency rule, regulation, adjudication, directive, or order being enforced."

105. Interview with Phil Metzger, EPA chief policy counsel, July 14, 1995.

106. "Dole bill markup rescheduled to give panel Democrats more time," *BNA Pensions & Benefits Daily,* April 3, 1995.

107. Reuters, August 8, 1995, "Dole Sees U.S. Senate Passing Reg Reform This Year."

108. Kenneth M. Ballen, "The Kochs Can Play Washington's Power Game," *National Journal,* May 16, 1992; the Senate Select Committee on Indian Affairs report, November 1989, p. 106.

109. Ibid.

110. Ibid.

111. Interview with Kenneth Ballen, July 19, 1995.

Bob Dornan

1. When asked in July 1995 about the gun, a staffer responded: "We have no comment."

2. Interview with Representative Bob Dornan, July 23, 1995.

3. R. H. Melton, "Record $54 Million in Giving Declared in Early Presidential Race," *Washington Post*, July 24, 1995, p. A7.

4. Center for Responsive Politics data from FEC.

5. John Aloysius, "Clinton to Set Ties to Vietnam Today," *Boston Globe*, July 11, 1995, p. 1.

6. Larry Makinson and Josh Goldstein, *Open Secrets*, (Washington, D.C.: Center for Responsive Politics, Congressional Quarterly, 1994), p. 59.

7. *Aerospace Daily*, December 31, 1992, p. 482.

8. United Press International, May 20, 1985, "Californians' Financial Worth Disclosed."

9. Ibid.

10. CRP data from FEC.

11. Ibid.

12. Ibid.

13. Harry Berkowitz and John Riley, "Tall Order: Rebuilding Kuwait," *Newsday*, February 28, 1991, p. D5.

14. Federal Election Commission, July 1995, "Report of Receipts and Disbursements."

Phil Gramm

1. Michael Barone and Grant Ujifusa, *Almanac of American Politics 1994* (Washington, D.C.: National Journal, Inc., 1993), p. 1,207.

2. Richard L. Berke, "Tough Texan Phil Gramm," *New York Times Magazine*, February 19, 1995, p. 27.

3. CBS News "60 Minutes," February 19, 1995, Vol. XXVII, No. 22.

4. Adam Myerson, *Policy Review* (Washington, D.C.: Heritage Foundation, October, 1989), p. 50.

5. John B. Judis, "The Porn Broker," *New Republic*, June 5, 1995, p. 14.

6. Much of this NRA section first appeared in a *Washington Post* Outlook article by Charles Lewis, entitled "Favorite Son of a Gun," May 28, 1995, p. C2.

7. Letter from Phil Gramm to potential contributors, July 1987.

8. Ross K. Baker, "The Adherent and the Apostate," *New Democrat,* May/June, 1995, p. 33.

9. R. G. Ratcliffe, "Gramm Ambitious from the Beginning; White House aspirations born in '70s," *Houston Post,* February 19, 1995.

10. Jeff Gerth and Dean Baquet, "The Senator and the Builder: A Special Report; Gramm's Homebuilding Bargain Raises Issue of Possible Conflict," *New York Times,* November 29, 1992, p. A1.

11. Ibid.

12. Michael Waldman, *Who Robbed America? A Citizen's Guide to the Savings and Loan Scandal* (New York: Random House, 1990), p. 230.

13. Interview with Edwin J. Gray, June 15, 1995.

14. James Ring Adams, *The Big Fix: Inside the S&L Scandal* (New York: John Wiley & Sons, 1990), p. 37.

15. Mary Fricker and Steve Pizzo, "S&L Scandal: The Gang's All Here," *New York Times,* op-ed.

16. James Ring Adams, "The S&L Debacle: What Taxpayers Should Know," The Heritage Lectures, no. 287 (Washington, D.C.: The Heritage Foundation, August 8, 1990).

17. Martin Mayer, *The Greatest Ever Bank Robbery,* (New York: Charles Scribner's Sons, 1990), p. 2.

18. Interview with Durward Curlee, July 6, 1995.

19. James Ring Adams, *The Big Fix: Inside the S&L Scandal* (New York: John Wiley and Sons, 1990), p. 37.

20. Stephen Pizzo, Mary Fricker, and Paul Muolo, *Inside Job* (New York: Harper Perennial, 1991), p. 455.

21. Ibid., pp. 246 and 298.

22. Adams, *The Big Fix,* p. 220.

23. Pizzo, Fricker, and Muolo, *Inside Job,* p. 431.

24. Martin Mayer, *The Greatest Ever Bank Robbery,* p. 177.

25. Jerry Knight, "Banker Influence Issue Could Tar Republicans, Too," *Washington Post,* May 31, 1988, p. D1.

26. Richard Whittle, "Papers offer rare view of Gramm," *Dallas Morning News,* July 25, 1993, p. 1.

27. Ibid., p. 12A.

28. Ibid.

29. Larry Makinson, *Open Secrets* (Washington, D.C.: Congressional Quarterly Inc., 1992), 2nd Edition, pp. 47 and 96.

30. Ibid., p. 12A.

31. Robert D. Hershey, Jr., "Business People; Deregulator Chosen for Commodity Post," *New York Times,* December 4, 1987, p. D2.

32. Ibid.

33. R. G. Ratcliffe, "Convention '92; Corporations paid for Gramm's convention parties," *Houston Chronicle,* August 21, 1992, p. B3.

34. Jerry Knight, "Energy Firm Finds Ally, Director in CFTC Ex-chief," *Washington Post,* April 17, 1993, p. B1.

35. Gramm campaign announcement dinner program.

36. Center for Public Integrity; John Harwood, "Meatpackers IBP's Ties to the Gramm Campaign Reflect Mutual Distrust of Economic Regulation," *Wall Street Journal,* August 15, 1995, p. A18.

37. "IBP Is Ordered to Pay Overtime to Workers; Amount is Undecided," *Wall Street Journal,* May 4, 1993, p. C18.

38. Roger Barnes, "Cumulative Trauma Injury Researched," *National Underwriter,* December 19, 1988, p. 90.

39. George Ruben, "Developments in Industrial Relationships," *Monthly Labor Review,* April 1989, p. 41.

40. John Harwood, "Meatpacker IBP's Ties to the Gramm Campaign," p. A18.

41. Ibid.; FEC.

42. Harwood, "Meatpacker IBP's Ties to the Gramm Campaign," p. 18.

43. Makinson, *Open Secrets,* pp. 256–57.

44. Fees from the Petroleum Manufacturers Association for speaking on April 6, 1992, were donated to charity.

45. S. C. Gwynne, "How Right Thou Art," *Time,* March 13, 1995, pp. 78–80.

Alan Keyes

1. Judith Colp, "Keyes' Race to Open Political Door," *Washington Times,* June 30, 1992, p. E1.

2. Michael Barone and Grant Ujifusa, *The Almanac of American Politics 1996,* (Washington, D.C.: National Journal, 1995), p. 607.

3. Ibid.

4. Alan Keyes, "My Race for the Senate," *Policy Review,* Spring, 1989, p. 3.

5. Alan Keyes, *Masters of the Dream* (New York: William Morrow, 1995), p. 126.

6. Ibid., p. 2.

7. Colp, "Keyes' Race to Open Political Door," p. E1.

8. Communications expenditures usually include mailings and phone calls on behalf of a candidate.

9. Nexis property tax file.

10. Richard Tapscott, "MD Candidate to Keep Taking Salary," *Washington Post,* May 16, 1992, p. A12.

11. Andy Lamey, "Odd Man In," *New Republic,* April 17, 1995, p. 16.

12. Richard O'Mara, "Alan Keyes for President?" *Baltimore Sun,* January 14, 1995, p. 2A.

13. Alan Keyes President '96 press release, July 27, 1995.

Richard Lugar

1. Margaret Carlson, "But Seriously, Folks," *Time,* March 13, 1995, p. 84.

2. Michael Barone and Grant Ujifusa, *The Almanac of American Politics 1996,* (Washington, D.C.: The National Journal, 1995), p. 470.

3. Phil Duncan, *Congressional Quarterly,* July 18, 1995.

4. George Stuteville, "The Nice Guy Who Finished FIRST," *Indianapolis Star,* April 16, 1995, p. D1.

5. *Hoover's Handbook Database,* (Austin: Reference Press, August 25, 1995).

6. Interview with Terry Holt, September 13, 1995.

7. Michael Brown, "The Lugar Club," *Indianapolis Business Journal,* November 6, 1989, p. 1A.

8. David Haase, "Giving Lugar Their All," *Indianapolis News,* February 18, 1995, p. B1.

9. Greta Shankle, "Health reform lobbying is no cheap chore," *Indianapolis Business Journal,* July 11, 1994, p. A1.

10. Judith Barra Austin, "Coats, Lugar Plan to Oppose Health Care Bill," Gannett News Service, August 5, 1994; and Senator Richard Lugar, "Health Care Debate," Congressional Press Releases, August 3, 1994, p. A1.

11. Juliet Eilperin, "Hoosiers Come to Washington to Protest Health Care Reform," States News Service, August 18, 1994.

12. AFX News, "Wall Street Today," November 11, 1994.

13. Michael F. Conlan, "S.2000 defeated, but Pryor to keep fighting price hikes," *Drug Topics,* April 6, 1992; *Chemical Marketing Reporter,* "Pharmaceutical credits preserved by Senate vote," March 16, 1992.

14. Business Wire, "Lilly constructing $65 million, 140,000 sq.-ft. expansion facility in Puerto Rico," February 28, 1992.

15. Jim Luther, "U.S. Pays Up to $156,000 for Each Puerto Rican Drug-Industry Job," Associated Press, May 14, 1992.

16. "Pryor's Drug Hike Penalty Proposal Gains Support," *Institutional Investor's Portfolio Letter,* February 3, 1992.

17. "Patents possible Brazilian U-turn worries U.S.," *The Financial Times Limited, Pharmaceutical Business News,* February 1, 1991.

18. United Press International, "Indiana News in Brief," March 7, 1986.

19. Ibid. "Indiana News in Brief," July 26, 1985.

20. Interview with Senator Richard Lugar, July 12, 1995.

21. Ibid.

22. Federal News Service, "Press Conference Senator Richard Lugar," August 29, 1989. Michael Moss, ibid., "Records Show Senator's String-Pulling at HUD," August 26, 1989.

23. "Letters from Readers" Response from Lugar in *Louisville Courier-Journal*, September 18, 1989.

24. Peter Key, "Auctionieer's gavel falls as Marott sold to satisfy loan," *Indianapolis Star*, January 27, 1994.

25. Federal News Service, August 29, 1989.

26. Michael Moss, "Records Show Senator's String-Pulling at HUD," August 26, 1989, p. 9.

27. "Lugar Defends Intervention For HUD Project," United Press International, August 29, 1989.

28. Common Cause press release, "Easy Money," February 10, 1989.

29. Common Cause press releases: "Taking It To the Limit," May 20, 1986; "71 U.S. Senators Kept a Total $2 Million in Honoraria For Personal Use in 1989, According to Common Cause Study" and "61 Current Senators Kept Total $1.4 Million in Honoraria For Personal Use in 1990," June 14, 1991.

30. Figures are compiled from Federal Election data, but do not include individual donations under $500 for the years 1989–94.

Arlen Specter

1. Interview with Arlen Specter, July 20, 1995.

2. Transcript of Specter announcement, March 30, 1995, p. 3.

3. Jane Mayer and Jill Abramson, *Strange Justice: The Selling of Clarence Thomas* (New York: Houghton Mifflin, 1994), p. 210.

4. Thomas B. Edsall, "Senator Specter, running against the grain; Jewish, Northeastern, Abortion-rights supporter seeks the GOP nomination," *Washington Post*, March 26, 1995, p. A6.

5. Ibid.

6. Ibid.

7. Donald L. Bartlett and James B. Steele, "Crime and Injustice" series, *Philadelphia Inquirer*, 1973.

8. Ibid.

9. Edsall, "Senator Specter, running against the grain," p. A6.

10. Terence Moran, "Specter's odyssey from showhorse to statesman; Senator alters the course of two careers—Bork's and his own," *Legal Times*, October 5, 1987, p. 7.

11. Ibid.

12. Mayer and Abramson, *Strange Justice*, p. 293.

13. Interview with Arlen Specter, July 20, 1995.

14. Michael Barone and Grant Ujifusa, *The Almanac of American Politics 1996*, (Washington, D.C.: National Journal Inc., 1995), p. 1128.

15. Larry Makinson and Joshua Goldstein, *Open Secrets, The Encyclopedia of Congressional Money and Politics, 1992* (Washington, D.C.: Congressional Quarterly, 1992), pp. 69 and 363.

16. Ibid., pp. 59 and 362.

17. Ibid., p. 69.

18. Citizen Action Report, "Unhealthy Money: $79 million Buries Health Care Reform; Part XIV," July 1995.

19. "Washington Talk: Briefing; Specter's Desserts," *New York Times*, March 11, 1987, p. 6.

20. Interview with the editorial board, "Arlen Specter stakes his claim to the presidency," *San Francisco Chronicle*, May 14, 1995.

Pete Wilson

1. William Safire, "Essay; Nixon on 1996," *New York Times*, May 12, 1994, p. A25.

2. Interview with Herb Klein, August 15, 1995.

3. Wilson eulogy at Nixon funeral, June 1, 1994.

4. Michael Barone and Grant Ujifusa, *The Almanac of American Politics 1996* (Washington, D.C.: National Journal Inc., 1995), pp. 86–87.

5. CNN "Larry King Live," June 22, 1995.

6. Ken Chavez, "Fund-raiser Draws Heat; Wilson Hosted Garbage Industry, Regulators," *Sacramento Bee*, June 5, 1993, p. A1.

7. Ibid.

8. Ibid.

9. Daniel Weintraub, "Groups With Stake in State Top Wilson's Donor List," *Los Angeles Times*, February 27, 1994, p. A1.

10. Glenn F. Bunting and Ralph Frammolino, "Fund-Raising Needs Create Ethics Dilemma for Wilson," *Los Angeles Times*, October 24, 1990, p. A1.

11. Bill Stall, "Feinstein, Wilson Differ On Approach For the Final Days," *Los Angeles Times*, November 3, 1990, p. A26.

12. Gordon Smith, "Crime measure seen as pricey proposition As 3-strikes criminals crowd prisons, costs become concern," *San Diego Union-Tribune*, October 16, 1994, p. A1.

13. George Skelton, "Family Drama Sears Wilson's Death Penalty View," *Los Angeles Times*, April 27, 1992, p. A3.

14. Ibid. See also United Press International, May 16, 1991 (BC cycle).

15. Stall, "Feinstein, Wilson Differ."

16. Skelton, "Family Drama."

17. Bunting and Frammolino, "Fund-Raising Needs Create Ethics Dilemma."

18. Mary Lynne Vellinga, "Guard Hits Jackpot with Overtime Pay," *Sacramento Bee,* April 23, 1995, p. A15.

19. John Hurst, "The Big House That Don Novey Built: Working the PR, Spreading Big Bucks, A Canny Union Boss Demands More Prisons and Top Pay for his Guards," *Los Angeles Times* Magazine, February 6, 1994, p. 16; interview with Don Novey, August 15, 1995.

20. Interview with Don Novey, August 15, 1995.

21. Smith, "Crime measure seen as pricey proposition."

22. Stephen Green, "State Pay Up 5% But More Jobs Left Open," *Sacramento Bee,* December 28, 1993, p. A1. See also Clark McKinley, "Study Calls Prison Spending 'Rogue Elephant,' " United Press International, June 23, 1993.

23. Caleb Foote, "The Prison Population Explosion: California's Rogue Elephant," report from The Center on Juvenile and Criminal Justice, June 1993; California Department of Corrections data, September 12, 1995.

24. Department of Corrections data, September 12, 1995.

25. Interview with Don Novey, August 15, 1995.

26. "Magic 13" Issues for Discussion Relative to Endorsement by the California Correctional Peace Officers Association (CCPOA) approved April 24, 1994 by the CCPOA State Board of Directors, obtained by the Center for Public Integrity.

27. Interview with Tom Hayden, September 27, 1995.

28. Dan Bernstein, "Need For More Prisons Questioned," *Sacramento Bee,* January 23, 1994, p. A1.

29. Proposition 103 Enforcement Project, headed by Harvey Rosenfield, October 1994.

30. Daniel M. Weintraub, "Insurance Industry Is Top Donor to Wilson Campaign," *Los Angeles Times,* November 1, 1994, p. A1.

31. Ibid.

32. Daniel Weintraub, "Groups With Stake in State Top Wilson's Donor List," *Los Angeles Times,* February 27, 1994, p. A1.

33. Ibid.

34. Larry Liebert, "What the PACs Gave California's Senators/Banks, S&Ls Were Big Donors to Both," *San Francisco Chronicle,* March 16, 1990, p. A20.

35. Bunting and Frammolino, "Fund-Raising Needs Create Ethics Dilemma."

36. Ibid.

37. Ibid.

38. Ibid.

39. Interview with Quarles, September 14, 1995.

40. Interview with Cunningham, September 22, 1995.

41. FEC records.

42. Bunting and Frammolino, "Fund-Raising Needs Create Ethics Dilemma."

43. Ibid.

44. Chris Chrystal, "Van de Kamp says Wilson should return honoraria," *United Press International,* January 11, 1990.

45. Bunting and Frammolino, "Fund-Raising Needs Create Ethics Dilemma."

46. "Wilson, special interests skirt law to pay for Asian trip," *San Diego Union-Tribune,* November 24, 1993, p. A8.

47. Letter to the Center for Public Integrity from Loren Kaye, undersecretary, California Trade and Commerce Agency, August 2, 1995.

48. "Wilson, special interests skirt law to pay for Asian trip," *San Diego Union-Tribune,* November 24, 1993, p. A8.

49. Dana Wilke, "Wilson talks austerity, lives prosperity, thanks to foundation," *San Diego Union-Tribune,* July 11, 1994, p. A3.

50. Greg Lucas, "Horse Group Loses, Wilson Donor Gains," *San Francisco Chronicle,* May 11, 1994, p. A15.

51. Greg Lucas, "Probe Urged of Wilson's L.A. Condo Critics say luxury residence a gift to governor, not state," *San Francisco Chronicle,* July 12, 1994, p. A13.

52. Wilke, "Wilson talks austerity"; and Robert B. Gunnison, "Names of L.A. Condo Donors Sought," *San Francisco Chronicle,* July 8, 1994, p. A21.

53. Gunnison, "Names of L.A. Condo Donors Sought."

54. Robert B. Gunnison, "Luxury Condo Leased in L.A. For Wilson, Arrangement raises ethical, legal questions for governor," *San Francisco Chronicle,* July 7, 1994, p. A1.

55. Dan Morain, "Wilson Faces Showdown on Choice for Regents," *Los Angeles Times,* March 3, 1993, p. A3.

56. Dana Wilkie, "Governor Appoints Davies as UC Regent," *San Diego Union-Tribune,* March 28, 1992, p. A3.

57. Morain, "Wilson Faces Showdown on Choice for Regents."

58. Wilson's 1994 Statement of Economic Interests form, dated February 28, 1995.

Wild Cards

1. Richard Benedetto, "Voters want independent in race," *USA Today,* August 11, 1995, p. 1A. 1,210 adults surveyed between August 4 and 7. Margin of error: +/−3 percentage points.

2. *New York Times*/CBS Poll, August 12, 1995. Survey of 1,478 adults between August 5 and 9. Margin of error: +/−3 percentage points.

3. *Washington Post*/ABC News Poll, August 11, 1995. 1,003 adults surveyed. Margin of error: +/−3 percentage points.

4. FEC records indicate that 273 candidates who each raised $5,000 or more were filed.

BILL BRADLEY

1. Al Hunt, "Dollar Bill's Best Games May Be Ahead," *Wall Street Journal*, August 17, 1995, p. A11.

2. Larry Makinson, Center for Responsive Politics, *Open Secrets*, 2nd edition (Washington, D.C.: Congressional Quarterly, 1992), p. 28.

3. Ibid.

4. The current state of election law is that bundling is legal as long as the organization in question does not direct its employees to donate. In the case of Prudential-Bache, the corporation did so. All numbers are from FEC data provided by the Center for Responsive Politics.

5. Associated Press, "NJ Senator to Refund Donation," December 23, 1994.

6. FEC.

7. Makinson, *Open Secrets*, p. 112.

8. Aaron Pressman, "The Street's 'Killer Year' in Congressional Elections," *Investment Dealers' Digest*, September 28, 1992, p. 18.

9. Eric Pianin, "Senate passes Tax Bill Opposed by Bush," *Washington Post*, September 30, 1992, p. A7.

10. Donald Bartlett and James Steele, *America: Who Really Pays the Taxes?* (New York: Touchstone, 1994), p. 17.

11. Makinson, *Open Secrets*, p. 73.

12. Government Accounting Office report, "Tax Policy: Puerto Rico and the Section 936 Tax Credit," (GAO/GGD-93-109) June 1993, p. 53.

13. Ibid., p. 48.

14. Bartlett and Steele, *America: Who Really Pays the Taxes?*, p. 240.

NEWT GINGRICH

1. Campaign statement by Newt Gingrich, April 8, 1974, on announcing his candidacy.

2. Larry Makinson and Joshua Goldstein, Center for Responsive Politics, *Open Secrets* (Washington, D.C.: Congresisonal Quarterly Press, 1994), p. 666; *Open Secrets*, 1992 edition, p. 658.

3. *Campaign Practices Reports*, "Congressmen Prepare a PAC Appreciation Day," February 13, 1984, p. 5.

4. Michael Ross, "Senate GOP Filibuster All but Kills Lobby Reform Bill," *Los Angeles Times*, October 7, 1994, p. A1.

5. Jeffrey Klein, "Newtiavelli," *Mother Jones*, January 1995.

6. Figures for 1993–1994 were not available in time to be included.

7. Editorial, "Read the fine print," *Atlanta Constitution*, October 19, 1994, p. A16.

8. George Lardner Jr., "Gingrich Promised NRA No Gun Control Legislation," *Washington Post*, August 1, 1995, p. A1.

9. Glenn Simpson, "In Professor Gingrich's Class, Money Talks," *Roll Call*, September 15, 1994, p. 1.

10. Ibid.

11. Common Cause report, "The X Files: Speaker Newt Gingrich's Financial Empire," February 1995.

12. Tim Curran, "Eight to Testify in Gingrich Probe," *Roll Call*, July 13, 1995.

13. Simpson, "In Professor Gingrich's Class."

14. Common Cause, "The X Files."

15. Ibid.

16. Makinson and Goldstein, *Open Secrets*, 2nd edition.

17. Citizen Action report, "Unhealthy Money: $79 Million Buries Health Care Reform; Part XIV; A Report by Citizens Fund," August 1995.

18. Phil Kuntz, "Gingrich Introduced Legislation to Aid Firm That Was Donor to Think Tank," *Wall Street Journal*, February 3, 1995, p. A14.

19. Interview with Rick O'Donnell, August 11, 1995.

20. See *The Public i*, the newsletter of the Center for Public Integrity, March 1995.

JESSE JACKSON

1. William Schneider, "The Democrats in '88; The party's possible candidates divide into four categories—rejuvenators, revisionists, reconstructionists, and revivalists," *Atlantic Monthly*, April, 1987, p. 36.

2. Robert Ajemian, "Campaign Portrait, Respect and Respectability, Jackson Tones Down His Style," *Time*, August 17, 1987, p. 16.

3. Andy Plattner, "The Preacher and His Programs," *U.S. News & World Report*, April 11, 1988, p. 30.

4. FEC report.

5. Interview with Frank Watkins, July 25, 1995.

6. Visit to National Rainbow Headquarters, July 25, 1995.

7. Ibid.

8. Elizabeth O. Colton, *The Jackson Phenomenon: The Man, The Power, The Message.* (New York: Doubleday, 1989), p. 4.

9. 1988 financial disclosure forms.

10. Interview with Frank Watkins, July 25, 1995.

11. Interview with Mike Carter, August 29, 1995. The coalition is a 501(c)(6), taxable, nonprofit organization which the IRS said is not required to disclose financial information if the group falls within certain net income criteria.

12. Interview with Chrystal Johnson, August 7, 1995.

13. Interview with Frank Watkins, July 25, 1995.

14. Operation PUSH pamphlet and materials.

15. James Kelly, "When PUSH Gives a Shove," *Time,* April 14, 1986, p. 88.

16. Phone call to Illinois Secretary of State, Department of Corporations. PUSH ITB was dissolved September 1, 1992; and Illinois Secretary of State certificate of dissolution for domestic corporation, file number N 5269-729-8.

17. Mark Hosenball, "Jesse's Business: a shakedown racket?" *New Republic,* May 9, 1988, p. 10*ff.*

18. Jacob Weisberg, "The Disorganization Man, PUSH's Troubles Could Hurt Jackson's Campaign," *Newsweek,* August 17, 1987, p. 19.

19. Ray Gibson and John Kass, "Operation PUSH in debt, calls emergency meeting," *Chicago Tribune,* January 26, 1991, p. 10.

ROSS PEROT

1. FEC records.

2. Lawrence I. Barrett, "Heckler in Chief," *Time,* March 29, 1993, p. 27.

3. Perot on NBC News "Meet the Press," August 13, 1995.

4. Sidney Blumenthal, "The Mission, Ross Perot's Vietnam Syndrome," *New Republic,* July 6, 1992, pp. 16–23.

5. Margaret Carlson, "Perot and His Presidents," *Time,* May 25, 1992, p. 34.

6. Ibid.

7. Information materials from the Maryland Perot Petition Committee.

8. Peter Elkind, "The Ross Perot You Don't Know, the things that would make him a dangerous president," *Washington Monthly,* May, 1992, pp. 14–18.

9. Carlson, "Perot and His Presidents," p. 34.

10. Ibid.

11. Albert R. Hunt, "Perot would gain $15 million benefit in tax panel's bill," *Wall Street Journal,* November 7, 1975, p. 1.

12. Carlson, "Perot and His Presidents," p. 34.

13. Bob Dart, "Lobbyist Recalls '75 Perot work," Cox News Service/*Chicago Tribune,* November 11, 1993, p. 7.

14. Elkind, "The Ross Periot You Don't Know," p. 14.

15. Michael Tackett, "Another Perot Run in '96?; His Bid Might Inspire 4th and 5th Candidates," *Chicago Tribune,* May 15, 1995, p. 7.

16. FEC records.

17. Ibid.

18. Hugh Aynesworth, "Perot implores his followers to mobilize to make 2-party system work for them," *Washington Times,* p. A9.

19. Walter Shapiro, "He's Ready, but is America Ready for President Perot?" *Time,* May 25, 1992, p. 27.

COLIN POWELL

1. Howard Means, *Colin Powell Soldier/Statesman—Statesman/Soldier* (New York: Donald I. Fine Inc., 1992), p. 143–144.

2. Major Colin Powell's memo to Adjutant General Lieutenant Colonel Bernard Callahan, December 11, 1968.

3. Charles Lane, "The Legend of Colin Powell, Anatomy of an Establishment Career," *New Republic,* April 17, 1995, p. 24.

4. David Roth, *Sacred Honor* (New York: HarperCollins, 1993), p. 132–33.

5. Interview with Lawrence Walsh, August 22, 1995.

6. Peter Cary, "Breaking Barriers in the Barracks," *U.S. News & World Report,* August 21, 1989, p. 26*ff.*

7. Eloise Sanholz, "Pragmatist at the Pentagon," *Newsweek,* August 2, 1989, p. 20.

8. John Ranelagh, "America's Black Eisenhower," *National Review,* April 1, 1991, pp. 26–28.

9. Lorna S. Jaffe, "The Development of the Base Force 1989–1992," Joint History Office, Office of the Joint Chiefs of Staff.

10. Interview with Lawrence Korb, July 31, 1995.

11. Jon Meacham, "How Colin Powell Plays the Game," *Washington Monthly,* December, 1994, p. 1.

12. Michael R. Gordon and Bernard E. Trainor, "Beltway Warrior," *New York Times Magazine,* August 27, 1995, p. 41.

13. Means, *Colin Powell,* p. 278.

14. Lane, "The Legend of Colin Powell," p. 20.

15. Howard Means, "President Powell?" *Washingtonian,* December 6, 1994, p. 23.

16. Maureen O'Brien, "Gen. Colin Powell Sells Memoirs To Random for $6.5 Million," *Publisher's Weekly,* August 23, 1993, p. 10.

17. Interview with Powell aide Bill Smullen, August 9, 1995.

18. Lawrence I. Barrett, Jeffrey H. Birnbaum, J.F.O. McAllister, and Mark Thompson, "Will He Run?" *Time,* July 10, 1995, p. 24ff.

19. Neal Allen, "Powell: 'No political ambitions' for '96,' " *DePauw,* November 4, 1994, p. 1.

Concluding Thoughts

1. Vaclav Havel, *et. al.,* edited by John Keane, *The Power of the Powerless,* (Armonk, New York: M.E. Sharpe, Inc., 1985), pp. 39–40.

2. Marty Jezer and Ellen Miller, "Money Politics: Campaign Finance and the Subversion of American Democracy," *Notre Dame Journal of Law, Ethics & Public Policy,* Vol. 8, No. 2, 1994.

3. Alan F. Kay, Hazel Henderson, Frederick T. Steeper, Stanley B. Greenberg, and Christopher Blunt, "Who Will Reconnect With The People: Republicans, Democrats, Or . . . None Of The Above?" Americans Talk Issues (ATI) Survey #28, August 14, 1995, p. 5.

4. Ibid., p. 6.

5. Albert R. Hunt, "The Best Congress Money Can Buy," *Wall Street Journal*, September 7, 1995, p. A15, citing a Common Cause study.

Author's Note

1. In the interest of full disclosure, the Center for Public Integrity is a nonprofit, 501(c)(3) tax exempt organization which has been funded by foundations, corporations, labor unions, individuals, revenue from the sale of publications and editorial consulting with news organizations. At least two entities, the AFL-CIO and Milliken & Company, mentioned in this book regarding specific presidential candidates, have also supported the Center in the past. For more detailed financial information about the Center, call 202-783-3900. What is written in this book does not necessarily reflect the views of individual members of the Center's Board of Directors or Advisory Board.

Index